CW00616060

# Mus~~harraf~~
# The Years in Power

Murtaza Razvi has a master's in ancient Indian and Islamic history from the University of the Punjab, Lahore, and a master's in political science from Villanova University, Pennsylvania. He is a journalist with Dawn Media Group and lives with his wife and three daughters in Karachi.

# Musharraf
## The Years in Power

*Murtaza Razvi*

HarperCollins *Publishers* India
*a joint venture with*

New Delhi

First published in India in 2009 by
HarperCollins *Publishers* India
*a joint venture with*
The India Today Group

Copyright © Murtaza Razvi 2009

ISBN: 978-81-7233-896-4

2 4 6 8 10 9 7 5 3 1

Murtaza Razvi asserts the moral
right to be identified as the author of this work.

**HarperCollins *Publishers***
A-53, Sector 57, Noida 201301, India
77-85 Fulham Palace Road, London W6 8JB, United Kingdom
Hazelton Lanes, 55 Avenue Road, Suite 2900, Toronto, Ontario M5R 3L2
*and* 1995 Markham Road, Scarborough, Ontario M1B 5M8, Canada
25 Ryde Road, Pymble, Sydney, NSW 2073, Australia
31 View Road, Glenfield, Auckland 10, New Zealand
10 East 53rd Street, New York NY 10022, USA

Typeset in 11/14 Sabon
InoSoft Systems

Printed and bound at
Thomson Press (India) Ltd.

*Dedicated to the hope that Pakistan will achieve
peace with itself and the world*

# Contents

# PART II

# Prologue

For many in Pakistan, it is too early to form a dispassionate opinion about General Pervez Musharraf since his resignation on 18 August 2008 and embark upon a discussion of his legacy. In a country where the surreal overwhelms the real, there are often many dimensions of reality: disagreements outnumber agreements by wide margins on any given issue, be it history, politics, democracy, or even the genesis of Pakistan. In this curious mix of perspectives on reality, conspiracy theories abound. Each group spins and nurtures its own version; some do it more in order to confound their opponents rather than validate their own argument. Getting to the essentials, stripped of their many interpretations, is a rarity. Musharraf and his years in power are no exception. Pakistanis are widely divided on his controversial persona, his style of governance, his motives, and the like. The man single-handedly ruled his country for eight years in what were, and arguably remain, trying times for Pakistan: a nuclear-armed power plunged deep into the throes of an economic crisis, a frontline state in the global war against terrorism and, of late, its battleground; a nation lacking political stability ... Musharraf presided over all these challenges faced by his country and ruled as if it were a personal fiefdom, as indeed do most autocrats.

The story of Musharraf's very turbulent years in power (1999–2008) cannot be told without contextualizing it in the peculiar Pakistani milieu in which it unfolded. When he came to power, his was a nation tormented by an economic meltdown and on the verge of a default on its international loan commitments. In the aftermath of the May 1998 nuclear tests and the abysmal governance of the despotic, even if democratically elected, Nawaz Sharif, Pakistan was diplomatically isolated. When Musharraf left the seat of power eight years later with what appeared to be a relatively comfortable treasury, an economic meltdown again began to take hold, but most seriously he left behind a nation badly fragmented along many fault-lines, not least the very raison d'être of Pakistan which began to be questioned again as state institutions eroded and miserably failed to address the many challenges facing Pakistan. One of his legacies is thus the resurfacing of old political conflicts within and new challenges from outside. The politically fragile state in which his eight-year rule has left Pakistan has led many, especially those from smaller ethnic nationalities and groups and even a section of civil society, to once again bring into question the very creation of Pakistan.

The existing fissures can be better understood by recalling here a brief summation of Pakistan's political history. The secular-minded have always held that the country came into being as a homeland for those seen as forming a marginalized community, the Indian subcontinent's Muslims; the religious right attributes Pakistan's inception to the great faith, Islam itself. Hence the Islamic Republic, as Pakistan was officially designated by its first (unelected) prime minister, Liaquat Ali Khan, in 1949, a year after the death of its founder, Mohammed Ali Jinnah. The founding father was said to be opposed to naming it as such: 'Pakistan shall not be a theocracy ruled by mullahs with a divine mission … religion shall have nothing to do with the business of the state,' was Jinnah's briefing to the first Constituent Assembly in Karachi on the eve of Independence. However, a troubled, prolonged period of political experimentation followed his death in 1948, as power changed hands among unelected leaders who failed to draft a constitution on the basis of which the new, just liberated, country carved out of a post-Independence India could be ruled. Subsequently, long years of dictatorial, military rule, starting as early as in 1958, did not allow democratic institutions, values and practices to take root.

When democracy was finally given a chance by the military, which belatedly held the country's first elections on the basis of adult franchise in 1970, the civil–military establishment refused to accept the election results. The majority from East Pakistan had voted for the Awami League, a Bengali nationalist party, but Islamabad (in hegemonic West Pakistan) refused to transfer power. A civil war, later to be christened as a war of independence by Bengali nationalists, led to Pakistan's dismemberment. The 1971 India–Pakistan war resulted in the surrender of largely West Pakistani forces in Dhaka and the emergence of the independent state of Bangladesh.

Back in what remained of Pakistan, Zulfikar Ali Bhutto, whose Pakistan People's Party (PPP) had secured the highest number of seats in the election to the erstwhile West Pakistan assembly, came to power. However, Bhutto's democratic rule too soon became controversial given his dictatorial proclivities, controversial nationalization of a war-battered economy, victimization of his political opponents and erratic governance. After the opposition parties' allegation of massive rigging in the 1977 election held under the Bhutto government, the chief of army staff Gen. Ziaul Haq overthrew Bhutto. Pakistan's first and thus far only elected prime minister was tried behind closed doors for the murder of a political opponent in an extremely controversial case, found guilty, and hanged to death, all appeals for clemency by world leaders being rejected. Another eleven long years of army rule followed, spreading alienation amongst the smaller provinces, especially Bhutto's home province, Sindh, which has only a minuscule representation in the armed forces, the bulk of the forces being recruited from Punjab, followed by the North West Frontier Province.

The Zia regime that overthrew Bhutto in 1977—the latter was no darling of the West because of his socialist leanings and because he was a popular leader who vowed to unite the Arab–Muslim world to counter Western hegemony over global resources—had the implicit backing of the CIA. Two years after the coup, in 1979, Soviet tanks rolled into neighbouring Afghanistan to back a communist-led government that overthrew King Zahir Shah; simultaneously, a radical Islamic Revolution in Iran led by Ayatollah Roohollah Moosavi Khomeini deposed Mohammed Reza Shah Pehlavi, the US's staunchest ally in the Muslim world. The changing scene warranted an American response to jack up its receding influence in the region. Pakistan, an old, if erstwhile cold-shouldered, ally of the US against its policy of containment of the Soviet Union, became a frontline state in the American scheme of things for the region. Washington began pumping in dollars and military hardware to fight America's proxy war through Pakistan against the Soviet occupation of Afghanistan. However, greater, long-lasting damage was inflicted on Pakistan as the CIA also provided funds to set up hundreds of Islamic seminaries to ideologically train young mujahideen to wage jihad against the communists in Afghanistan. US support for radical Sunni mujahideen in Afghanistan also helped counter Shia Iran's revolutionary battle-cry: that America was out to subjugate the Muslim world, and it had to be resisted. Pakistan's support for the US's anti-Soviet agenda in Afghanistan, and the resulting campaign's puritan Sunni overtones, did not go down well with a revolutionary, Shia Iran. The Ayatollah leading the revolution saw Sunni puritanism as practised, and now backed, by Saudi Arabia as a tool of ideological expansion in the region via jihad against the Soviets in Afghanistan, and as running counter to his revolutionary ideals. Iran under the new revolutionary Islamic leadership and Pakistan under a Saudi–American-backed jihad in Afghanistan had for the first time a divergence of interests in the region. This in turn led to heightened sectarian tensions and clashes in Pakistan between the majority Sunni and minority Shia Muslims under the Zia regime.

The Soviet forces' withdrawal from Afghanistan finally began in April 1988, following the Geneva accords. Gen. Zia's mysterious death in a plane crash occurred in August that year. His removal from the scene and the waning interest of the US in Pakistan, which was no longer the frontline state against a crumbling Soviet empire, left Pakistan exposed to the dangers posed by thousands of well-trained mujahideen who would not settle for anything less than the establishment of a radical, medieval Muslim state in the region. With the Pakistani army's backing, such a state was eventually proclaimed by the Taliban in Afghanistan in 1995 after much infighting between the Darri-speaking warlords of the north and the Pashto-speaking Taliban of the south. However, between the Soviet forces' withdrawal in 1988 and 1995, the Pakistani military establishment, given its experience of covert operations in Afghanistan during the preceding decade, had come to regard Afghanistan as a country which could give Pakistan 'strategic depth' vis-à-vis India, seen as the arch-rival. Under pressure from the Pakistani army, Zia's democratic successors, Benazir Bhutto and Nawaz Sharif, could do little to disengage the army from this questionable, national-security doctrine which went as follows: If a pro-Pakistan government was installed and maintained in power in Kabul, it would secure the country's western borders by checking India's influence over Afghanistan's traditionally hostile policy towards Pakistan. Islamabad had inherited the British empire's dispute with Afghanistan on the Durand Line, the over 1000-mile-long but very porous border between the two countries. The pre-1979 imperial Afghanistan was also blamed for fuelling separatist passions among Pakistan's Pashtun population residing alongside its border with Afghanistan. The desire to keep a grip on Afghanistan through a friendly Taliban government at Kabul played itself out at a time when, ironically, another era of democratic rule was dawning in Pakistan in the aftermath of the end of the Zia dictatorship.

Zulfikar Ali Bhutto's daughter, Benazir Bhutto, and Gen. Zia's erstwhile protégé from Punjab, Mian Mohammad Nawaz Sharif, respectively, had two terms each in office between 1988 and 1999. Both Bhutto and Sharif had to go along with and support the army's Afghanistan policy; it was considered a no-go area for elected governments and remained the sole preserve of the Pakistani army's high command. As part of this bargain, Bhutto and Sharif were left free by the army to mutually engage in political musical chairs. They did this not just by challenging each other to mudslinging matches but also by taking practical steps aimed at decimating the other, to the utter neglect of governance and a sliding economy. While Bhutto was more subtle and somewhat restrained in her exercise of vitriolic, Sharif, during his two stints in power, went the whole hog and filed a range of corruption cases against her and her husband Asif Ali Zardari. The ruling couple was accused of siphoning off ill-gotten wealth and huge amounts in kickbacks from national projects to their offshore bank accounts.

As for his second stint in power (1997–99), Sharif had begun flexing his muscles equally forcefully against the civil–military establishment. Having appointed and retired army chiefs out of turn at his fancy, he had also moved a bill in parliament to virtually declare himself Amirul Momineen (commander of the faithful), a medieval title adopted by Islamic caliphs who ruled unchallenged unto death. On the heels of this political brinkmanship came the May 1998 nuclear tests in response to India's nuclear bomb, inviting widespread condemnation from the world, and economic sanctions that virtually crippled Pakistan. Given the dire straits of the economy and heightened political polarization between Sharif and his opponents, on the one hand, and Sharif and the armed forces, on the other, he stood utterly discredited in the public eye. Benazir Bhutto fared no better on the popularity index. Twice over, the two had taken turns at governing Pakistan; they were widely and equally blamed for their corrupt practices and bad governance when in power.

It was against this backdrop that the military coup of 12 October 1999 took place. The army chief, Gen. Pervez Musharraf, was hailed by many as Pakistan's saviour who would steer the country back to safety from the brink of the economic precipice to which it had been taken by a decade of misrule by the Nawaz Sharif and Benazir Bhutto combine.

It is in this context that Musharraf's eventful years in power (1999–2008) must be seen and analysed. This is necessary in order to be fair not just to him but to documenting Pakistan's political history as it unfolded in those years. This book is an attempt at doing just that.

# PART I

# 1

# The Enigma

Today, since his resignation in August 2008 under pressure from the selfsame political forces that had stood publicly discredited a decade earlier, Musharraf remains an enigma to friends and foes alike.

To friends, speaking with the benefit of hindsight, his reign was yet another opportunity lost for Pakistan to rise from the depths of political, social and cultural obscurantism. They say it was not he who failed, but the powers that be that failed him. To them, his is the story of a highly rated soldier who by circumstances beyond his control was confronted by barrages of bi-directional fire: that of balancing his professional responsibilities as the head of a nuclear-armed Pakistani army as well as politically steering his country, which he was as its head of state under oath to defend, out of troubled waters.

According to his supporters, beginning on 12 October 1999, Musharraf donned the mantle of a saviour. He overcame a 'coup' instigated against him by an elected prime minister who, though he enjoyed a two-thirds majority in parliament, was tarnished by corruption charges and lack of spine at home and abroad, and thus extremely unpopular. After coming to power, many believed that Musharraf took the high road by pardoning his self-styled enemy who had possibly tried to kill him (and dozens of others on board the commercial flight) by refusing the plane in which he was travelling permission to land in Pakistan. Once he assumed office, Musharraf set about rearranging politics to address the challenges left behind by the so-called democratic rulers, promising to lead Pakistan out of its predicaments and charting its path towards sustainable democracy. Making peace with India became the cornerstone of Musharraf's vision for a prosperous, economically vibrant and politically stable Pakistan.

In the post-9/11 context, Musharraf's also became the story of Pakistan's survival as a sovereign nation; a state poised on the brink of failure, it had only a single individual to thank or blame for the actions taken in the context of a rapidly changing international situation and diplomacy. The about-turn Pakistan took on the Taliban regime, the subsequent presence of US-led forces in Afghanistan, the growing extremism at home, and India's posturing to extract advantage out of the emerging scenario, by offering to help the US in fighting the war against global terrorism before Pakistan committed to it, stared Musharraf in the face, say the general's friends. He was the man of the hour; Pakistan would not have been the same without him.

Thus, settling in his new role as the chief executive of the country, Musharraf was beset with multiple problems, including a looming economic disaster which had to be contained; he not only did that but during his subsequent eight years in power transformed it into an apparent economic boom. Just then politics began to catch up with him. Major political forces, Benazir Bhutto's People's Party and Nawaz Sharif's Pakistan Muslim League, the former having been kept at arm's length and the latter having been given the boot by the general, joined hands to plot his overthrow. The US and the UK backing Bhutto, and the Saudis backing Sharif, eventually persuaded Musharraf to let the two exiled leaders return to Pakistan in a spirit of accommodation and reconciliation.

Musharraf's supporters contend that by this time the West had realized that it could not extract any further concessions from Musharraf to further its 'war on terror' agenda and began banking on Pakistan's tried, tested, even though failed, political leadership to do its bidding. A section of Pakistani civil society, not quite knowing its role, says that Musharraf's supporters got sucked into the agenda of deposing him and derailing the political system he had put in place. The anti-Musharraf lawyers were pumped up by Nawaz Sharif, and they rallied behind the sacked chief justice who was harming rather than safeguarding the interests of Pakistan by entertaining, for instance, petitions of 'missing persons', many of whom were involved in and wanted for terrorist activities by the US.

His supporters go on to say that Musharraf must be credited with holding the fairest election since 1970. In the face of this, the PPP, the very party which depended on Musharraf's generosity and spirit of reconciliation, turned on him, with the help of its Western backers, while Sharif kept the heat on the general to settle his own vendetta. In August 2008, Musharraf stepped down to avoid further political polarization and violence among his countrymen, though his conscience told him that doing so at the time might not best serve the interests of his country, maintain his supporters.

He was a clean man, though not made of the same stuff as politicians are; nobody can accuse him of any financial wrongdoing. All his actions, right or wrong, were undertaken in good faith and in the cause of Pakistan. He will be remembered as someone who gave unprecedented freedoms to the media, which in turn contributed to his downfall. More than that, it was the Americans who finally wanted Musharraf out and got their way. He tried to lift Pakistan out of its quagmire but was failed by the powers that be. The rest is history.

\* \* \*

This by and large is the opinion of Musharraf's supporters on his tumultuous years in power. Those who have been personally close to the general almost unanimously say they would like to remain anonymous for fear of hurting their 'friend's' feelings by going public, especially with a Pakistani journalist like myself, a breed the general had learnt to distrust. In the course of my research for this book, people who have been closely associated with Musharraf, including his family, either refused to speak up unless they received explicit permission to do so from the general, or they conveyed their 'No' by promising to consider my request for an interview and then ignoring it altogether. Others just tried to buy time, putting it off without having to say 'No'. Whilst they may not have much to hide about Musharraf, many of his supporters that I spoke to blamed the media, which they said he had so liberalized, for his downfall. Anger seeps through their implicit refusal to talk; some expressly ask not to be named lest the information they divulged were used to Musharraf's detriment. However, no one was rude, but they didn't want to be seen 'talking' to someone the general wouldn't have wished. His friends' loyalty to him is total.

\* \* \*

Musharraf's opponents can be divided into two categories: those who were directly affected by his rule and those who disagreed with his policies. Amongst the former are the Sharif brothers, who since their return from exile have rallied for his accountability. When I went to see the younger brother, Shahbaz Sharif, now the chief minister of Punjab, he said he would have to consult the elder Sharif before he said anything about Musharraf, and promised to get back later with an appointment. Despite reminders, the request was not granted. The Sharifs' opponents say they have a lot to hide, i.e., how they were exiled, what actually happened on 12 October1999, and the terms under which they were allowed back from exile.

For most of Musharraf's opponents who share their thoughts on him, the same events and watersheds in his years in power are used to negate any association of goodness and lofty ideals with the man. They say the general was a reckless soldier who undertook the Kargil misadventure, which resulted in a military, political and diplomatic debacle for Pakistan. He was ambitious, and had put a plan in place to mount a coup d'état against the elected government given the slightest provocation, and he did. He held a bogus referendum in 2002 and got it indemnified by the Supreme Court, which, fearing his displeasure, had also given him the mandate to amend the constitution. He humiliated the nation by going to the Agra Summit in July 2001, offering India more than Pakistan had ever bargained for; the Indians called his bluff by sending him back empty-handed.

He then set about furthering the US agenda in the wake of 9/11 just so that he could stay on in power, and the latter from then on became his sole objective. He presided over bogus elections in 2002, handpicking his deputies to pack a parliament which would never debate any policy but act only as a rubber stamp to an all-powerful president who had usurped most of parliament's and the prime minister's powers. Pakistan was placed at the mercy of the US and military action initiated against its own people, and America's 'war on terror' objectives took precedence over the country's own good.

By 2007 the people had had enough. The firing of some sixty higher court judges, the president's illegal re-election by an outgoing parliament, and the 3 November 2007 declaration of emergency rule became inevitable acts of commission for the dictator on his way out. Benazir Bhutto's murder the following December and the 18 February 2008 election results made it clear that the nation had had enough and Musharraf had to go. He would not have resigned on 18 August had the new coalition government not initiated impeachment proceedings against him, and had it not become patently clear to him that his days in power were numbered. His rule will be remembered at best as an aberration in the democratic process.

\* \* \*

The truth perhaps lies somewhere in between the two extremes. Musharraf, say his friends and foes alike, was a very isolated man in his last months in power. Those who still nurture a soft corner for him only venture so far as to say that he would not listen to anyone, save perhaps to a narrowing circle of advisers and 'friends' with whom he had surrounded himself. Most of the general's diehard friends remain tight-lipped on what brought about his downfall, except to speak in wider terms, pointing their fingers at the Americans and the People's Party.

The beginning of Musharraf's decline in power, some say, began on 9 March 2007, when he made the chief justice of Pakistan, Iftikhar Mohammed Chaudhry, non-functional. Others say it was the imposition of emergency rule on 3 November 2007. Yet others believe that it was 15 November 2007, when he doffed his military uniform. The conspiracy theorists pre-date the beginning of the general's fall to his US visit during September 2006; his gung-ho interviews with the American media, his faux pas on the rise of rape incidents in Pakistan, the killing of the Baloch nationalist leader Nawab Akbar Bugti, and the like.

Last but not least is a fantastic story of the general's visit to a Dallas suburb, Paris, Texas, while on his trip to the US in 2006, which came up during an interview with someone who calls himself Musharraf's friend. The general had been advised by the Pakistani embassy in Washington to go to Dallas for a medical check-up during the US visit. It started a rumour back home that he had had a heart attack while on the tour and that the military high command was being readied to take charge. The story was promptly trashed by both the foreign office and the Pakistani embassy in Washington. It is, however, said that after that check-up the president began complaining of choking, to such a degree that on one occasion he nearly fainted. The check-up could have been an attempt at inducing a heart attack, or leaving him with traces of something that might cause an attack some time in the immediate future. However, those behind the sinister plan waited and waited ... and nothing happened. Then they decided to remove him from office by putting into motion a political plan, in which the new pawns were the failed leaders waiting in the wings, like Bhutto and Sharif.

Musharraf's opponents, however, insist it was the general's miscalculations about himself and about the people he so heroically wanted to lead but for whom he had done little to command any respect or loyalty that finally saw him out of office. They say his alienation from the people and real-life events brought about his downfall, in the classical, clichéd sense.

# 2

## The Accidental Dictator

Tuesday, 12 October 1999 was for many in Pakistan a day spent on tenterhooks, on the ground and in the air. While army chief General Pervez Musharraf was on board a PIA flight to Karachi from Colombo, Prime Minister Nawaz Sharif in Islamabad was entertaining thoughts that would bring him down before the day was over. The countdown to Sharif's dethroning began with a morning spent closeted with his closest deputies, drafting a speech to be aired over national radio and TV later that afternoon, announcing that he had retired Musharraf. There was to be no justification given for the abrupt sacking; the self-proclaimed Lion of Punjab had done it before, boasting an impressive history of differences with former army chiefs Aslam Beg, Asif Nawaz, Waheed Kakar and Jehangir Karamat in the course of his two somewhat brief stints as prime minister. General Karamat was forced to resign in October the year before, after he issued a political statement at a military academy which had not gone down well with Sharif. This was the first time in the chequered politics of Pakistan that the top general was forced to step down by an elected prime minister. The general had developed differences with Sharif over activating the controversial Council for Defence and National Security. The council, comprising the forces' chiefs and provincial chief executives, was the creation of President Farooq Leghari, and aimed at checking 'abuse' of power by the prime minister. Sharif had already pressurized Leghari into resigning earlier, and planted one of his former employees, Rafiq Tarar, his industrial empire's erstwhile legal adviser, in the presidency. Sharif's next target was the then chief justice of Pakistan, Sajjad Ali Shah, who presided over a full court bench hearing petitions against Sharif's abuse of power. President Leghari had resisted the prime minister's advice to remove the chief justice, but with the induction of Tarar as president, the chief justice was removed with a mere stroke of the presidential pen. Thus, enjoying a two-thirds majority in parliament, and after clearing all the impediments in his way, Sharif was all set to reign unhindered and unchecked. A bill to further Islamize Pakistan's laws, which also sought that the prime minister henceforth be called the Amirul Momineen (commander of the faithful), had already been tabled in parliament. Critics of the bill say that if it were passed, the bill would have enabled Sharif to issue summary orders as the chief executive, as was the custom during the medieval Muslim caliphate period, when caliphs exercised all powers as commanders of the faithful. His choice for the next army chief was Musharraf, one of Pakistan's top commandos, an Urdu speaker from Karachi who perhaps would not have a strong following among the mostly Punjabi and Pathan army top brass.

However, as was the prime minister's wont, differences with the new army chief also began to surface within weeks of Musharraf's appointment. These were principally over the prime minister's unilateral appointments and promotions in the armed forces. Musharraf was expected to go along but he put his foot down.

Amidst all this, and some six months into office, Musharraf had launched the ill-conceived Kargil operation which, Sharif openly alleged, had caught him unawares. 'While I was signing the Lahore Declaration with Prime Minister Vajpayee, he [Musharraf] stabbed the peace process in the back,' Sharif was reported to have said. However, Musharraf's account of the Kargil episode, as narrated in his memoirs, is at variance with Sharif's. The general has insisted all along that everyone, including the prime minister, was 'on board' his Kargil plan. Thus publicly falling out with his army chief, Sharif would not confirm Musharraf as chairman, Joint Chiefs of Staff Committee in the aftermath of Kargil, even though the general's appointment as chief of army staff (COAS) was a fait accompli. By the end of September 1999, the disastrous Kargil operation having undermined Sharif's efforts to mend fences with India and embarrassed his government thoroughly, relations between the prime minister and the army chief were at their lowest ebb. Islamabad buzzed with rumours, as the economic crisis which began in the wake of Pakistan's nuclear tests in May 1998, also worsened. The country could not afford a political tussle and instability, yet one of the two men simply had to go, said analysts. Zafar Abbas wrote in the news monthly *Herald* that Sharif's younger brother and chief minister of Punjab, Shahbaz Sharif, and his minister, Nisar Ali Khan, met Musharraf in a last-ditch effort to bridge the differences between the prime minister and the COAS. Then, one fine day, Musharraf declared: 'I am not going anywhere.'

Nawaz Sharif's two-thirds majority in parliament was believed to be the result of the rigged February 1997 elections that followed the sacking of Benazir Bhutto's government by President Leghari. It is generally held that elections in Pakistan cannot be rigged without a helping hand from the all-powerful army, especially its mighty intelligence wings, the Inter-Services Intelligence (ISI) and Military Intelligence (MI), which maintained political cells tasked with spying on politicians until after the February 2008 elections. The democratic government only recently dismantled the political cells of the intelligence agencies.

On the eve of the October 1999 coup, the *Herald* commented:

If one were to go by the book, Prime Minister Nawaz Sharif faces no real threat, from inside or outside parliament. But if one were to go by the spate of rumours currently doing the rounds in the political and social circles of Islamabad, and the nearby garrison city of Rawalpindi, the meltdown may actually have begun.

This transpired to be no less than prophesy.

Armed with his heavy public mandate, which had helped Sharif concentrate all powers in his hands to hire and fire heads of institutions, the prime minister struck at the time of his own choosing without so much as an inkling that this would be the last time he would be in a position to exercise his freedom of choice. As Musharraf's plane approached Pakistani airspace, the pilot was told to divert the flight, even if it were to a nearby Indian airport, because the fired COAS would not be allowed to land at Karachi. A civilian government-backed coup had been staged against the army chief, but without taking the army high command on board. While Gen. Ziauddin Butt was being crowned as the new COAS, in Islamabad, a counter-coup was already under way, with Musharraf's loyal deputies having swung to action within minutes of PTV broadcasting the news of his sacking and the appointment of a new army chief.

The *Herald* thus logs the day's hectic events blow by blow:

**10 a.m.:** Prime Minister Nawaz Sharif leaves for Shujaabad [near Multan] accompanied by his son Hussain Nawaz, speechwriters including Nazir Naji, Minister Javed Hashmi, PTV chairman Pervez Rashid and HBFC chairman and former press secretary to the prime minister, Siddiqul Farooq. The media team and other people are dropped from the entourage at the last minute. The people with the PM reportedly finalize a draft for the speech to be given by Sharif after sacking General Pervez Musharraf.

**2 p.m.:** The prime minister returns to his official residence. The meeting regarding the sacking of General Pervez Musharraf commences.

**3:30 p.m.:** ISI chief, Lieutenant General Khawaja Ziauddin Butt, meets the prime minister at his residence.

**3:40 p.m.:** Nawaz Sharif appoints General Ziauddin as the new chief of army staff.

**4:00 p.m.:** The PTV news controller receives a telephone call from PTV chairman Pervez Rashid to make arrangements for a special bulletin. The chairman, however, does not reveal the contents of this bulletin.

**4:45 p.m.:** The news controller receives a fax from Pervez Rashid containing the announcement that Nawaz Sharif has sacked General Pervez Musharraf. The news controller hands the fax to the Kashmiri newscaster.

**4:48 p.m.:** A tellip runs on the PTV screen saying that Chief of Army Staff Pervez Musharraf has been retired by the prime minister. This is followed by a special bulletin announcing that Prime Minister Nawaz Sharif has retired General Musharraf as chief of army staff, and that Lieutenant General Ziauddin has been made the new army chief as well as been promoted to the rank of general by the PM.

**5:05 p.m.:** Army movement begins.

**5:30 p.m.:** The news bulletin is repeated, in which Nawaz Sharif is shown sitting with Lieutenant General Ziauddin at the Prime Minister House.

**5:45 p.m.:** Major Nisar of the Azad Kashmir Regiment, along with fifteen jawans, forcibly makes his way inside the PTV station. The major enters the control room and orders the PTV staff to not include the news of General Musharraf's sacking in the regular English bulletin at 6:00 p.m.

**6:00 p.m.:** The English news bulletin begins and carries no mention of General Musharraf's sacking in the headlines.

The army takes over Shalimar Television Network (STN) and the news bulletin on PTV World is disrupted abruptly.

**6:05 p.m.:** Corps Commander Rawalpindi, General Mehmood Ahmed, along with Brigade 111 troops, leaves for the Prime Minister House.

**6:10 p.m.:** Military secretary to the prime minister, Brigadier Javed Malik, accompanied by men from the Punjab Elite Force heads towards the PTV station from the Prime Minister House.

**6:15 p.m.:** PTV chairman, Pervez Rashid, and the prime minister's security officer, Pervez Rathore, enter the control room and order Major Nisar to leave immediately. Major Nisar declines. In the meantime, Brigadier Javed Malik, military secretary to the PM, rushes in and orders Major Nisar to disarm. To defuse the situation, Major Nisar and his jawans throw down their weapons. They are then locked in a room. The Punjab Elite Force jawans are ordered to guard the entrance of the PTV station and not allow anyone to enter the building.

**6:20 p.m.:** Pervez Rashid enters the newsroom and hands a piece of paper to the newscaster. At the end of the English bulletin, after the weather report, newscaster Shaista Zaid reads out the news of Pervez Musharraf's 'retirement' by Nawaz Sharif.

**6:30 p.m.:** Senator Safdar Abbasi of the PPP calls the party media office, informing that the airports have been taken over by the army and all flights are cancelled. Meanwhile, troops led by Lieutenant General Mehmood Ahmed enter the Prime Minister House and Prime Minister Nawaz Sharif, his brother the Punjab Chief Minister Shahbaz Sharif and

Lieutenant General Ziauddin are taken into custody. After a few minutes, they are taken to Chaklala, a cantonment area near Rawalpindi. Sharif's son, Hussain Nawaz, his speechwriter Nazir Naji, and the staff of the PM House are also detained.

**6:40 p.m.:** A major of the Punjab Regiment, along with five armed soldiers, arrives at the PTV station. They approach the main gate and ask the Elite Force jawans to let them through, but the jawans refuse. The major leaves.

**7:05 p.m.:** The major returns with an army truck loaded with soldiers. Once again, he asks the Elite Force men to let the troops enter the building, but the men do not open the gate. The major orders the troops to climb over the main gate. The Elite Force men surrender their weapons within minutes and the troops enter the building.

**7:15 p.m.:** PTV transmission is suspended.

**7:30 p.m.:** A massive crowd, including several journalists, gathers in front of the PTV station. The troops deployed at the gate refuse to answer the queries of the media men.

**7:47 p.m.:** General Musharraf lands at Karachi airport.

**8:00 p.m.:** The army completes takeover of all airports, PTV stations, radio stations, telephone exchanges and residences of the federal ministers. No one is allowed to enter the ministers' colony. Meanwhile, hundreds of people throng Constitution Avenue and the PTV building. Most of the people are chanting slogans welcoming the army. The telephone lines to the Prime Minister House, Presidency, ministers' colony, their private residences and those of important government functionaries are cut.

**8:15 p.m.:** People gather in front of the Prime Minister House, but troops do not permit anyone to come near the gate. A photographer of a local daily is manhandled by a soldier for taking pictures of the troops. He is taken inside. Rumours start to spread like wildfire, but no one is available to confirm them.

**10:15 p.m.:** PTV transmission is resumed. A tellip is running on the screen saying that the government of Nawaz Sharif has been dismissed, and that the chief of army staff and chairman of the Joint Chiefs of Staff Committee, General Pervez Musharraf, will address the nation shortly.

**13 October, 2:50 a.m.:** General Pervez Musharraf addresses the nation and announces the dismissal of the Nawaz Sharif government and the establishment of military rule in the country.

**3:40 a.m.:** The PTV Islamabad staff are allowed to leave the building. [Mubashir Zaidi]

The events surrounding the takeover of the PTV building in Islamabad and the high drama unfolding there were corroborated by the gatekeeper on duty, Shaukat Ali, an ex-serviceman hailing from a village near Rawalpindi. Now in his mid-fifties, he fits the typical profile of most assigned such jobs in Pakistan. Ali recalls:

It was around late afternoon, the pre-dusk prayer time, when we heard the news as it travelled through the station, that Gen. Ziauddin was being made the next army chief. Soon, a vanload of army men arrived at the station. One of them stepped out and introduced himself. 'Salam Aleikum, I am Major Nisar,' he said. I returned the greeting. He requested me to let him and his people in. I called my security officer Mr Mohammed Ali on the intercom and asked for permission for them to enter the building. They were allowed in. The next I heard was that Major Nisar had taken control of the broadcasting floor and ordered that the news of Gen. Ziauddin's appointment as the army chief was not to be repeated in the next hourly news bulletin. He also deployed the few people he had brought with him elsewhere in the building, in the technical area, at the gate, at the entrance, etc. By this time we knew there was some commotion brewing. PTV chairman Pervez Rashid and Managing Director Mirza Yusuf Beg had also arrived on the scene.

Soon thereafter, Brigadier Javed Malik came in with his Punjab Elite Force, armed with Kalashnikovs and quite a bit of police reinforcement. They were there at the behest of the prime minister. Brigadier Malik and Major Nisar had an exchange of hot words; so much so that they pointed their guns at each other. But the brigadier had a bigger and better armed force to back him, so he succeeded in disarming Major Nisar and his few men who were present there in army uniform. The latter were promptly locked up in a room. The brigadier also deployed some of his men at the gate. By now we knew the commotion was big.

Then, suddenly I saw the Chairman [PTV] Pervez Rashid walking up to me at the gate. He told me that the brigadier's men deployed there would decide who comes in and who goes out. Then I panicked. I asked my security officer what to do. I didn't want to be caught in a crossfire; I had children and responsibilities to fulfil, you know. My officer said there was nothing he could do under the circumstances; that I would have to fend for myself as best I could. Just then came the brigadier to me at the gate; I knew it was very serious, whatever it was, so I came to my feet and saluted him. The chairman was right behind him. The brigadier pulled up his pistol and waved it straight in my face. 'Listen to me, you!' he yelled. 'You have to obey my men around here. You open the gate only when they say, got it?' I nodded hysterically. Soon after that he went away in a vehicle with the surrendered arms his men had taken from Major Nisar's men.

By then [a] flood of journalists had gathered at the gate, out of nowhere; among them were the regular intelligence people in their civvies, you could tell. They insisted I open the gate. Meanwhile, an army lieutenant also stepped forward and asked me to open the gate. I kept mum. He turned away. I panicked and called my security officer again. I said there was big commotion out here; what to do? I've just refused entry to an army chap; he's bound to come back with his people. My officer told me again I was on my own, and to do what I felt fit. Then I saw Captain [or Major] Safdar pass by the gate with some of his men in a vehicle. I recognized him because he's from Chakri, near my village, and the nephew of the former army chief, Asif Nawaz Janjua. He was stopped from proceeding any further by an intelligence colonel who told him that armymen were being held hostage inside the TV station while he went about his business. Captain Safdar took a swift about-turn and screeched his jeep's brakes right outside the gate. I knew then that I had to save my backside. He ordered loudly, 'Open the gate. I say open it, now!' I didn't know what to say but managed to murmur that I didn't have the key. He yelled, 'Up' and the men in khaki began climbing up the gate instantly. They were about ten or eleven in all. Just then one of the Elite Force men fired in the air. The captain and his men were furious. They made straight for the force's men, Nawaz Sharif's loyalists. Within no time they beat them up black and blue with their rifle butts.

I didn't want to be caught in the mêlée that ensued, so I ran from my post at the gate to hide behind a tree. From there I saw the handful of Captain Safdar's men assume charge of the building. They dragged the police and the Elite Force men out one after the other, disarmed them and then locked them all up. This happened within minutes. They cut off the phone lines, pulled out the plug of the TV transmission, and even locked up the chairman and the MD. One of Nawaz Sharif's key men present there, and who was seen giving orders earlier, ran and hid under a table. Captain Safdar dragged him out and beat him up badly.

Then the captain came to the gate. Here there still stood a police constable. The captain asked him, 'What are you doing here?' The cop said he was on duty. 'You're dismissed. Go!' he ordered. The guy pleaded that the gate be opened. 'Go as you came,' the captain yelled, and then ordered his men to beat up the cop until he climbed up the gate and was out of the building. This was done ruthlessly; the constable cried for mercy as he struggled to climb up the steel gate.

Then, the gate was somehow opened, the people outside made way, and truckload upon truckload of troops started to roll into the station. It was way past eight o'clock in the evening by then. The troops took up positions inside and outside the building. They were soon in complete control. No one was allowed to come in or leave until way past three in the morning when Gen. Musharraf made his speech to the nation on national TV. That was done from Karachi, I believe.

The troops stayed in the building for a good many weeks thereafter. Later, one of the army officers summoned me and asked me where I had been at the time of the commotion. I explained that I was hiding behind a tree to avoid taking sides, having to obey one party against the directives of the other. He said I had done the wise thing.

So, left largely incommunicado aboard his plane to Karachi from Colombo on the afternoon of 12 October 1999, Gen. Musharraf did not know in great detail how his loyal colleagues had foiled

Nawaz Sharif's attempt at staging what the general called a 'coup' against him. Of the 'counter-coup' he says his men in khaki mounted to keep him as their army chief, he knew even less, as the dramatic events unfolded on the ground while his plane, gliding at critically low fuel levels, nearly crashed prior to landing.

Had the crash taken place, it would have in all probability been declared an accident, with or without Sharif being brought to a trial by the army. That it did not gave Pakistan its first 'accidental' dictator for the next eight years.

# 3

## The Game Plan

After taking charge as the leader of the 12 October 1999 coup, Gen Musharraf addressed the nation on 17 October, outlining in some detail his plans for the future. He promised a 'true' democracy as opposed to the one he had just abolished. The state of the economy and national disunity remained the mainstay of his lengthy address, like those of all his military predecessors who had enforced martial law in the past. They all began their speeches with the ubiquitous '*Mere aziz hamwatano ...*' (My dear countrymen), before informing them that they had suspended the constitution and fundamental rights, imposed emergency rule and censorship, deployed troops at all 'sensitive' government buildings and installations, sealed airports and the border crossings to prevent those who had looted national wealth from escaping abroad—all, of course, in the national interest. Then they would indulge in a long tirade against the ruler they had just deposed and paint a very bleak picture of the country just before they had risen to the occasion as soldiers who were duty bound to answer the call of the nation and defend it from any threat, internal or external.

Pakistanis had heard it all, in 1958 from Gen. Ayub Khan, in 1969 from Gen. Yahya Khan, in 1971 from the first civilian chief martial law administrator, Zulfikar Ali Bhutto, and then from Gen. Ziaul Haq in 1977. After Zia's plane crash in 1988, the people also heard democratically elected presidents, Ghulam Ishaq Khan (twice) and Farooq Ahmed Khan Leghari, make similar speeches when they, armed with their constitutional powers under Article 58(2)b (a reminder of Gen. Zia's tinkering with the constitution), dismissed the first and the second Benazir Bhutto governments and the first Nawaz Sharif government. Though martial law was not imposed by the indirectly elected presidents after they summarily dismissed directly elected governments as there was no necessity to suspend the constitution which permitted them to do so legally.

Musharraf also seemed to have been reading from the same script, meant for a general staging a coup and not a civilian president, with minor changes thrown in for the sake of novelty. For instance, he said, his takeover was leading to no imposition of martial law (there was in effect no need for it because of the absence of any tangible pro-Nawaz Sharif sentiment in the country at the time and hence no threat to public law and order; in Lahore, Sharif's own home town, people actually greeted his overthrow by distributing sweets). Musharraf decreed that only parts of the constitution were to be held in abeyance until further orders. Then he went on to present the gloomy picture of the country and a charge sheet of Sharif's political and financial wrongdoings in graphic detail, which again more or less mirrored the public sentiment at the time.

This was Pakistanis' first brush with a general in eleven long years at a time when no one believed any longer that a military coup could still be a possibility. The world had changed: Nelson Mandela's struggle for democratic self-rule had brought an end to the apartheid regime in South Africa, the Israelis had begun talking to Arafat, the British Commonwealth had made democracy one of the key qualifying requirements for all its member states, and the United Nations had set the New Millennium development goals, among which democracy was a defining feature, for all further human development. Here therefore we were on the eve of the millennium, with a self-appointed head of state who had just thrown out an elected, howsoever ineffective, government which had failed to live up to the people's expectations.

Though Musharraf later became known for candidly sharing his opinion, including on controversial issues, back then he knew that the people he planned to lead did not know that very deeply ingrained personality trait of his. This was no time for flamboyance; that could await other occasions. The nation he addressed that day also needed collective self-reassurance. Consequently, the general indulged in little extempore pronouncements for which he became famous in the months and years that followed. He stuck to the written text (as archived by BBC Online), very well aware of the occasion that had necessitated that speech, as fate (and Nawaz Sharif) would have it:

> Today we have reached a stage where our economy has crumbled, our credibility is lost, state institutions lie demolished. Inter-provincial disharmony has caused fissures in the federation of Pakistan and people are at each other's throats. We have lost our honour, dignity and respect ... Is this the way to enter the new millennium? ... But I am an optimist.

He then went on to explain the circumstances that forced him to take action:

> I took over in extremely unusual circumstances not of my own making. It is unbelievable and indeed unfortunate that a few at the helm of affairs in the last government were intriguing to destroy the last institution of stability in Pakistan by creating dissension in the ranks of the armed forces ...

This indeed was a rare admission coming from the army chief about possible infighting that might have resulted from Sharif's rash decision to anoint Gen. Ziauddin Butt, a fellow Kashmiri long settled in Punjab like the Sharif family itself, as the army chief after summarily dismissing the existing chief in absentia without due process. The PM's dismissal order's notification had not been issued when the pro-Musharraf army high command struck back. The army chief's dismissal thus never became an official executive order under the law, as Musharraf also argues in his memoirs. This argument, however, came from someone who would place the constitution in abeyance to assume power and hold it for eight years; there was no way he could do so lawfully.

However, having thus made a case for Sharif's overthrow, he assured the people that he had not taken over of his own free will, but had been obliged to do so under the very extraordinary circumstances resulting from a prime minister's rash decision to fire him in absentia. 'What if my plane running out of fuel had crashed and so many more innocent people [had] died with me?' he asked. This again went down rather well with the people; no coup leader in the past had taken such pains to explain his action citing such irrefutable circumstantial evidence in his support.

The general then moved on to reveal his game plan, calling the military coup not an extended martial law but 'only another path towards democracy' (the speechwriter must be given full marks, but knowing Musharraf in subsequent years he probably put those words in his own mouth). Then he trotted out the customary assurance given by his predecessors: 'The armed forces have no intention to stay in charge any longer than is absolutely necessary to pave the way for true democracy to flourish in Pakistan.'

Though this was widely hailed by a media still confused as to which side of the fence it stood at the time, that is, democracy versus military rule, there was some, guarded, criticism at least in theory without directing it at the person of the army chief. In the same speech, Musharraf went out of his way, as judged against those of his predecessors, to placate the media; but in reality he also gave the media what it had never even dreamt of getting from a coup leader: 'I have great regard and respect for the media. I trust it to play a positive and constructive role. I am

a firm believer in freedom of the press and I am even considering
to liberalize the policy on the establishment of private television
and radio channels ...'

This was definitely one promise that saw prompt and complete
fulfilment. Within months of the army takeover, independent
parties interested in opening up TV and radio channels were
encouraged to apply for broadcasting licences. The regime was
so liberalized that within a span of only a few years, a revolution
of sorts took place in the electronic media sector. Today there are
some hundred TV channels, many broadcasting news and views
live or even outsourcing current affairs programming, including
hourly news bulletins in Urdu from Western media organizations
as part of their daily transmissions.

'There would have been little of this allowed under either
Nawaz Sharif's or Benazir Bhutto's democratic governments.
Neither had the tolerance of criticism that could match Gen.
Musharraf's,' says an Islamabad-based editor of a national
daily, who had had the chance to interview the two leaders
on several occasions. Other political observers in similar key
capacities at their respective institutions agree, notwithstanding
the crackdown on the media in the wake of the six-week
emergency rule that Musharraf imposed at the tail end of his stint
in power in November 2007. However, as soon as the emergency
was lifted, the media bounced back, rather boomeranged,
on the general with a vengeance until his resignation the
following August.

This was unprecedented in a country where editors under
previous military regimes had to send the actual pasted copies of
newspapers to the authorities for clearance before being sent to
be printed. It was also unprecedented in a country where elected
prime ministers had gone all out to gag the press, threatened and
closed down publications critical of them; they even had editors
picked up by intelligence agencies, tortured, and held for days
without due process. Both Zulfikar Ali Bhutto, arguably the
father of populism and democracy in Pakistan as it exists today,

and Nawaz Sharif, were guilty of such practices. Sharif had Najam Sethi, the then editor of the English-language weekly *The Friday Times*, picked up and held by army intelligence personnel without due process in 1999. Musharraf in his memoirs says he had instructed his men to hold the editor in protective custody and not to hand him over to the prime minister's men; later, the general says, he told the prime minister that the editor would have to be freed because they couldn't hold him without due process. Sharif had also tormented the country's media giant, the Jang Group, threatening its owners with the closure of their printing press if their publications did not fall in line and ceased all criticism of his policies. Neither Sharif nor Zulfikar Ali Bhutto before him had allowed the judiciary any independence; Sharif's men, including his party MPs, had stormed the Supreme Court and nearly manhandled the then chief justice Sajjad Ali Shah, who was finally impeached by fellow judges acting at the behest of the prime minister, and duly sanctioned by Sharif's loyalist president, Rafiq Tarar. The judiciary was kept in check by both Bhutto and Sharif in order to plug the possibility of the wronged parties going to court against their respective governments. Musharraf's belated action against some sixty higher court judges and Chief Justice Iftikhar Chaudhry after he imposed emergency rule in November 2003 was not unprecedented in the judiciary's history in Pakistan. It was only the wholesale sacking of so many judges who refused to take a fresh oath under a provisional constitution order that was unparalleled.

Meanwhile, immediate steps taken in the aftermath of the Musharraf-led coup in October 1999 had a ring of extraordinary caution on the part of the army. This clearly spelt a break from the handling of affairs by past military dictators. The composition of the new government was an apt example of Gen. Musharraf insisting on doing things his own way. Nawaz Sharif's overly loyalist and lame-duck president, Rafiq Tarar, was retained by the general to avoid making changes in the existing system just for the sake of change and thereby adding to the existing

political instability. In fact, the general in his 17 October 1999
speech thanked the president, saying he had 'very kindly agreed
to stay [on]'. A National Security Council headed by Musharraf
as the chief executive was formed, with the air and navy chiefs
as key members. The six-member council was also to have 'a
specialist each in legal, finance, foreign policy and national
affairs'. Furthermore, it was promised that 'a think tank of
experts shall be formed as adjunct to the National Security
Council to provide institutional advice and input', and finally
'a cabinet of ministers who will work under the guidance of the
National Security Council'.

Having thus explained the composition of his government,
Musharraf went on to list his seven policy objectives:

1.  To rebuild national confidence and morale,
2.  To strengthen the federation, remove inter-provincial
    disharmony and restore national cohesion,
3.  To revive the economy and restore investor confidence,
4.  To ensure law and order and provision of speedy justice,
5.  To depoliticize state institutions,
6.  To devolve power to the grass-roots level, and
7.  To ensure accountability.

In the years that followed it would be largely on the basis of
these promises that an empowered media and the people, whose
confidence in Pakistan's own media was restored, would hold
Musharraf accountable. The overall consensus today seems to
be that his failures dwarfed his successes, though he did try to
break new ground in certain policy areas and forced a rethink.
For instance, it was for the first time that a leader, elected or
unelected, had so openly spoken of inter-provincial disharmony
and lack of national cohesion. Leaders before him, even Zulfikar
Ali Bhutto, after the break up of the country in 1971, would
not phrase in such a frank lexicon the problems that fanned
disharmony among ethnically drawn provinces. By contrast,

here was a military leader who was not only acknowledging the existence of the issue but also promising to do something about it. The subject had remained taboo throughout the short political history of Pakistan, with successive governments being in a state of denial. A lack of national cohesion plagued the state right from its inception, with bad blood among the provinces manifesting itself as one of the major symptoms of the disease, but no effort was made to own the diagnosis, leave aside doing something about it. Consequently, the problem was only compounded with the passage of time.

Since 1947 a strong and all-powerful central government has coerced the provinces into surrendering their resources to it. The national pool thus created has not been equitably distributed, with Punjab, the most populous and the best developed of the provinces, claiming the lion's share. Sindh, the Frontier and Balochistan have had to live with much heartburn despite the fact that Sindh, as the country's financial hub and home to the key port city of Karachi, contributes roughly 70 per cent of the total revenue to the national exchequer; the Frontier province provides a major share of hydroelectric power to the national grid and Balochistan supplies the bulk of its immense wealth of natural resources, including minerals and natural gas, to the rest of the country. Punjab's claim to being the hand that feeds by virtue of its agricultural produce has receded in the past as the country has had to import even the basic, staple foodgrains and vegetables for its growing needs as population growth outpaces the supply of essential commodities. On the other hand, consumption patterns in Punjab are much higher as it has been rapidly developing its industrial sector. Since the last years of the Zia regime, a trend of flight of capital from Karachi to Punjab and the movement of multinational companies' head offices also began after the industrial-cum-port city plunged into political chaos. Benazir Bhutto's and Nawaz Sharif's regimes made little effort to restore peace or stability to the volatile city, often dubbed as mini-Pakistan because it attracts skilled and unskilled labourers, blue- and white-collar workers alike from across the country, thanks to its ever-expanding commercial potential despite its many problems, and a more rapidly growing job market.

The two mainstream political parties today, the People's Party and the Nawaz-led Muslim League, however, made no effort to give Karachi a sense of belonging. It was because the presence of their opponent, the locally popular Muttahida Qaumi Movement (MQM: United National Movement)—which derives its appeal from the city's long-settled middle class comprising urban, post-Independence settlers from India forming the single largest ethnic group among its sixteen million inhabitants—would not allow them the opportunity of making any meaningful political inroads that could translate into a vote bank for them. Thus, neither Bhutto nor Sharif could hope to derive any immediate political mileage out of setting things right in Karachi; both lacked the vision that could have allowed them to invest in the future, howsoever near or distant. While in power, both Bhutto and Sharif sought only to superficially and expeditiously work with the MQM but found the party more demanding than they had bargained for. Subsequently, both launched clean-up operations against the MQM workers in Karachi. The political alienation from the national mainstream of cosmopolitan Karachi, which is home to nearly 10 per cent of the multi-ethnic total population of Pakistan, has considerably added to inter-provincial disharmony. Islamabad's entrenched suspicion of the MQM, of Sindhi, Baloch and Pashtun nationalist parties has undergone little change over the years. The rural Sindh-based People's Party governments of the Bhuttos or those of the military dictators from Punjab or the Frontier have been no exception to the rule of singling out Karachi. It was Ayub Khan's government in the 1960s that shifted the capital from Karachi to the wilderness close to the army headquarters in the garrison town of Rawalpindi that is today Islamabad. Ayub's dislike of Karachi and his military action against dissidents in the city were unmatched. Karachi residents had in the 1960s thrown their weight behind Fatima Jinnah, the sister of Mohammed Ali Jinnah, and the military dictator's fiercest opponent. Thus, Karachi had to be punished. The city's alienation from the political mainstream goes back nearly four decades.

Perhaps it was Musharraf's Karachi background that helped him realize the gravity of the problem and the need to address it rather than further denying and thereby compounding the issue (lack of national cohesion and provincial disharmony). In an attempt to placate Karachi, he inducted in his core team qualified advisers and aides from the city. The way forward was to alleviate the sense of alienation that the people of Karachi in particular felt as a result of the political discrimination that they had been subjected to. This could only be done by talking to the MQM, which, of all the country's political forces, least carried the baggage of having supported either Nawaz Sharif or Benazir Bhutto. In 1999, both the leaders were the army establishment's bêtes noires. As for its links with the army, the MQM was believed to have been created by Gen. Ziaul Haq's intelligence agencies in the 1980s, originally as the Mohajir Qaumi Movement (post-1947 Indian Immigrants' National Movement). The party assumed the new, more inclusive name of 'United' National Movement because it had to focus on a city as its power base where people of Indian immigrant origins were on their way to becoming a minority in the years ahead due to the high influx of new immigrant workers from the rest of Pakistan. Nawaz Sharif in the early 1990s, after falling out with the MQM led by its exiled leader Altaf Husain, helped keep the original party alive under its 'Mohajir' nomenclature by sheltering its dissidents in Punjab. Originally, back in the 1980s, by helping to create the MQM, Gen. Ziaul Haq sought to build on the wedge that existed between a largely non-Sindhi-speaking urban Sindh and a predominantly Sindhi-speaking rural Sindh. The latter was and is a slave to the magic that the word 'Bhutto' invokes, the former regards it as anathema, because it evokes, among other things, bad memories. The MQM paid back its de-facto 'co-founder' Gen. Ziaul Haq posthumously by holding mammoth roadside prayer meetings in Karachi for weeks after Zia was killed in a plane crash in 1988. At the time, the MQM's real rival, the People's Party under Benazir Bhutto's leadership, looked all set to win and it did win the post-Zia 1988 election.

In the aftermath of the 1999 coup a decade later, Musharraf as an army ruler did eventually manage to reach out to and win back the confidence and the support of the MQM leadership for his rule. From the army establishment's point of view, he was dealing with a party that was of the army's own creation. Even if this was only partially true now under an all-new, evolved MQM, there was no harm seen in re-embracing an old friend while one was in need; from the MQM's perspective, Musharraf was acceptable to the party leadership for the same reason and also perhaps because he himself came from the same immigrant background. The party trusted him because he understood at first hand the frustrations inherent in sustaining the MQM's popularity in Karachi. Musharraf thus succeeded in restoring some semblance of order in the very important, if politically fragmented, city that also happened to be the economic nerve centre of the country. The immediate dividend of the change in Islamabad's mindset towards Karachi was the arrest of the flight of capital and multinational businesses from Karachi to Punjab or Islamabad.

However, before Musharraf transferred any power to the MQM, he had to ensure that the party would support him in the bigger game ahead: the national election. While a deal was being worked out, the MQM was prevailed upon or decided on its own (less likely) not to take part in the planned local government elections for the Karachi city government in 2001. The right-wing, clerical Jamaat-i-Islami (JI) which could claim a sizeable and thus credible vote bank in Karachi second only to the MQM, came to power, even though officially the local government elections were held on a non-party basis to maintain the façade that the Musharraf regime favoured no one political party over another. Musharraf had also aligned the JI, a protégé of Ziaul Haq's military regime, for forming another political alliance of religio-political parties representing various Muslim sects to fill the vacuum created by Bhutto's and Sharif's mainstream parties that he wished to restrict from capturing the popular vote.

As for Karachi, the devolution plan promised and put in place by Musharraf also gave the city, among other metropolises from the rest of the three provinces, a popularly elected city government ahead of the 2002 national election—an upgrade from an elected municipal services management system to more independently exercisable managerial powers, including policy-making, use of the (then) directly devolved financial resources, and the autonomy to use them under the general's Devolution of Power Plan. Here, for the first time, was a military ruler trying to share and devolve power to the people at the grass roots. This was something that the democratically elected governments before Musharraf had not only felt no need to do, but had actively resisted. They saw any devolution of power to a lower rung of governance as erosion of their own absolute power.

In retrospect, however, while Karachi's grievances were partially addressed under the devolution plan, Balochistan and the Frontier, the former much more than the latter, continued to suffer from neglect under the military regime and subsequently under the quasi-democratic order which Musharraf put in place after the 2002 national election. The establishment of cantonments in Balochistan whereby the army appropriated huge chunks of land became the rallying cry for Baloch nationalists. The PML-Q-led government under Musharraf tried to reach out to Baloch leaders for a settlement by offering incentives to the Baloch, but the army never allowed the plan to be implemented. A full-blown insurgency in Balochistan by secular nationalists ensued, and brute force was used to suppress it, with the nationalist leadership moving underground or going into exile.

Veteran Baloch leader, the former governor and chief minister of the province, Nawab Akbar Khan Bugti, who had a history of 'on again', 'off again' relations with Islamabad, was pursued into his mountain hideout and killed. The killing further fanned the sentiment of alienation among Baloch tribes. The nationalist parties boycotted the February 2007 polls, and similarly, the radical Islamists in the Frontier holding sway over large swathes of land, too, are part of the consequences of Musharraf's failure to take the two most underdeveloped provinces along on his reform agenda.

Back in October 1999, the general's priority number three, i.e., the revival of the economy and restoration of investor confidence would have to wait for a post-9/11 (2001) world in which some economic relief finally began coming to Pakistan. Restoring law and order, the provision of speedy justice, depoliticization of state institutions, and ensuring the accountability of corrupt politicians and bureaucrats remained just promises. While law and order was arguably at its lowest throughout Musharraf's tenure in power, his arm-twisting and finally the wholesale sacking of the senior judiciary in November 2007 did not help the cause of providing speedy justice. Ensuring the accountability of corrupt public office holders was a non-starter from the outset; it was at best applied selectively to political opponents in the initial years, but even then many were taken off the hook after their loyalties were bought, and then the accountability regime was allowed to die a slow death. Musharraf's post-2002 election cabinet included ministers and even chief ministers who were bank defaulters but whose loans were written off, and even pending criminal cases were withdrawn against them in return for their defection from Bhutto's and Sharif's parties. Finally, the Bhutto–Zardari and the MQM-specific National Reconciliation Ordinance (NRO) of 2007 proved the proverbial last nail in the coffin of the so-called National Accountability Bureau and its mandate to arrest the corrupt and recover looted public money from them. That said, a moral ground could still be found for the NRO and its beneficiaries: Zardari had spent a total of some eleven years behind bars facing criminal and corruption charges, and notwithstanding the state's determination to prove him guilty, he was not convicted on even one of the many charges levelled against him.

# 4

## Two Long Years in the Wilderness

The period prior to 11 September 2001 constituted Musharraf's time in international diplomatic wilderness and in the throes of a growing political alienation at home. Initial public sentiment of relief at Nawaz Sharif being catapulted from absolute power began to die down as the general's accountability regime began losing credibility. The Commonwealth ceased Pakistan's membership following the coup, the Saudis as the country's traditional 'friends in need' were wary of Musharraf as he looked set to punish their erstwhile friend Nawaz Sharif. Demands from civil society and the media for a road map to democracy became more vocal as a sense of déjà vu began to spread about the general's plan, as with his predecessors who had seized power by extra-constitutional means, to stay on for the long haul.

From the very outset, Musharraf made little secret of his abhorrence of Pakistan's two largest parties led by Benazir Bhutto and Nawaz Sharif. While his extreme enmity with the latter was understandable, his equally forceful attempts at alienating, if not actively marginalizing, Bhutto's People's Party, were understood only by a few—those who stood to gain in the just resuscitated PML-Q, the king's party, from the absence of the two popular parties from the political mainstream. Then there were other partners, if rivals, waiting to jump on to the Musharraf bandwagon, the Muttahida Qaumi Movement (MQM) and the religious right. Both had a history of being favourites with the establishment from time to time and as required.

Musharraf's wholehearted embrace of the MQM's leader in exile, Altaf Hussain, who was a proclaimed offender and an absconder from law, and of the religious right, while at the same time revelling in being photographed with his pet dogs (an affront to Muslim sensibilities) were also factors that led to a growing suspicion of him among the masses as a leader with a clear vision for his nation. To many observers this also meant instituting a divisive, as opposed to inclusive, politics by a leader who was accountable only to himself.

On the regional and international fronts, there was little solace to be drawn from battered relations with India in the aftermath of the Kargil crisis, which was more of Musharraf's own making rather than the political government's. Relations with Iran were strained given Pakistan's unqualified backing of the Taliban regime in Afghanistan; even those with China were arguably at a low after Pakistan's failure to check infiltration by militant Islamist missionaries into the neighbouring Muslim-majority Chinese province of Xing Kiang. A Taliban-led, isolated and internationally pariah Afghanistan was the only country with which the military-led regime enjoyed good rapport; and this to the considerable chagrin of the US. The Clinton administration had tied the easing of any of the economic sanctions imposed on Pakistan in the aftermath of the May 1998 nuclear tests to Pakistan's exertion of pressure on the Taliban to hand over Osama bin Laden and to the Taliban's cessation of support to various Muslim terrorist groups, including those active in the former Central Asian Soviet republics and in Chechnya. The US embassy bombings in August 1998 in Kenya and Tanzania were also traced back to bin Laden's Al Qaeda network operating out of Afghanistan. Musharraf, like his predecessor, General Jehangir Karamat, made little effort to distance himself from the Taliban.

Strobe Talbott, the then US deputy secretary of state for South Asia and the man selected by Clinton to engage with India vis-à-vis its emerging nuclear regime in South Asia, details, in his

book *Engaging India: Diplomacy, Democracy and the Bomb*, the
hurdles that the US felt lay between a military-led Pakistan and
Washington. Though Nawaz Sharif was the prime minister at the
time, the Americans found his helplessness, especially during the
Kargil episode, in reining in his army chief from implementing
his own agenda quite shocking and unnerving. On his famous
panic-propelled trip to Washington on 4 July 1999, Sharif had
told Clinton and his aides that he would not feel safe in his
own country should he fall foul of his army chief, Musharraf.
As Sharif begged Clinton to intervene to defuse the Kargil crisis
with India, he even expressed his possible inability to return to
Pakistan and survive as prime minister should Clinton refuse to
help him. The Clinton administration squarely put the blame for
the Kargil crisis on the Pakistani army, and helped only after
Sharif reluctantly agreed to order an unconditional withdrawal
of troops from Kargil—even if that meant humiliation for his
army; and perhaps particularly for its chief, General Musharraf,
whose brainchild the operation was.

Then in October, writes Talbott:

> Nawaz Sharif committed his final blunder as the Prime
> Minister of Pakistan: he provided a pretext for the military
> coup that he so feared—and that Jaswant [Singh] had
> predicted ... [Sharif] was charged with attempted murder
> on the grounds that the plane [carrying Musharraf] could
> have crashed and sentenced to death. Clinton instructed the
> [US] National Security Council staff to marshal whatever
> influence the US government had to persuade Musharraf
> to commute [Sharif's] sentence ... (p. 176)

Talbott goes on to sum up the kind of tense relations that
developed between Musharraf and the Clinton presidency:

> Rick Inderfurth, the then assistant secretary for South Asia,
> was the first high-ranking official from Washington in

January 2000 to make a trip to Pakistan since the military coup ... Rick took with him Michael Sheehan, a State Department official responsible for counter-terrorism, which had replaced non-proliferation as Topic A on the agenda with Pakistan. (p. 190)

Inderfurth at this point was given no clear guarantees by Musharraf that he would rein in the Taliban or stop infiltration into Kashmir, which disappointed the Americans. According to Talbott, Inderfurth told Musharraf that unless progress was made on these issues, Clinton might not include Pakistan in his forthcoming visit to South Asia in March 2000. Musharraf argued back that doing so would strengthen militancy in the region. Meanwhile, back in Washington, both the State Department and the CIA tried to dissuade Clinton from going to Islamabad, but Clinton turned down the suggestion. 'I'm not going to Pakistan for my health, for God's sake! I'm going to try to keep us in the play there—both for what happens inside that country and for getting them to cut out the bad stuff they're doing in the region, and that means Kashmir and Afghanistan [p. 192],' he argued back forcefully, and made that trip in March as he had planned it.

There couldn't have been a greater contrast between the American president's visit to New Delhi and to Islamabad. While he mingled freely in India and was shown wining and dining there, in Islamabad it was just a sneak visit for a couple of hours that took him from the airport to the presidency in a helicopter and back. No media coverage was allowed, not even pictures taken of Clinton meeting Musharraf, because that would have sent the general and the people of Pakistan a wrong signal. A recorded message by the US president was played back on TV screens in which he pledged American support to the people of Pakistan if they chose 'the path of democracy and progress instead of one of terrorism and regress'.

The Americans had ensured that Musharraf was not able to take advantage of the Clinton visit and use it as a stamp of approval for his coup. US–Pakistan relations were not easy by any stretch of the imagination. It would take Clinton's Republican successor, George W. Bush, and the 11 September 2001 attacks on the US to alter for the better that bilateral equation between the US and Pakistan. Pakistan's diplomatic isolation was never as complete as it was at the time.

The veteran Bharatiya Janata Party (BJP) leader and the former deputy prime minister of India, L.K. Advani, who is known for his right-wing, hardline approach to relations with Pakistan, writes in his autobiography, *My Country, My Life*, that Pakistan was never as badly isolated diplomatically as it was during his party's second stint in power in India, which began simultaneously with Musharraf taking over the reins in Islamabad: '... we broadened our diplomatic offensive to make the world community understand both the reality of the Kargil war and Pakistan's continued support for terrorism in India' (p. 696).

India had refused to engage Pakistan in any formal talks or dialogue since the disintegration of the Lahore Declaration (February 1999) for peaceful settlement of all outstanding issues that was signed between the two countries by prime ministers Nawaz Sharif and Atal Bihari Vajpayee. Musharraf's Kargil adventure had wholly destroyed for months any trust that might have then been built between New Delhi and Islamabad. India now attached the precondition that Pakistan condemn the violence in Kashmir and halt all assistance to terrorist activities inside Indian borders—a condition based on charges that Pakistan denied.

Meanwhile, just weeks after the Clinton visit, Nawaz Sharif was found guilty in April 2000 by an anti-terrorism court of conspiring to kill the army chief. He was sentenced to life imprisonment. The following month, Musharraf got the Supreme Court of Pakistan to validate his coup of October 1999. The court gave him an unprecedented three years in which to put the country back on the road to democracy and also to review the extraordinary powers vested in him to amend the constitution in order to usher in a new representative system of governance. In December 2000, Musharraf struck an amnesty-cum-exile deal with Nawaz Sharif, with the Saudis underwriting it. The Sharifs' assets were seized, but the entire extended family was exiled to Saudi Arabia.

Thus, having comfortably settled in the saddle, Musharraf approached New Delhi via back-door diplomacy, hinting at his willingness to be flexible in order to ease tensions with India. The effort was aimed at ending Pakistan's global diplomatic isolation. On receipt of such signals from Pakistan, Lal Krishna Advani says in his autobiography that it was he who convinced Prime Minister Vajpayee to respond to the overtures for peace made by the Pakistani general who was only answerable to himself for his actions. Advani says that he then began talking to senior Pakistani diplomats through an intermediary for a thaw in India and Pakistan's strained bilateral relations since the Kargil conflict. India announced a unilateral ceasefire against the separatists in Kashmir in November 2000 on the eve of the Muslim fasting month of Ramzan; Pakistan welcomed the move. Prime Minister Atal Bihari Vajpayee then hinted at what he called his desire to turn a new leaf with Pakistan, putting the sordid Kargil episode behind. Musharraf was invited for a summit meeting with the Indian leader in Agra in July 2001, and he wholeheartedly embraced the invitation.

However, before leaving for India, he got President Rafiq Tarar to resign in June 2001. Then he declared himself the president without having to relinquish the office of army chief. The move did not win the general any approval from the world at large but India kept a low profile on the issue, declining to comment either way. New Delhi was now prepared to receive the general on his first state visit to India. The symbolism inherent in the entire affair was significant. Indian armed forces were to present a guard of honour to their arch-rival's army chief, and one who had been the architect of the Kargil war just two years earlier.

The much-hyped Agra Summit, however, came to naught as India and Pakistan failed to resolve their differences over the status of Kashmir and Pakistan's alleged support for terrorism inside Indian borders. Failing to agree even on a joint statement at the end of the three-day marathon visit to India, Musharraf in his flamboyant style left for home in a huff. At the press conference held by Indian officials, it was claimed that the two sides had agreed to keep talking to each other and that Prime Minister Vajpayee's earlier acceptance of the invitation by President Musharraf to visit Islamabad later in the year remained unaltered.

The media, both in India and Pakistan, was disappointed. Some in India had hailed the summit as a step to bringing down the 'Berlin Wall' in South Asia. In Pakistan, Musharraf's Sunday breakfast meeting with senior Indian editors, which was broadcast live and in which he held forth in great detail on his vision of a South Asia free from conflict, was the high point of the visit, but it was also the event that derailed his negotiations with the Indian leadership. Indian editors and analysts were seen and heard under full media glare comparing their less articulate leaders with a media-savvy Musharraf who clearly won their hearts and minds. In retrospect, however, a section of the Indian media did blame Musharraf for hogging the media limelight and speaking out his mind while the Indian leader remained tight-lipped on the agenda under discussion between the two leaders. 'They broke the ice, then froze,' was the *Indian Express* banner. The *Economic Times* headline lamented: 'The breakfast that broke the table.' Pakistan's *Dawn* blamed the failure of the summit on the deep-rooted mistrust between the two countries. The *Hindu* ominously wrote: '… relations may now get worse before they get better' and that's precisely what happened in the months that followed the failed Agra Summit.

For his part, Musharraf in his memoirs all too obviously blamed the then Indian home minister Lal Krishna Advani, albeit without taking any names, for the failure of the summit. Advani in his autobiography more than adequately responds to that charge, shifting the blame back on Musharraf for a failed outcome, saying it was the general's obsession with what he called a freedom struggle in Kashmir while India insisted on Pakistan owning up to and desisting from acts of cross-border terrorism. Advani goes on to add:

> Seeing, perhaps, that he would not be able to take home an Agra Declaration, Musharraf precipitated the second unhelpful development in the form of his audacious attempt to conduct the remaining part of his summit talks with India through the media. On the morning of 16 July, he turned what was meant to be an informal breakfast meeting at his hotel with about thirty-five prominent Indian journalists into a virtual hour-long press conference. Apart from arranging its telecast on Pakistan's government-run PTV, he also allowed a leading Indian channel to telecast it fully. Thus, we in the Indian delegation, had the extraordinary spectacle of watching the Pakistani President articulate his rather combative views on Kashmir and cross-border terrorism, even as he was, at that very time, holding closed door talks with the Indian Prime Minister. (p. 703)

In that interaction with senior Indian editors, broadcast live in both the countries, Musharraf had also dwelt very candidly on India's military victories and alleged support for separatists in Pakistan, including the Bengali separatist movement that led to the creation of Bangladesh in 1971. If Kargil and what was happening in Kashmir hurt the Indians, Indian offensives in Siachen and the former East Pakistan also hurt the Pakistanis, he had argued, like a schoolboy out to score a brownie point while at a rival school.

The Indian media and the viewing public were, however, much enamoured by Musharraf's openness to lay all bare, even if they disagreed with what he said. In the purely political context, and given the troubled history of India–Pakistan relations, this was brinkmanship, as opposed to statesmanship that was required of the leaders on both sides. Consequently, the trip to India achieved little besides giving an opportunity to Pakistan's first couple to avail themselves of photo-shoots at Musharraf's ancestral Neherwali Haveli in Delhi and at the Taj Mahal in Agra. The blessings that India and Pakistan needed, to move on from their differences, of the great saint at Ajmer whose shrine Musharraf wanted to visit for thanksgiving after signing the Agra Declaration, eluded them.

# 5

## Do or Die

Pakistan's diplomatic isolation ended in the wake of Gen. Musharraf's decision to assist the US in hunting down Osama bin Laden and Al Qaeda operatives for whose blood Washington bayed after the 11 September 2001 attacks. In his memoirs, Musharraf has dwelt at length on his decision to turn his back on the Taliban, arguing that he had little choice given the way the Americans had sought his commitment to fight alongside them or be ready to be 'bombed back to the stone age'. In the words of the former Pakistani foreign secretary, Shamshad Ahmed, writing in *Dawn* with the benefit of hindsight (13 May 2007):

> The Bush administration officials made it clear that they would 'not be satisfied with condolences and boilerplate offers of help from Pakistan'. The choice was between being a target or a partner. It was a moment of reckoning for Pakistan which, because of its known links with Afghanistan's Taliban regime was in the line of fire. In General Musharraf's own words, 9/11 'came as a thunderbolt ...' He was right in claiming that he had to absorb external pressure and mould domestic opinion in readjusting Pakistan's policies ... He chose, perhaps rightly, to avoid [being on] the 'wrong side' of a 'wounded' superpower, and made Pakistan a vital ally in the US-led anti-terrorism coalition ... According to Musharraf, 'Powell was quite candid' in making it clear that 'you were either

with us or against us'. He took it as a 'blatant ultimatum'
to which his spontaneous response was: 'We are with the
United States against terrorism and would fight along with
your country against it.' Musharraf took no time in pledging
the needed support and cooperation.

Former US Secretary of State Colin Powell, deposing before the
National Commission on Terrorist Attacks Upon the United
States, in Washington on 23 March 2004 had this to say:

> Two days after 9/11, Deputy Secretary [of State] Armitage
> told Pakistan's Intelligence Chief, who was in Washington
> on an official visit, exactly what we expected of his country,
> listing seven requirements. The next day I called President
> Musharraf to get his answer. [He] agreed and turned away
> from the Taliban ... President Musharraf has been a strong
> partner ever since.

Taking the nation into confidence on his decision to join the
war on terror as late as on 19 September 2001, Musharraf said
that he had pledged support to the US in three principal areas:
sharing intelligence, use of Pakistan's airspace, and provision of
logistical support. According to Shamshad Ahmed:

> ... as a follow up to Colin Powell's conversation with
> Musharraf, [the] US ambassador [in Islamabad] delivered
> to him a list of seven demands asking Pakistan inter alia
> to seal its border with Afghanistan, cut off fuel supplies
> to the Taliban, block any operations or movement of
> Al Qaeda members and provide 'blanket over-flight and
> landing rights as well as access to Pakistan's naval and
> airbases and borders ...' According to a senior US official
> [not named], Pakistan was told that 'it ain't what you say,
> it's what you do'.

This is quite credible given the level of frustration the US had with Pakistan since the American embassy bombings in East Africa in August 1998, and on the need for Islamabad to stop backing the Taliban regime, something that Strobe Talbott consistently speaks about in his book *Engaging India*. The Clinton administration was forced to make that the top item in its agenda of interaction with Musharraf, relegating American concerns over nuclear proliferation to a second level. Though Musharraf understood exactly what the Americans wanted him to do even then, he continued to play ball with them, perhaps partly because the Clinton administration did not see the need to get tougher than it felt it already was on Pakistan by having imposed crippling economic sanctions after Islamabad went nuclear, and refusing to lift these unconditionally. The Bush presidency saw little need for change in US policy towards Pakistan before 9/11; it missed no opportunity of sending Musharraf the message that he should isolate the Taliban and stop Al Qaeda operatives from exporting terrorism, as was evident from Colin Powell's lengthy briefing cited above before the US National Commission on Terrorist Attacks. Powell referred to US officials' meeting days before 9/11 with the visiting ISI chief in Washington: 'On September 5 ... we told him that Pakistan needed to take immediate, concrete, visible steps alongside the United States to choke off terrorist threats emanating from Afghanistan.' Powell also spoke of US assistant secretary of state for South Asia Christina Rocca's earlier meeting in July with Musharraf 'to emphasize that we wanted to re-engage Pakistan but that the Taliban [factor] was the single biggest issue standing between us'.

With these facts as the context, it is not difficult to understand the American posture and the tone and tenor of American officials talking to Musharraf and other high-ranking Pakistani officials immediately after 9/11. It also becomes understandable why Musharraf took no time in unconditionally pledging his support to the US. There was little ground left for Islamabad to insist on Washington providing proof of the Taliban's involvement with or backing of Al Qaeda in its terrorist designs on the West, particularly the US, the consistent argument advanced by Pakistani officials while discussing Afghanistan with the Americans. Also, Musharraf must have known that this was no time to advance the same tired argument given the Americans' clear message to him which only demanded one thing of him: do or die. He chose the former. Besides, there were dividends for him and for Pakistan in the months ahead.

By 2004, the Bush administration was all praise for Musharraf, at least in public. Privately the Americans must have kept cajoling him to do more, but the façade they maintained was one of amity and trust. Colin Powell informed the National Commission that

> Pakistan's support [was] absolutely vital to our fight against the Taliban ... [it] led to more than two-thirds of Al Qaeda's top leadership being killed or captured, most significantly 9/11 mastermind Khalid Shaikh Muhammad and key plotters Ramzi bin al-Shibh and Abu Zubaydah—all captured in Pakistan. Continuing with our strategic moves, we have put in place an entirely new relationship with Pakistan ... Some view this ... as a temporary marriage of convenience. I do not. President Bush does not ... President Bush's proposed five-year $3 billion aid package for Pakistan embodies America's abiding commitment to Pakistan.

On 13 May 2007, Shamshad Ahmed wrote in *Dawn*:

> Pakistan's post-9/11 quick policy turnaround made it a pivotal player in the US-led global war on terror, and gave it prominence in the international community that helped the military regime in its quest for legitimacy. It started receiving special attention in Washington and European capitals. In a

US effort to shore up the Musharraf government, sanctions relating to Pakistan's 1998 nuclear tests and 1999 military coup were quickly waived. In October 2001 large amounts of US aid began flowing in ... besides extending grants to Pakistan totalling a billion dollars in the three years after 9/11, the US also wrote off an equal amount in debt ... in June 2004, President Bush designated Pakistan as a major non-Nato ally ... in March 2005 [he] authorized the sale of F-16 fighter jets to Pakistan.

As for the fallout of the decision to join the war on terror on the home front, Musharraf had to face fierce opposition from nearly all quarters. The religious right and the old guard in the ISI aside, which had helped 'put together', as it were, the Taliban, and even the liberal democrats were opposed at least to the unilateral way in which the decision had been taken. Among the mainstream, popular political forces which Musharraf had pushed to the wall, Bhutto's People's Party and Sharif's Muslim League, termed it a divisive decision and one that lacked consensus and thus credibility with the people of Pakistan. It need not have been effected in the way it was but for Musharraf's one-man rule, they argued.

Radical militants, with or without links to the Al Qaeda, who were on the run in Afghanistan and Pakistan soon after the American invasion of Afghanistan, also turned their wrath on Pakistan. Musharraf was now their number 1 hate personality. He escaped two well-planned assassination attempts in December 2003, which left many bystanders dead. A third and a fourth suspected attempt on his life followed, though he escaped both by a long margin due to the improved presidential security and intelligence after the first two attacks on his life.

Musharraf emerged as daredevil from Pakistan's post-9/11 turnaround on Afghanistan, bringing in the wake of his solitary action a remarkable reversal in the country's fortunes. He had done it again after the misadventure in Kargil which, from his point of view, went foul only because of Sharif's involvement in it and his lack of political decision-making. Left to his own devices in the post-9/11 world, Musharraf went it alone, this time with success, even if only as a transitory phase in his career as a leader who never shied from leading from the front.

# 6

# Boxing India (and Democracy)

After the failure of the Agra Summit in July 2001, border skirmishes with India intensified once again in October along the Line of Control in Kashmir, the bloodiest since the Kargil conflict two years earlier. India again accused Pakistan of infiltration in the restive Muslim-majority state under its control since 1948; Musharraf vehemently denied the staple charge although he knew by now that his denial would cut little ice with the world and the US. He also, however, knew that now Pakistan was on the right side of the fence with the Americans, having offered all that Washington needed to fight Al Qaeda and the Taliban in Afghanistan. An element of brinkmanship with New Delhi now would not invite the kind of wrath from the Americans that he had had to live with since ousting Nawaz Sharif.

In December 2001 the attack on the Indian parliament by two Islamic militant groups allegedly operating out of Pakistan shattered all hopes of a dialogue for peace between the two countries, scuttling any prospect of Vajpayee's visit to Islamabad as agreed at Agra in July. The BJP-led government termed it as 'our 9/11'. India suspended overflight rights for Pakistani commercial planes, banned any trade or social exchanges with Pakistan, and ordered its troops to the western border. Pakistan retaliated with similar measures. The two countries deployed nearly a million-strong force, eyeball to eyeball, along their border. India made the following demands of Musharraf, as detailed by L.K. Advani in his autobiography:

1. Hand over to India twenty terrorists whose names along with evidence of their criminal acts against India had been supplied to the government of Pakistan.
2. Closure of facilities, training camps, arms supply, funding, and all other manner of direct and indirect assistance to terrorists.
3. Stoppage of infiltration of arms and men from Pakistan into Jammu & Kashmir and elsewhere in India.
4. A categorical and unambiguous renunciation of terrorism in all its manifestations and wherever it exists, irrespective of the cause it seeks to further. (p. 648)

This was more in the nature of a charge sheet against the Musharraf-led regime wrapped in demands. The general denied all the charges contained in the list, and went so far as to mock the so-called list of the twenty individuals India said were its most wanted and living in Pakistan. The list included the Pakistan-based Jaish-i-Muhammad and Lashkar-i-Taiba masterminds alleged to have carried out terrorist acts in India; these were also the groups and individuals—including Maulana Masood Azhar, who was exchanged for the release of the hijacked Indian Airlines plane from Kathmandu to Delhi in 1999—accused by India of planning and carrying out the assault on its parliament. The list also mentioned Indian terrorists, including figures from the Indian underworld and some Sikh separatist leaders from Indian Punjab.

In his categorical response to the demands, Musharraf said that no Pakistani national would ever be handed over to India; as for the wanted Indian nationals, he denied their presence in Pakistan. Meanwhile, the hardliner militant Masood Azhar roamed free, holding meetings and rallies across Pakistan still advocating jihad in Kashmir. When confronted by the media regarding his conduct and inaction against him, Musharraf put on a poker face and replied that the cleric was a free citizen and no charges had been brought against him in a Pakistani court of law to warrant his arrest. In January 2002 at a SAARC summit in Kathmandu, Musharraf once again pledged his country's moral and diplomatic support for what he called 'freedom fighters in Kashmir'. This and other such blatant acts were seen as open hostility on the part of the general which further infuriated the Indian leadership.

However, Indian Home Minister Advani's diplomatic offensive against the Musharraf regime, which took him to the US, also fell short of India's expectations. It failed to yield the direct pressure Advani sought to have Washington apply on Musharraf in his dealings with India. While the Bush administration sincerely sympathized with India over the outrageous attack on its parliament, it refused in so many words to condemn Musharraf as the facilitator of terrorism inside Indian borders, advising instead that New Delhi resolve the matter with Islamabad through a dialogue and using peaceful means.

During his meeting at the White House, Advani quotes Bush as having told him in private that 'his administration expected Pakistan to "abandon terror as an instrument of state policy"'.

> He [Bush] conveyed to me that he expected Gen Musharraf 'to take all necessary steps' in fighting terror. 'He [Musharraf] has done it in the case of the Taliban, and I expect him to do it in the case of India also. I have told him to take appropriate steps against extremists operating in and from Pakistan.' He also stressed the importance of solving the Indo-Pakistan 'differences' through diplomatic and political means.

There was no official word on such a hard position taken by America although this may have been conveyed to Musharraf in private. Even if this were so, he yielded to American expectations

by banning only two militant organizations, the Jaish and the
Lashkar, later in January 2002, vowing his resolve to curb
religious extremism in Pakistan. While this was not enough from
India's point of view, his action invited much praise from the
American and European capitals. Buoyed by this encouragement,
Musharraf announced his road map for reinstating democracy
in Pakistan by promising to hold elections in October 2002,
which, too, won him more praise from the same quarters. Thus
having offered two carrots to his opponents in civil society at
home and friendly governments abroad, he held a referendum
in April to win a five-year term in the presidency in the run-up
to the October elections. The referendum was deeply flawed,
one-sided, doctored and held little credibility with the people
of Pakistan, but that was of little concern to the general who
wanted some legitimacy for his rule, if only on paper. He went
so far as to admit to the public that certain excesses might have
been committed by those overseeing the referendum, but he was
personally never a part of any such scheme or wished it to happen
that way, because he was after all and remained a very popular
leader. Nonetheless, civil society and the opposition political
parties pinned their hopes on the general holding a relatively
fair election and a new parliament that could put a stop to his
unilateral decision-making, though there was little on the ground
to indicate that this would translate into reality.

All this, while the standoff with India continued along the
border. Musharraf never let himself be bogged down by the
dangerous prospect of the two nuclear-armed neighbours going
to war. Such concerns were left to friendly Western governments,
inviting them to play the role the general expected of them: to
intervene and intercede on his behalf, to convince India to back
off while he maintained his offensive posture in the face of
heightened tensions along the border. In May he test-fired three
nuclear-capable, surface to surface, medium-range missiles, and
told the nation over television that Pakistan did not want a war
with India but that it would respond with full force and fury if

forced into it. His fiery rhetoric led Britain and America to step up their efforts to calm the war-mongering sentiment emanating from both sides. The following month, the two Western nations launched what they called their diplomatic offensive to lessen tensions between India and Pakistan. They made it clear to the two sides that they meant business by issuing travel advisories to their citizens against visiting either country, and even by asking those present there to leave India and Pakistan.

Still, Musharraf paid little heed to the gravity of the situation besides assuring British and American officials that Pakistan would not initiate war; the assurance of no first use of nuclear weapons was held back as a bargaining chip. Simultaneously, Musharraf continued to pursue the goal of strengthening his own rule. It is clear from his memoirs that he saw himself as the sole messiah of a nation that was facing many internal and external challenges, though least of all was the lack of legitimacy of his own regime, the absence of political stability, and a national consensus on vital issues. Terrorist attacks backed by Islamist militants were on the rise in Pakistan itself as the US-led war on terror and Musharraf's support for it continued. The *Wall Street Journal* correspondent to South Asia Daniel Pearl, suspected of being an undercover CIA agent by Al Qaeda, was abducted in January 2002 and gruesomely murdered in February. The terrorists tried to get the release of Muslim prisoners handed over by the Musharraf regime to the US and incarcerated at the Guantanamo Bay prison in Cuba as their key demand for the release of Daniel Pearl. The US refused to accede, resulting in the beheading of Pearl at the hands of Khalid Shaikh Mohammed, believed to be number 3 in the chain of command at Al Qaeda. Mohammed, after his arrest, confessed to the US authorities of his murder of Pearl in Karachi. In May, some eleven French technicians building a nuclear-capable submarine with the Pakistani navy in Karachi were targeted and killed in a suicide attack; hate-motivated suicide attacks against the minority Shia Muslims and the latter's tit-for-tat responses had become the norm; rival sectarian and turf-securing, politically motivated attacks also continued among various militant factions and groups. In June, the US consulate in Karachi was once again targeted in a suicide attack that left twelve bystanders, though no US citizen, dead.

Amidst this internal mayhem in the cities and external threat of a war with India, Musharraf continued to acquire more and lasting powers for himself in preparation for staying on and to stay on top of an elected parliament that would come in as a result of the promised elections in October. Promulgating a presidential ordinance under the sweeping powers given to him by a coerced Supreme Court, he resurrected the infamous Article 58(2)b of the constitution, the brainchild of the previous military dictator Ziaul Haq, which allowed the president to summarily dismiss an elected government and dissolve parliament at his discretion. He also disqualified both Nawaz Sharif and Benazir Bhutto from contesting the October election, though neither of the leaders living in exile wished to contest what they called 'a sham election under the shadow of a dictatorship'.

In his memoirs, Musharraf describes in great detail how he felt the urge to sideline both Nawaz Sharif and Benazir Bhutto so as to make them irrelevant to the new democratic political dispensation he wanted to put in place. For this, he chose the Chaudhry cousins of Gujrat in Punjab to spearhead a new, pro-Musharraf Pakistan Muslim League, comprising primarily those members of the Sharif-led League who were willing to switch loyalties. Shujaat Husain, the elder of the Chaudhry cousins, was Sharif's interior minister; the younger, Parvez Elahi, had served as a provincial minister under Sharif in Punjab. As it transpired, there were many other turncoats like them in the Muslim League who were apparently waiting in the wings to be asked to ditch their exiled leader. The PML has a long history of members and leaders defecting to join hands with new rulers, democrats or dictators. The Chaudhrys did the needful for the general and were rewarded for their effort. The elder cousin was nominated the head of the new Muslim League while the younger reigned over Punjab as the chief minister for the following five years. The family, not particularly known for its political acumen and much less for intellect, saw a ballooning of its fortunes, and not just in the political sense.

Alongside, changes were also made in the election rules, to support Musharraf's doctrine of 'Enlightened Moderation', providing that parliament must have at least 30 per cent women representation for reserved seats, and abolishing the discriminatory practice of separate electorates for Muslim and non-Muslim voters—an abominable anomaly introduced by Ziaul Haq but retained by the Bhutto and Sharif governments that followed. These two changes to election regulations were widely welcomed across the board, in Pakistan and abroad.

The October 2002 election did take place against the predictions made by certain quarters that the general would postpone it on the pretext of the internal security situation and the standoff with India. However, the election resulted in a hung parliament despite the People's Party and the Muslim League (Nawaz) accusing the government machinery of conducting massive pre-election rigging and of doctoring results on the election day itself. A rightist Islamic parties' coalition, traditionally seen as being close to the military since Ziaul Haq's time, secured an unprecedented number of seats. In the Frontier province, with its tribal areas bordering Afghanistan, the Islamic parties made a clean sweep. Civil society groups, secular politicians and political observers termed it another coup by Musharraf abetted by the mullah brigade which was brought in through the backdoor by the army. He was now ready to cobble together a government of his own hand-picked individuals, culled from his favoured Pakistan Muslim League (Q)—so named after the Quaid-i-Azam, Mohammed Ali Jinnah, as opposed to the erstwhile PML (Nawaz)—and a coterie of Musharraf supporters who contested the election as independent candidates. A month later, elections to the Senate, the upper house of parliament, also saw the induction of a majority of pro-Musharraf men and women. The Muttahida Majlis-i-Amal (MMA), the six-party religious alliance, however, chose to sit in the opposition. Observers believed that it was just a façade, for when the time came the MMA was instrumental in supporting the 17th Amendment to the constitution which gave a blanket cover to all the actions taken by Musharraf since the 1999 coup and also vested more powers in the president which he had amassed under the provisional constitution order passed by him soon after he toppled the Sharif government and thereafter. The supposed quid pro quo that the MMA got him to agree to in return for its support was that he would relinquish the post of army chief within a year, a promise he flouted. The MMA was also 'given' an unprecedented, sizeable 'mandate' in the 2002 election to scare the Americans: their sweeping the polls in the two western provinces of the Frontier and Balochistan, and 'winning' a few urban seats in Punjab and Sindh was meant to send the signal that were it not Musharraf with his 'Enlightened Moderation' that the West was willing to support, Pakistanis would put the mullahs in power through the ballot. The ruse seemed to work, and the West continued to throw its weight behind the 'liberal' dictator.

However, far from being boastful that he had conducted an election and therefore restored democracy in Pakistan, Musharraf was candid enough to term his effort as 'a transition to democracy'. Perhaps he did not want to give too much credibility to the political non-starters and sycophants he had brought to the government and who owed their presence at the helm to him alone. The precedent of Mohammad Khan Junejo rising to the office of prime minister under Ziaul Haq and then breaking loose of that general's noose to assert his political authority must have informed Musharraf's view of his own deputies in the power-sharing gambit. The political lackeys he chose for the jobs he wished to delegate to them proved themselves to be just that in the years ahead.

# 7

# Enlightened Moderation

In the aftermath of the October 2002 elections an ineffective government headed by a lame-duck prime minister Mir Zafarullah Jamali, a mild-tempered, easy-go-lucky tribal sardar from Balochistan, took charge under Musharraf's stewardship. Musharraf made the new government the custodian of his doctrine of 'Enlightened Moderation'—a forward-looking and progressive interpretation of Islam which he wanted to see prevail in Pakistan. There was no room for bigotry and intolerance in the great faith, he argued, and those who subscribed to a more puritan interpretation were welcome to do so but they had no right to impose their views on others in the name of Islam. The interpretation went down well with the majority of Pakistanis, especially those associated with the performing arts; the PML(Q)-led government never quite embraced it as its own due to the party's largely feudal, tribal and conservative complexion. However, under the general's orders (and he continued to call the shots), restrictions placed on dance in live theatrical performances were lifted, giving a new lease of life to that rapidly disappearing art form since the time of Ziaul Haq, and one that had only just managed to survive in Lahore, having been decimated in other large cities. A whole new generation had grown up since the 1979 coup by Gen. Zia under the shadow of a highly intolerant and obscurantist version of Islam. Most performing, and even some forms of the visual arts, had begun to be regarded as un-Islamic and thus impermissible in public life in an Islamic republic, though they continued to exist and flourish in a restricted environment. The lifting of many restrictions imposed earlier on the performing arts culminated in the president setting up a National Academy of Performing Arts in Karachi, which started professional training in many fields of the performing arts and staged performances of its own. Before Musharraf assumed power, merrymaking too had begun to be regarded as un-Islamic and successive governments had banned the celebration of New Year's Eve at public places, including posh hotels; however, private parties were beyond the purview of the ban. With the cultural opening up of society, Valentine's Day too was put on the national calendar, and youngsters began to celebrate it in public places; hotels and restaurants offered special deals on the occasion. This amounted to no less than a sea change in public life as lived under previous regimes.

Meanwhile, the MMA-led religious coalition parties' government in the Frontier province passed the Hasba Bill, declaring the enforcement of Islamic Sharia law throughout the province. The move placed great stress on the Quranic injunction of 'adjuring to do the good and forbid the evil'. However, when put into effect, this meant little other than the imposition of further restrictions on women, who were already a marginalized section of the largely Pashtun society. Billboards and advertising hoardings displaying women models were taken down throughout the province, girls in schools and colleges were told to observe the Muslim veil as a mandatory dress code, music and video shops were threatened with closure if they did not stop selling vulgar CDs, the revitalized public-sector Abaseen Arts Council theatre in Peshawar was virtually shut down. Performing artistes from the Frontier made a beeline out of Peshawar for Lahore where they could hope to continue making a living after all such prospects were killed in their home province.

This, while Musharraf was promising greater freedoms and empowerment to Pakistani women, the minorities and performing artistes. The federal government was told in no uncertain terms to challenge the Frontier government's attempt at creating a state within the state. A review petition was filed with the Supreme Court which, after referring the matter to the Federal Sharia (Islamic) Court (a largely ineffective hangover from Gen. Zia's time) and the Council of Islamic Ideology, struck down the Hasba Bill as unconstitutional. The MMA government was furious but there was nothing it could do to implement its agenda if it fell outside the constitution of Pakistan. A watered-down, non-binding bill was later approved by the Frontier government which only provided recommendations for observing Islamic law in the public sphere. By 2004, the MMA officially fell out with Gen. Musharraf when he refused to honour the pledge to doff his military uniform after the MMA had supported the 17th Amendment to strengthen his grip on power.

With his 'Enlightened Moderation' agenda put in action, and the official mullah-backed party in parliament and in the Frontier province sidelined, state-run television continued broadcasting dance recitals, both classical and popular forms in which principally women participated; something that had been taboo long before Musharraf came to power. In 1989, for instance, PTV was seen to have committed blasphemy when it presented a pop music show featuring the siblings and pop icons Nazia and Zohaib Hasan who swung on the stage while singing their popular numbers together. The then prime minister Benazir Bhutto had to ban the two from making any appearance on the stage together or to be seen dancing on TV. Musharraf had come a long way in challenging and defeating that mindset. There was now no turning back the clock, and he was least apologetic in implementing his cultural policy, with or without the support of the government under him. He and other high-ranking government officials were regularly shown on TV watching live performances by women singing and dancing, some with men. The presidency also began holding an annual pop music concert in its backyard on the eve of Independence Day, presided over by Musharraf, and broadcast to a national audience live. Independent TV channels competed with PTV to stage their own entertainment shows featuring dances. Basant Panchami, the kite-flying festival traditionally marked in the city of Lahore to herald spring, became a national media event. TV screens were filled with song and dance as inalienable parts of the festival. Other cities also began celebrating Basant and the event became a month-long period of festive activity. Musharraf himself took part in the festivities, flaunting them as his major contribution aimed at bringing about social change and fostering tolerance for pluralism in society. The International Performing Arts Festival, another privately initiated annual local event in Lahore, also received official patronage and grew into a mega affair over the years. Karachi launched its own international KaraFilm Festival, the first in the country, and promising to become an annual event.

Musharraf's cultural revolution of sorts was launched in the wake of Pakistan's continued military standoff with India. The general perceived and used it as an opportunity to show the world that there was more to Pakistan than a country that was a hotbed of terrorist activities and Al Qaeda's training grounds. It was an effort to improve the image of the country, which was to become a preoccupation with the general in the years ahead. The policy, however, did wonders for improving Musharraf's own image in the West as an enlightened, progressive leader who had a vision for his people and the country and plans to extricate it from an obscurantist, stifling version of Islam.

The opening up of society in the wake of 'Enlightened Moderation' put in action worked. The Americans, on the one hand, and Prime Minister Vajpayee in India on the other, as we learn through the horse's mouth, were once again convinced that Musharraf deserved to be given another chance. Strobe Talbott writes in *Engaging India*:

In 2003, the Bush administration—especially Powell, Armitage and Rocca—worked quietly behind the scene to nudge India and Pakistan toward a revival of the peace process. Bill Clinton chipped in as well ... During a period of heightened tension between India and Pakistan, Clinton received a phone call from Musharraf asking for help in restarting discussions with Vajpayee. Clinton replied he would not be party to any such approach unless he was certain that Musharraf recognized that a demand for India to give up Kashmir could not be part of the deal. Musharraf said he would be back in touch. Clinton heard nothing more for nearly nine months ... In November 2003 ... in a private meeting with Vajpayee [in Delhi], Vajpayee cautiously raised the possibility of resuming talks with Musharraf. When Clinton told him about the call he had received from the Pakistani leader earlier in the year, Vajpayee asked him to get back in touch with Musharraf and convey a simple message: Vajpayee was determined, if possible, to remove once and for all the 'burden' that the India-Pakistan dispute imposed on both countries; he was prepared to reopen a channel to Islamabad without advance commitments on either side, but only if he was confident he would not be embarrassed as he had been after Lahore [Declaration, signed between him and Sharif in 1999] ... Two days after the Clinton trip, India and Pakistan announced they had agreed to a ceasefire along the Line of Control. The talks led to a resumption of overflight rights and air links that had been suspended in the wake of the attack on the Indian parliament two years before.

Less than two months later, in January 2004, Vajpayee attended the SAARC summit in Islamabad. What transpired there made up for everything that had been lost at the Agra Summit in July 2001 between an overenthusiastic, flamboyant and media-savvy Musharraf and a calculating, reluctant Vajpayee. Both now donned the mantle of statesmen, having been sobered perhaps by the prospects of an all-out destructive war that could have been sparked off by the two countries' military posturings along the border during the past year. Unlike what Clinton had said to Musharraf early in 2003, Vajpayee agreed to discuss all bilateral issues, including Kashmir, which was seen as a major concession by most in Pakistan. The breakthrough laid the foundation of the composite dialogue for peace that Islamabad and New Delhi then pursued until the standoff in the wake of the November 2008 terrorist attacks in Mumbai, for which the Congress-led Indian government blamed Pakistan.

Back in January 2004, India and Pakistan looked set to give a sustained dialogue between them a chance without being in a great hurry to resolve their long-standing disputes over a cup of tea, as was the case at Agra, for instance. But even back then the efforts at dialogue did not go down well with a section of the so-called hawkish elements in Pakistan (as perhaps in India too), including some hard-core elements in the army itself. Musharraf narrowly escaped a bombing attack aimed at his motorcade in Rawalpindi cantonment, which was believed to be an insider job. Low-ranking army personnel were apprehended, tried and convicted.

Another major development that took place in the wake of Musharraf's 'Enlightened Moderation' in practice was the opening up of an honest side of the general, though scepticism persisted on its veracity among certain Pakistani and Western analysts. The father of Pakistan's nuclear programme, Dr Abdul Qadeer Khan, was prevailed upon to confess on TV his involvement in nuclear proliferation activities and of passing on the technology to build the bomb to the Libyans, the Iranians and the North Koreans until as late as in February 2004—long after 9/11. Then, making a case for the scientist's heroic status with the people of Pakistan, Musharraf swiftly pardoned and dismissed him. Dr Khan was placed under house arrest in Islamabad, as Musharraf rejected the possibility of allowing the American authorities to independently interrogate him. The Bush administration nonetheless welcomed the development, and Musharraf's resolve to henceforth abandon the practice of permitting any individual unrestricted access to Pakistan's nuclear components or secrets. Musharraf assured the world that he would strengthen his command-and-control regime over Pakistan's nuclear weapons, rejecting the possibility that the weapons could ever fall into the hands of Islamist terrorists.

In February 2009, however, the Islamabad High Court (the institution was created by a stroke of the pen by Musharraf after imposing emergency rule in November 2007 and virtually firing some sixty high court and Supreme Court judges) annulled Dr Khan's house arrest after the PPP-led government relented under public pressure, and sought to remove restrictions placed on him by the Musharraf regime. Khan remains a popular figure in Pakistan despite his reported 'fall from grace', as phrased by the Western media. According to a BBC Online analyst, Dr Khan told the Pakistani media in July 2008 that 'Pakistan had transported uranium-enrichment equipment to North Korea in 2000 with the full knowledge of the country's army, then headed by Gen. Musharraf'. Musharraf has repeatedly and vehemently denied any knowledge of Khan's purportedly secret and illegal proliferation activities, both whilst he (Musharraf) was in power and during his lecturing tour to the US as recently as in January 2009. Dr Khan after being set free by the high court told journalists at his residence in Islamabad that his position had been vindicated by the court's annulment order, and that Musharraf had lied about not being in the loop about his activities. These, he alleged, were carried out with the general being fully in the picture. Meanwhile, the US had again requested access to Dr Khan in July 2008 for questioning him about sharing nuclear technology with North Korea in February 2004; the request was turned down by the PPP-led government which, curiously like Musharraf, said it considered the matter closed. Dr Khan's release has not gone down well with the US and Britain. A US senator responded to the move by saying that his country must reconsider the economic and military aid worth $1.5 billion per annum for the next five years that the Obama administration has pledged to Pakistan.

Back in April 2004, after putting Dr Khan in the dock, then hastily pardoning him and placing him under house arrest, Musharraf had got parliament to put a stamp of approval on his National Security Council, a supra-parliamentary forum headed by him and comprising the air force and the navy chiefs along with the prime minister. The move was an effort on the general's part to formalize the army's role in policy-making and running the country. Rights activists deplored the approval of the council by parliament, supposedly a sovereign institution in a parliamentary democracy. In June 2004, Pakistan and India formally began their composite dialogue after the army had cracked down on suspected Al Qaeda militants in the Fata region, and over 200 terrorists were reported to have been killed in the operation. This was the first major offensive against Al Qaeda. Two months later, Musharraf decided to make a change at the top executive level. Prime Minister Zafarullah Jamali was asked to step down. In his place, Finance Minister Shaukat Aziz, an expatriate Pakistani banker who had come on secondment to help Musharraf manage the country's finances and who had brought in foreign investment and averted default, was elevated to premiership.

By the end of the year, the general was ready to announce that he was not prepared to doff his military uniform just then, against what he had promised the religious parties' alliance, the MMA, which then formally fell out with him. The reason given was simple: extremism that had manifested itself in the form of terrorist attacks in the northern and western parts of the country, and sectarian warfare which had reared its ugly head again in the large cities did not allow him to relinquish his post as army chief. He would not leave the job of wiping out extremists, which had only just begun, halfway. He said his political opponents, now including those in the MMA who had joined hands with Sharif's supporters, were trying to destabilize the country and the democratic system he had put in place. Terming them as regressive elements who were sincere neither in their thinking nor actions, the general vowed to stay on as army chief until such time that he was convinced that there would be no rolling back of the process he had got going. He cited the reinstatement of Pakistan as a Commonwealth member earlier in the year as proof of his democratic credentials. There was no immediate public uproar against Musharraf's refusal to doff his military uniform. However, the best the opposition was able to do was to stage a demonstration in Lahore, and even that some three months after the general's announcement that he would stay on as army chief.

Meanwhile, the composite dialogue begun with India continued on the path of building bridges, as India certified that infiltration from Pakistan into Indian-administered Kashmir had fallen significantly. In what was called a ground-breaking confidence-building concession, India agreed to open a bus route between Srinagar and Muzaffarabad on the Pakistani side of the Line of Control, without insisting that Kashmiris allowed to travel back and forth to meet their divided families should carry Indian or Pakistani passports. For the people of Kashmir this heralded the real melting of the ice that had separated them from their kith and kin since the first Kashmir war between India and Pakistan in 1948. The move was hailed by all, including Britain which has a huge Kashmiri diaspora based there.

Then came the London 7.7. 2005 bombings. When the British intelligence traced three of the bombers involved in the attack to having links to some seminaries in Pakistan, and implied that more British Pakistanis, because of their background, might be among the suspects, Musharraf was flabbergasted. He almost lost his composure and hit back, blaming British society for the alienation of and discrimination against a section of its own nationals who sought acceptance elsewhere because they were denied it in their own country. This was the flip side of Musharraf's 'Enlightened Moderation' which called on the

West to show respect for cultural differences and for an end to discrimination against Muslims to avoid alienating them. This to him was one of the basic weapons that had to be used to succeed in the global 'war on terror'. The independent stance taken by the general went down well with British Asians and a huge section of Pakistanis at home.

The 8 October earthquake that struck across Pakistan-administered Kashmir and virtually levelled the territory's administrative capital, Muzaffarabad, along with parts of the adjoining Frontier Province, focused the world's attention on Pakistan once again—this time to assist it in dealing with the tragedy. The number of dead crossed the 70,000 figure, and millions of survivors were left homeless. The aid and assistance reaching Pakistan in kind and cash were unprecedented. India too chipped in generously by sending in essential supplies by plane and truck loads, and even helping out with clearing the rubble in areas where Pakistani rescue teams were unable to reach in the immediate aftermath of the tragedy.

The overwhelming world response and the sympathy that was generated for the victims of the natural disaster also helped improve Pakistan's image as being home to a largely moderate people as opposed to radicalized, West- and India-hating fanatics. The thousands of Western volunteers and media crews that came to cover the tragedy lent credence to Musharraf's claim that the vast majority of his people actually practised an enlightened and moderate form of Islam in their day-to-day lives as naturally as Muslims living elsewhere in the diaspora.

Following the devastating earthquake, suicide bombings and attacks against government installations and personnel also took a back seat. Ordinary Pakistanis from across the many dividing fault lines came together in a rare show of solidarity. Musharraf's one-man rule ceased to be a preoccupation with the public and civil society at this time of national tragedy. He was no longer regarded as the bad guy leading an institution blamed for overthrowing elected governments and as being a burden on the economy. The worst of his opponents stepped forward to do whatever they could to help the army with the relief operations. Moreover, in the course of the months that followed the tragedy, the handling of the mammoth relief and rehabilitation effort was not riddled with any noticeable charges of corruption levelled against the army-managed organization in charge of it. However, because being a politician was not in his grain, Musharraf did not try to take any advantage of this massive default public approval of his administration's effective handling of the gravest of natural disasters to have ever struck Pakistan. That he thought he did not need any public approval for his actions, right or wrong, could be the other reason why he did not build on the popular goodwill that existed for him after the tragedy struck. This was another opportunity lost at building on the public goodwill that came Musharraf's way since the staging of the coup d'etat by the army in October 1999.

Rarely does an autocrat get a chance of garnering public approval, but here was a man who denied ever having made any mistakes, let aside learning from them. While lecturing in America in January 2009, he repeatedly asserted having no regrets for whatever he did. Upon his return to Pakistan in early February, he boasted to *Dawn* that he was readying himself for his next lecturing tour to India where, in the aftermath of the Mumbai attacks, he said he wanted 'to confront India on its home ground'. As on India, his views on democracy in Pakistan have also remained unchanged as he reasserted his position that the British model of democracy did not suit his country. Democracy here would have to evolve and take its own form and shape, he philosophized. While in power, he used to allude to the Malaysia and Singapore models, but in practical terms he did little to either ensure law and order or reform the foreign direct investment regime to make Pakistan an attractive destination for investors—something that forms the cornerstone of the so-called Malaysian/Singaporean models. The economic stability, sustained growth and development that the two nations have enjoyed over the decades have somewhat compensated for the lack of many democratic freedoms.

In the same recent interview, Musharraf rejected the notion that he had any political agenda in the months ahead. Curiously enough, he evaded questions about his resignation and refrained from making any negative statements about the sitting PPP-led government. He seemed very settled in his new role as the self-appointed ambassador-at-large of Pakistan, a role which is now taking him around the world on lucrative lecture tours. While his doctrine of 'Enlightened Moderation' remains very much in currency with him, with the world still willing to listen to him expounding the theory at great length, there is little attention paid to the mess he has left behind in the form of home-grown terrorism, which is now a full-blown monster that threatens to strike beyond Pakistan's borders. The gap between what the general said when he was in power (and still says) and what he did, or rather did not do to match his words, is a point that eludes his eager audiences in ace institutions abroad. But it works just as well for the general; he had it good in power; he still doesn't have it bad, all considered. He holds forth on national and international issues before a captivated international audience, as it were, while back home his sprawling farmhouse bungalow in the hillside estate near Islamabad that he allotted himself while in power is being decorated with imported fixtures. The Army House, the army chief's official residence in the nearby garrison city of Rawalpindi, remains his residence, with a security protocol that matches the president's.

# 8

# Battleground Home Front

Notwithstanding its widespread appeal to the vast majority of Pakistanis who received it as a breath of fresh air, Musharraf's 'Enlightened Moderation' in effect did little to curb the growing scourge of extremism at home. Conversely, it can be argued that extremist forces reacted to its many manifestations, like song and dance and the general opening up of society, as if they had found a reason to resist what they saw as Western and therefore alien values brought right to their doorstep. The Islamists believed that if they succeeded in 'capturing' a nuclear-capable Pakistan there was greater hope of their survival as a force, and that even if it could not reshape the world, it could still avenge the wrongs perpetrated against Muslims by a Christian West, a Jewish Israel and a Hindu India. This is very much an ideology based on hate, and akin to that which drives Al Qaeda and its surrogates in Pakistan and Afghanistan, the Taliban. Such a xenophobic world view is beyond redemption in that it leaves no prospect of an engagement or a dialogue with an entrenched mindset. Musharraf either failed to understand that or had reasons that held him back from going the whole hog against the militants. Now that he is no more heading the government, he advocates a full-blown military action against militants holding the state hostage in the north-west and in the Swat region of the Frontier province. The army should be fully equipped and readied to deal with the internal threat posed to Pakistan's security and stability, even if that means rolling out tanks to re-establish the writ of the state, he told *Dawn* in February in a first-ever interview to a Pakistani paper since stepping down in August 2008.

A number of suicide bombings and other attacks were carried out between 2004 and 2008 across Pakistan, claiming several hundred lives, but a clear policy and strategy against containing and combating home-grown terrorism remained conspicuous by its absence. Fire-fighting measures, such as cordoning off certain roads with foreign missions located on them, increasing the level of security provided to VIPs, and the like failed to check the menace from growing and spreading. The army and paramilitary forces acted only in self-defence rather than pursuing the terrorists. This was because there was no well-thought-out plan in place, nor a central controlling mechanism devised to effectively root out the scourge of terrorism.

The general at the top of the power pyramid remained ambivalent to the very end, believing perhaps that his policy of 'Enlightened Moderation' would build enough public pressure on the militants to achieve what military action against them might not. However, more important, perhaps, he also looked at the world beyond America's disengagement from Afghanistan. The army having invested so much in the erstwhile Taliban regime would again need it there to check what the army perceived as India's growing influence along Pakistan's western border. If in the process of securing what Musharraf and his generals viewed as the national interest, Afghanistan bore the brunt and became an inverse image of an enlightened, moderate and an economically vibrant Pakistan, then so be it. As the cliché goes, all is fair in love and war, and Pakistan has long had a love–hate relationship with its north-western neighbour. When the Taliban were in power, the army loved Afghanistan; when a hostile (to Pakistan) regime replaced the Taliban, it began loathing that country again.

That is perhaps why Musharraf went easy on the Taliban and even looked the other way when they allegedly returned to Afghanistan from Pakistan to conduct assaults against

Karzai and those associated with his regime, or even the NATO-led international forces deployed in that country. The Bush administration perhaps made it clear to Gen. Musharraf, officially by its statements in support of the Karzai regime and otherwise unofficially, that it did not envisage a role for Pakistan army or its intelligence agencies inside Afghanistan. This was because the US-backed Karzai regime and its partners in the Northern Alliance in particular were fiercely opposed to any such role for Pakistan. Musharraf's assertion throughout was that Afghanistan would remain a game wide open and a country far from stability unless the Pashtun majority there represented by the Taliban was given a stake in governance. Failing this, the Taliban would continue to seek shelter in Pakistan and perhaps keep infiltrating from across the porous border which it is not practicable to seal.

The logical outcome of all this escaped Musharraf: the Taliban's presence in Pakistan, because of their marginalization under the new, emerging political dispensation in Afghanistan, would push them closer to Al Qaeda and also radicalize their fellow Pashtuns in Pakistan into holding the state hostage. Instead, he increasingly spent his time and energy trying to convince the Americans that they and he together should go only after the Al Qaeda leadership (largely of Arab and Central Asian rather than of Afghan or Pakistani origin) and not the Taliban. As in Kargil, he miscalculated yet again.

Al Qaeda would not be decimated any time soon, the Taliban would not turn their backs on it like Musharraf did on them, and American troops would not leave the job in Afghanistan unfinished to return home just because of public pressure back home. President Barack Obama's decision to scale down and eventually pull out American troops from Iraq, but reinforce American and NATO military presence in Afghanistan for a longer haul was a possibility that Musharraf and his know-all deputies in the army top brass had not made any room for in their strategic thinking. Since Clinton's cold-shouldering

of Islamabad and his proactive embracing of India, Pakistani
military and foreign office pundits have remained weary of the
Democratic Party. As wishful thinking would have it, most of the
Pakistan–US relations prognoses in Rawalpindi and Islamabad
have revolved round the hypothesis of a Republican president
occupying the White House. Now that this has not happened,
and Obama has categorically stated that the US forces would
stay in Afghanistan, the new elected government in Islamabad
and the new army chief at the army headquarters in Rawalpindi
will have a lot of neglected homework to finish.

Even under the Bush administration, with which Musharraf
fancied himself as having a lot of leeway, the American position
on and Washington's plan in Afghanistan rested on its longer-
term objectives in the region, i.e., to weed out terrorism and
support for it in that country and elsewhere where it might go
from there—read Pakistan. Musharraf and his military and
foreign policy strategists missed reading between the lines the
American policy in Afghanistan as it was subtly stated by the
Republicans time and again. After all, there is nearly always
a minimum bipartisan consensus that exists between the
Republicans and Democrats on critical areas of the US foreign
policy. The proof of this came readily after Barack Obama's
victory in the November 2008 election; even as the president-elect
he had vowed to bolster the number of US troops in Afghanistan
while showing a willingness to reduce them in Iraq. What
Musharraf failed to understand was that the longer he gave the
Taliban the cushion to stay in Pakistan and operate from there
against the Kabul regime, as the latter alleged, the more wary
the Americans would become of him as a reliable partner in the
war against terrorism. Furthermore, from Pakistan's own internal
security point of view, the presence of the Taliban on its soil
would radicalize Pakistani Pashtun tribesmen, and indoctrinate
and conscript to their cause youth from utterly impoverished
areas of the country, extending deep beyond the Pashtun belt
into southern Punjab. This is precisely what has occurred. Many

fighting alongside the Taliban in the north and north-west of the country are what the local people in the mountains call 'Punjabi Taliban', who come from the underdeveloped districts of southern Punjab reeling under a medieval feudal/tribal social set-up that leaves the people there with little hope.

The case of the full-blown Islamist insurgency in the Swat district of the Frontier province is a classic example. In this fairly developed summertime tourist hotspot and the only place with a proper skiing facility in Pakistan in winter, a local cleric, Maulana Sufi Mohammad, who as early as during Benazir Bhutto's second tenure in office in 1996 had emerged as a de facto recruiting agent for the Taliban's 'jihad' against the Northern Alliance in Afghanistan, began flexing his muscles again. This was principally because what he was doing also complemented the Pakistani army's objective of strengthening the Taliban in Afghanistan (and the radical militants in Kashmir fighting against Indian rule as and when required); the cleric fully understood that. Musharraf, he believed, would only open one front at a time, either along his eastern border with India or that along the western border with Afghanistan. Having tamed India in 2004 and begun a composite dialogue, Musharraf refocused his strategic thinking on what Pakistan needed to do to secure a friendly Afghanistan. Considering himself the man of the moment, as he claims in his memoirs, he says he had to keep himself on top of the changing political landscape in Afghanistan. Because that country was not blessed with a matching clairvoyant he fancied himself to be, it was he who had to do the thinking for Kabul too.

The Pakistani army's military doctrine on Afghanistan had withstood the 'vicissitudes of time' (which is a euphemism for it remaining unchanged), come democratic or direct military rule. The Benazir Bhutto government was forced to look the other way with regard to Maulana Sufi Mohammad's activities so long as he did not turn on her government. She even placated the mullah by allowing his illegally raised militia to go around enforcing Islamic law, of the kind the MMA government sought to implement throughout the Frontier Province, in Swat's neighbouring Malakand Agency, a tribal area that was the cleric's home base. The Bhutto government went the extra mile and got the then Frontier assembly to legislate in order to approve the selective imposition of Sharia law in the Malakand Agency. Under Musharraf's rule, apparently disgruntled by his policy, the cleric expanded his activities to the neighbouring, scenic Swat valley. Because the main highway to Swat district passed through the mullah's Malakand Agency, he began enforcing weird rules on passing vehicles: they must switch sides and drive on the right because driving on the left was un-Islamic (the left hand is supposedly dirty, because Muslims clean themselves up after defecating using that hand, and a tradition of the Prophet Muhammad recommends that you eat with your right hand; hence it followed that driving on the right was more Islamic than driving on the left). The mullah's men enforcing the driving rule also began enforcing the veil on women tourists heading out to Swat with their families to vacation there, tourism being the valley's erstwhile economic lifeline. The harassment brought all tourism traffic to Swat to a complete halt.

Once that was accomplished, the mullah launched his own FM radio station (and came to be known as 'Maulana Radio'), which threatened the people in Swat to mend their un-Islamic ways of catering to men and women with a Western lifestyle who came to their valley for recreation and merrymaking. The Musharraf regime did nothing to arrest the mullah in his tracks. When finally some action was taken against him under American pressure to stop him from recruiting young men for jihad in Afghanistan against the Karzai regime, it was only half-hearted. The mullah was arrested but released after assurances that he would end his activities. Meanwhile, his son-in-law, cleric Fazlullah, defied the government and holed up with his armed militia in Swat, enforcing Sharia law everywhere he went in his trek northwards. His intransigence and unceasing attacks on government installations, administrative buildings and girls' schools and colleges in particular finally led the government to mount a military operation to dislodge him and his men after he rendered the Swat (Saidu Sharif) airport unusable and blew up the ski-lift and resort in the valley. Meanwhile, the militants' siege of Swat played havoc with the people's lives and livelihoods; the valley remains virtually out of bounds for Pakistani and foreign tourists alike. Fazlullah's men have destroyed many rock engravings and historical sites in Swat in retaliation for the ongoing military action against his militia.

The carvings destroyed or defaced by Fazlullah's zealots date back to the Buddhist period from 200 BC to CE 600; the outrage is reminiscent of the Taliban's strikes on the giant Buddha statues in Bamiyan, Afghanistan, in 2001. A dawn-to-dusk curfew is the norm in the now utterly impoverished scenic valley as military action continues to oust Fazlullah's militia. In any respite that the terrorists get from the military action they ensure that they blow up more girls' schools and colleges and prevent any semblance of normality from returning to the valley. The local people, a whopping half a million souls inhabiting the 100-mile-long stretch of the valley through which runs the River Svastu on whose banks the *Rig Veda* and the Puranas were written, are forced to eke out a subsistence-level living, relying largely on a seasonal crop of maize and produce from the fruit orchards that fortunately abound. They blame Musharraf for allowing their valley to descend into chaos by not acting against the lawlessness to which the two clerics subjected it.

As for the semi-autonomous tribal areas called the Federally Administered Tribal Areas (FATA) and Provincially Administered Tribal Areas (PATA), adjoining the North West Frontier Province, these were allowed to become a hotbed of Taliban-cum-Al Qaeda-sponsored-and-perpetrated terrorism that aimed at Pakistan and 'Muslim lands' beyond its borders. Darra Adam Khel (a manufacturing and market hub for locally produced firearms and equally effective replicas of sophisticated international weaponry), the Mohmand, Bajaur, Orakzai and

Khyber agencies are virtual battlegrounds today, with those affected by the ongoing war between religious militants and paramilitary forces fleeing their homes and taking refuge in shelters set up outside the 'war zone'. The Khyber Agency is a mammoth marketplace for imported goods, including durables, as duty-free transit trade items to Afghanistan that never reach their destination across the border. It was also the scene of the recent blowing up of the transport vehicles' depot which was set up to facilitate the Afghan land transit trade and the bulk of NATO and American forces' supplies. Bordering the provincial capital, Peshawar, Khyber became home to the operating bases of the local Taliban-inspired bands of extremists during Musharraf's years in power. The military action to dislodge the militants in Bajaur was undertaken only after Musharraf resigned in August 2008. The more distant regions of North and South Waziristan are areas where Baitullah Mehsud, the terrorist accused of being behind the murder of Benazir Bhutto, and his armed militia virtually hold complete sway. A substantial number of young men and boys in the impoverished southern Punjab have also joined the Pashtun militants there, who now call their scattered groups as forming the Tehrik-e-Taliban Pakistan. The movement is neither yet united in a cohesive organizational set-up nor operates under a centralized leadership. There is, however, an ideology that has certainly grown under Musharraf's rule.

In the neighbouring Kurram Agency next to North Waziristan back in FATA, the Taliban power has asserted itself by assuming sectarian overtones: the original Shia Muslim-majority residents were turned into a minority by the influx of Afghan refugees who settled there after the Soviet invasion of their country in 1979; but the balance decisively tipped in favour of the puritan, militant Sunni creed following 9/11 when the Taliban on the run entered the area and stayed on. Sectarian killings and hate crimes since then have become the norm, pitting the two Muslim sects against each other in Kurram with a dangerous spillover of sectarian fires to the neighbouring settled areas of Bannu, Tank, Hangu and the city of Dera Ismail Khan in the Frontier province.

Deep inside North and South Waziristan the only hope of dislodging the militants with any success are precision strikes by American Predator drones. The frequency of such strikes may have increased after Musharraf bowed out, but the precision of the strikes has not, which creates a bigger mess for the democratically elected government. Civilian casualties are high and politically hard to sustain by Islamabad, which has given tacit approval to the Americans to carry out such strikes in areas where the Pakistani army had rather not or could not venture. The army at no point would want to be seen as acting against its own people at the behest of a foreign power. The army's belated military action in Swat and in the tribal areas bordering the Frontier capital Peshawar came only in the wake of suicide attacks carried out by the Taliban against the politicians of the ruling Frontier coalition. The military action in Swat was mounted at the request of the provincial government, not the US. That it was again the provincial government which backed out of it will be seen as the failure of the political government to act with any determination, as has traditionally been the case in Pakistan's history.

The Taliban were allowed during the Musharraf regime to spread their wings into the Frontier's settled districts like Charsadda, a smaller twin city of Peshawar by the same name and home to the leftist, secular Awami National Party's (ANP) central leadership. The neighbouring districts of Mardan, Swabi and Nowshera are equally infested with the Taliban's presence. Musharraf's interior minister, Aftab Sherpao, and lately the ANP chief Asfandyar Wali Khan, the grandson of the secular and (Indian) unionist Khan Abdul Ghaffar Khan, barely survived suicide attacks in Charsadda. In both semi-autonomous tribal and settled districts of the Frontier province, local Taliban became a force to reckon with so long as Musharraf remained in office. They went around unchecked, shutting down music and video shops, threatening barbers with closure of their business if

they did not stop offering the 'un-Islamic' services of trimming
or shaving men's beards, and threatening women teachers and
girls, asking them to stop attending schools and colleges. Some
institutions' buildings were blown up or occupied by the local
Taliban to drive their point home, but the Musharraf-led regime
did little besides offering to negotiate with such terrorists in
an attempt to get them to reach an understanding with the
government.

This was obviously done so as not to discourage or disarm the
local Taliban or their Afghan counterparts seeking refuge with
them. They too were perhaps waiting to return to Afghanistan
with the backing of the Pakistani army once the Americans left
that country, just as Musharraf himself believed. That it would
not happen while Musharraf managed to stay in power was
beyond the general's inflated sense of his own self-assessment as
a visionary and a messiah who would lead his people to safety in
troubled times. Perhaps the argument that he and his army could
not fight against their own people was a case of they 'would' not
fight those they considered to be their own people. The distinction
needs to be understood not only from a soldier's point of view
but more so from a general-turned-autocratic-ruler's perspective
who thought he was aware of the bigger picture in terms of his
immediate war strategy and the objectives that extended beyond
that: perhaps an offensive later after a strategic retreat now to
retain de-facto control of Afghanistan.

Thus, Musharraf's soft-pedalling on the threat posed by
encroaching Talibanization to his enlightened and moderate state-
in-the-making was based on another, and greater miscalculation:
that so long as he stayed in power, and that would be for a long
time to come, he would wriggle out of the threat by redirecting it
at a pro-India regime in Afghanistan whose lifespan in turn would
be short and end as soon as the Americans left that country. That
there were at least one too many assumptions there on his part,
and that the Americans would not leave Afghanistan at least
whilst Musharraf remained in power, never crossed the general's

mind, with the result that large swathes of Pakistan itself were, as a practical fait accompli, made over to the Taliban.

Any and all military actions taken against the militants under Musharraf's reign were limited to apprehending or taking out largely what he called 'foreign elements (Arabs, Tajiks, Uzbeks and Chechens) who had links to Al Qaeda'. He never implicitly or explicitly ascribed any such 'proven' Al Qaeda links to the Afghan Taliban or their home-grown Pakistani cells, though he admitted that both shared a similar world view but maintained that while Al Qaeda sought to change the world, the Taliban could be content with enforcing their ideology as a basis of their own state in Afghanistan. Musharraf drew little distinction between Taliban of Pakistani and Afghan origins, as both would supposedly serve the army's purpose well in an Afghanistan soon to be abandoned by the Americans. The result was that this grossly faulty and self-deluding view allowed pockets of extremism to grow and become virtual states within the state of Pakistan.

While certain tribal areas and settled districts of the Frontier became Taliban-controlled territories by the end of the general's eight-year-long one-man rule, larger cities, notably Karachi, Lahore and the capital Islamabad, were also not beyond the grip of the growing scourge of extremist militarism in action. The Karachi corps commander's convoy was targeted in the heart of the city's upscale Clifton Cantonment in June 2004 in which eleven people were killed. Though he escaped narrowly, the city was declared out of bounds for diplomats stationed elsewhere in Pakistan. Roads leading to Western consulates in Karachi were barricaded and some entirely closed to vehicles. In Lahore, notable for its thriving cultural activities, shopping and eating out, a city that had largely escaped the onslaught of extremism, suicide bombers struck government buildings and institutions, including the regional headquarters of the Federal Investigation Agency, which purportedly works closely with Western intelligence agencies, and a navy training college. The story of terrorists and suicide bombers holding Islamabad hostage is longer and more staggering.

# 9

## Schools of Bigotry

As the immediate fallout of the Afghan jihad in the 1980s, Pakistan began brimming with madrassa seminaries teaching the Quran and instilling the fear of Allah in the hearts and minds of the people. From a total of only a few hundred estimated madrassas that existed in the country until 1977, their number today has grown to thousands. Gen. Zia, encouraged by the Americans' need to support the Afghan jihad, allowed petro-dollars from Saudi Arabia and the UAE to roll in to set up madrassas of all sizes, many with the dual purpose of teaching the Quran and Islamic law as well as to ready the Afghan refugee youth to take to armed jihad against the Soviet infidels encroaching on 'Muslim land'. The euphemism was all too obviously meant to be applied to Afghanistan under Soviet occupation, but given Islam's universality in its spread and thought, it also encompassed 'lands' as distant as Palestine, Chechnya and Bosnia, and as close to the hearts of Pakistanis as Kashmir under Indian administration just next door in the opposite geographical direction.

With the establishment of large numbers of madrassas funded by generous sums of money donated by God-fearing, rich sheikhs from the Persian Gulf, who were also requested by a friendly West to fund Saddam Hussein's war against radical, Shia Iran for their own good, madrassas became the most notable and conspicuous presence in Pakistan under Ziaul Haq. Not to be left behind, Iran too pumped in some funds to raise and reinforce

Shia madrassas to counter the threat of a growing, puritan Wahabi creed that began engulfing Pakistan. Graduation, if not conversion, to the puritan school of thought began largely among the majority, non-puritan Sunnis, who for centuries had enjoyed their qawwali, song and dance at Sufi saints' shrines as an integral part of their religious rituals and worship. In the aftermath of the first Gulf war in the 1990s, when Saddam's relations soured with Kuwait and Saudi Arabia, Iraq too began funding the more traditional, generally non-belligerent, mainstream Sunni seminaries in Pakistan. Even Libya pumped in its wealth to back similar groups as Iraq in its defiance of the West's Arab friends in the Persian Gulf.

Gen. Ziaul Haq, on his part, also extended state patronage and annual monetary grants to madrassas without bringing them under the net of public accountability or even annual audits of received funds and their expenditure. While this gave birth to a new kind of rather lucrative, evangelical competition among various schools of religious thought, it also divided Pakistani society along hardened sectarian grandstanding which continued as a hangover of Zia's dubious Islamization process. The entire gambit was funded in large part by Pakistan's benefactors from the Gulf so as to contain Iran's influence in Pakistan. The Taliban were very much the product of this aggressive madrassa onslaught which used Pakistan not only as its launching pad but also, which has since become clear, as a breeding ground for fanaticism.

In a span of two decades, Pakistani society as a whole underwent a radical change. Mosques were generally the poor man's Mecca, certainly not known for their décor, and had bare minimal facilities for ablution and prayers. The better off seldom rubbed shoulders with their plebeian counterparts, except perhaps at annual Eid prayers. With the petro-dollars rolling in, the appearance of the mosques also began to change. When just facelifts were not adequate, additional land adjacent to a mosque was grabbed or even purchased for expansion of the premises. In time many mosques began to resemble compounds, with custom-made madrassas built on the pattern of boarding schools and the faculty's residential quarters. The now affluent madrassas also invited and enrolled foreign students by the hundreds from across the Islamic world and the Muslim diaspora in non-Muslim countries. From Bosnia and Morocco in the West to Indonesia and China in the East, Pakistani madrassas began boasting a cosmopolitan student profile, if cosmopolitan it can be called. Many mosques began being decked with wall-to-wall carpeting, equipped with state-of-the-art public address systems, and even air conditioning—the Gulf model of houses of Islamic worship was on the rise. Thus refurbished, the mosque also began catering to the well to do. Today, on a given Friday, you can see the latest models of cars, sedans and SUVs parked outside a neighbourhood mosque in any posh locality in a large city. Thanksgiving trips to Mecca, other than at the time of the annual Hajj pilgrimage, also became the norm for the better off.

Pakistan's Wall Street, I.I. Chundrigar Road in Karachi, is closed to traffic during the midday Friday prayers as young shirt-and-tie clad executives leave their office blocks to join the massive prayer gathering on the road. Obviously, this was not part of the culture prior to Gen. Zia's period in power, or else provision for mosques would have been made in and around the business district as the city was built up over the years. In the fasting month of Ramzan, affluent areas of Karachi, especially, present another sight that was not part of the culture a generation ago. Wealthy businessmen arrange lengthy and well-attended late-night prayers on their lawns. At dusk, many just feed the poor as the less fortunate come to line up to break their fast.

Many highly qualified young professionals today take time off from work, up to forty days annually, to go on voluntary preaching missions inside Pakistan and abroad. Some doctors and others with paramedical training also join the missionaries in territories where Muslims may be seen as waging jihad against non-Muslims or even their fellow Muslims, say, a secular Muslim regime and the like. The missionaries include by and large the better educated, urban professionals from nearly all walks of life. Starting in the late 1990s, many pop and rock band singers and cricketers too have joined the faithful in their quest, not so much for spirituality but for piety and the zeal to convert non-Muslims and 'lesser' Muslims to Islam. This was hardly the Pakistan envisioned by Jinnah or one that someone like Musharraf would be at ease with, as public space for secular activities and pastimes shrank significantly from what it had been a generation ago. For an entire new generation that grew up in the wake of this enormous social change, a new culture of religiosity and association of wealth with religion and its generous distribution amongst the needy is a fact of life; what was just a niche, specialized religious discourse yesterday is the mainstream today, and those who grew up with the change have never known it to be any different.

Until the ouster of the Taliban following 9/11 it was not uncommon for a disgruntled, uninspired, or a failed young man from a middle-class, urban, educated background to talk of going for jihad in the way of God to make any sense of his existence. Many with professional degrees, in, say, engineering or medicine, and without a job went in for some basic military training at one or the other madrassa-sponsored training camp for a couple of weeks on their way to active jihad or as a volunteer to help out with the 'cause' in Afghanistan, Kashmir or Bosnia. It was not unheard of that a businessman or a professional would 'donate' one of his sons to a madrassa and let him be used in the way of God while that child's other siblings would pursue normal, modern education to ready themselves for career jobs. For every one family that could afford to provide all their children good education but gave one child away in the name of God, there were hundreds from among the teeming millions of poor who could and would send their children, perhaps all six of them, only to a madrassa.

In many madrassas, boarding and lodging are on the house; even in the madrassas offering only day classes, food is free and no fees are charged for teaching the pupils to read and write, principally the Quran, or preparing them to be men of God even if they don't send them out on jihad. The madrassa culture has come to stay. Even with a halt to the Afghan war-related jihad, funding from abroad, or that by the Saddam regime and the Libyans, donations made to madrassas by individuals and organizations are phenomenally high today, and there's little accountability relating to the use of such funds going to madrassas. Thus the duly empowered neighbourhood mullah, who used to be a poor man of God unaware of worldliness a generation ago, now assumed the title of *alim* (scholar; *ulema*: plural) as never before. Nawaz Sharif's family, whose fortunes multiplied under Gen. Ziaul Haq's regime and the kind of Islamization of state institutions and society that took place under it, also supported one such creed of ulema, hence the family's personal ties with the Saudi rulers. This was the radically altered, culturally remapped, new Pakistan whose reins Musharraf took and then sought to reorient it back to its pre-Afghan jihad and pre-Ziaul Haq social ethos.

He began well, with the introduction of a madrassa reform plan which recognized the madrassas' utility as basic, free-education providers but also the need to plug them into the public sector school and higher education systems. The plan proposed that alongside the teaching of the Quran and Islamic studies, madrassas also impart some practical knowledge, such as basic school-level science and arithmetic besides Urdu and English-language teaching so as to enable a madrassa-qualified student to exercise the option of pursuing higher studies in a university if he or she so desired. The registration of madrassas, whether they received state grants or not, was made mandatory. However, very few complied with the directive. Most questioned the need for it and refused to register. The few less inclined to tread the path of belligerence argued for the need for initiating a dialogue with the government on how best to 'resolve the problem'.

Having got such mixed signals from the so-called stakeholders and those leading the government who would only reluctantly, if at all, enforce the new policy, Musharraf responded by saying that the registration of the madrassas would be voluntary as opposed to mandatory. Rights activists believe that the original plan proposed by Musharraf cut through what has traditionally been a military–mullah alliance against democratic, secular forces in Pakistan. It was this alliance, trying to protect its turf, which was eventually responsible for the death of the entire plan.

The powerful civil–military bureaucracy which had re-embraced Islam as state ideology under the Zia regime was the new stumbling block in bringing the madrassas under any form of surveillance or public accountability.

Starting in 2005, two cleric brothers on the government payroll, Abdul Aziz and Abdur Rashid Ghazi who ran Quranic madrassa seminaries for girls and boys adjacent to Islamabad's Lal Masjid, a landmark in the middle of the capital, began flexing their muscles. The two boarding school madrassas housed hundreds of students, local and foreign, and were constantly running out of space. Over the years, since Gen. Ziaul Haq had allotted an additional few hundred square yards next to the mosque to build a madrassa, the two brothers had been using their influence within the Islamabad administration and the federal bureaucracy to acquire more and more land which they brought into their expanding madrassa compound. The mosque was notorious for its hate-filled speeches and, as some in the intelligence agencies alleged, hiding Al Qaeda sympathizers, even though the chief cleric of the mosque was a government employee. However, given their personal contacts among the serving and retired civil and army officials, no one in the government would touch the two clerics with a bargepole. As the Americans forced Musharraf to 'do more' in the war on terror, and some Al Qaeda men were

picked up and handed over to the Americans, the clerics declared
their own war against the general and his supporters, those seen
as liberal-minded and the like.

The clerics began their mission of purging society of all evil
by making inflammatory speeches against Musharraf's social
liberalization policies, using the public address system to deliver
the weekly midday Friday prayer sermons, demanding that
government change what they called its anti-Islam course or
be ready for retaliatory action by the faithful. Meanwhile, the
Islamabad municipality, the Capital Development Authority
(CDA), announced its crackdown against illegally raised
buildings, including several mosques built on green belts and
plots intended for public amenities. This was just the excuse
the firebrand clerics were apparently waiting for. As illegally
constructed mosques began to be demolished, the sermons and
threats from the Lal Masjid grew in their ferocity. To make their
point, the two clerics ordered their seminary students, armed with
sticks, to take to the streets of the capital to stage their protest,
which became a regular Friday event. Next, the students went
around not just stopping vehicular traffic but trying to enforce
the Islamic veil on women drivers and passengers held up on
the roads. No action was taken against the clerics despite such
provocation for weeks and months. In late 2006, bands of male
and female student vigilantes from the Lal Masjid seminaries
began raiding nearby markets, forcing shopkeepers to remove
music and film CDs. With no action forthcoming from the
authorities, the students looted and burnt music CDs which
were piled up in a heap outside the mosque. Next, the women
seminary students broke into and occupied the adjacent CDA-
managed children's library. Books inside the library not deemed
sufficiently Islamic met the same fate as the CDs. Still there was
no action. On the contrary, Gen. Zia's son and a minister in the
Musharraf-led government's cabinet, Ejazul Haq, was allowed
to go to meet the two clerics and to try to persuade them to
cease their illegal activities in exchange for the government's

assurance that their demands would be considered. The clerics refused to back down.

Seeing the government on the defensive, they announced their plans to enforce the Sharia law in the Islamabad federal territory and invited other seminaries elsewhere in the country to follow their lead. Consequently, Lal Masjid students armed with guns and sticks went around the capital warning the sinful to desist from vice or face their wrath. Wholesale harassment of citizens, especially independent women running businesses, followed, amidst claims that the Lal Masjid 'brigade' had reformed many women who had repented and promised not to indulge in un-Islamic activities. A mother and daughter, with children, were picked up and held hostage for allegedly indulging in sex trade. In one such attempt, seminary students forcefully entered a Chinese-owned spa and held seven Chinese masseuses hostage for indulging in un-Islamic activities. The assault led to the Chinese government officially protesting to Musharraf. Even then no action was taken against the Lal Masjid clerics. High officials volunteered to intervene and brought the matter to a peaceful end, with the Islamabad administration officially promising the clerics to crack down on massage parlours and other businesses suspected of indulging in sex trade if the seminary students would inform the police rather than act on their own. This was unprecedented in terms of showing tolerance of utter lawlessness in the heart of the capital by the Musharraf regime. All this while, veiled girl students kept occupying the children's library, refusing to vacate, while their male counterparts virtually closed the main artery in front of the Lal Masjid to traffic.

As the continued rhetoric emanating from the mosque's loudspeakers refused to cease and the people were called upon to rise and overthrow an un-Islamic regime, the government came under increasing public and media pressure to enforce its writ on the errant mullahs. Musharraf in his weekly broadcast, in-camera sessions with college students, assured the nation that he was prepared to take action against the mullahs' lawlessness

if the media promised not to show bodies. This had the effect
of spraying fuel over fire. The seminary students went all out,
resorting to aerial firing and declaring the entire area out of
bounds for the security forces. As the police tried to close in,
armed clashes ensued in all earnestness. Before the troops were
called out to assist the police, seminary students had vandalized
and set ablaze several government buildings and ministry offices
and banks in the area. Thus began a final standoff on 3 July 2007,
with sporadic firing from both sides shattering the proverbial
calm of Islamabad and confining the residents of the area to
their homes.

The images of the clashes being broadcast twenty-four hours
a day by the independent media jolted the nation. It is said that
the turning point came after army personnel were killed by
firing from the opposite side. By now the media was fully on to
the story, including those developing on the sidelines. In a role
reversal, after weeks of lawlessness, it was now paramilitary
forces using loudspeakers to warn the clerics holed up inside the
Lal Masjid compound to lay down their arms and surrender. The
warnings became clearer in their intent after a few days. Now the
authorities were asking the clerics to let the innocent girls and
boys (students) go and they might be given amnesty, as parents
of the students had begun gathering outside the compound to
urge their release. The clerics were clearly using them as human
shields. A few of the children were released in order to raise
the possibility of a dialogue which would secure safe passage
for the clerics and their militant companions who had allegedly
collected a stockpile of ammunition inside the compound and
seemed determined to fight to the finish unless they were granted
safe passage.

All this while, the right-wing MMA party and other clerics
from across the country volunteered to hold negotiations with
the mullahs and the militants. Despite the militant clerics and
their armed brigade holding Islamabad hostage for days, no
one who came to mediate was denied permission by Musharraf.

Among those who offered and were allowed to intervene at this critical juncture were politicians from the religious alliance, the MMA, and Musharraf's so-called trusted loyalist Chaudhry Shujaat Husain, the head of the military-backed ruling party, the PML-Q.

On the eve of the final day of the siege, the elder cleric brother and the firebrand prayer leader Abdul Aziz was caught by security forces trying to escape to safety as he came out covered from head to toe in a black veil posing as a woman. The images were broadcast live from outside the Lal Masjid by TV crews present there. He was taken straight to PTV, and still dressed in the veil, he uncovered his face, saying he had decided to come out and negotiate everyone's release. Thus having made a complete fool of himself and having caused deaths in the process by now, he was arrested. His wife, who headed the girls' madrassa, and daughters also followed Abdul Aziz's exit out of the besieged compound. The paramilitary forces then began pounding the premises with mortar mercilessly. By 11 July 2007, when all firing from the compound ceased, the troops entered the premises. A total of some hundred people had been killed in the operation, the younger cleric Abdur Rashid Ghazi among them. Heavy shelling and explosions captured by TV cameras from ammunitions stored inside had charred many of the bodies beyond recognition.

Although the media was not allowed to show the bodies, the debate on TV on the fate met by the militants began to turn sympathetic. This was the opportunity opposition leaders of all hues and political leanings had been eagerly awaiting. On the other hand, Taliban rebels in Waziristan who were holding a dialogue with the government on reaching some accommodation, called off the process in retaliation for the military action against Lal Masjid.

More intriguingly, even if unsurprisingly, the ruling PML-Q leaders Chaudhry Shujaat Husain and his cousin Parvez Elahi, the chief minister of Punjab, who both claimed to be Musharraf's most trusted allies, rushed forward to announce that they would institute a fund offering lifetime stipends for the upkeep of the affected families who had suffered a loss in the operation. Hundreds of adults and children were enlisted for financial help, while the two cousins kept appealing to Musharraf to show clemency and let the arrested cleric walk free. Thus, while a sordid, gory chapter in the history of Islamabad came to an end, another one had just begun.

The survivors of the Lal Masjid siege, which the media was now calling a national tragedy, vowed revenge through suicide bombings against targets everywhere. Islamabad would never be the same peaceful, if unexciting and dull, place for which it was equally cherished and derided.

Clearly, the PML-Q-led government under the pro-military establishment Chaudhry cousins from Punjab also had their traditional loyalties elsewhere which ran counter to Musharraf's vision. Unlike Nawaz Sharif before them, under Gen. Ziaul Haq, who largely shared the general's Islamization vision, the Chaudhrys did not share any of Musharraf's progressive ideas. They were only interested in raking in the benefits of supporting the general they took as their master without having to practically support his progressive social agenda. Their popularity and election to key public offices rode the wave of absolute power exercised by Musharraf, feeding on the droppings thrown their way. The PML-Q's rout in the February 2008 election amply drove that point home. The elder Chaudhry, Shujaat Husain, went around meeting diplomats in Islamabad days before the election, boasting that his party was set to win a two-thirds majority, and that it had been decided at a high-level meeting chaired by Musharraf only weeks earlier. On election day, however, the plan was never put into action because the army in the nick of time decided to sit back and give a level playing field to all contestants. The election was fair, except perhaps in a few constituencies in Karachi where the MQM had a field day. It was so fair elsewhere that no one disputed its results.

As for what came to be known as the Lal Masjid tragedy, weeks later, under court orders, the Islamabad administration was told to unlock the mosque and open it for prayers. A renovated mosque was handed over to a new cleric, who was beaten up by the old cleric's goons and made to run for his life. The court also ordered that the seminaries be restored and handed back to their old administration.

This takes us to Musharraf's other ongoing battle on the home front, one against an independent judiciary headed by the then chief justice of Pakistan, Iftikhar Mohammed Chaudhry.

# 10

## Justice Denied

The legal crisis began on 9 March 2007, with Musharraf summoning the chief justice to his camp office at Army House in Rawalpindi Cantonment. Also present on the occasion were his Military Intelligence chiefs and some other officers. The chief justice was asked to resign, citing allegations of misuse of power while in office. Justice Chaudhry refused. He was allegedly intimidated and threatened with consequences, but he stood his ground. When detaining him at Army House for several hours to exert pressure on him did not work, he was reluctantly permitted to go home; he was denied entrance to the Supreme Court and an announcement of his suspension from office was made by President Musharraf.

At the time of his appointment to the Supreme Court in June 2005, Justice Chaudhry was seen and perceived as Gen. Musharraf's man of trust and thus entrusted with the key position. However, over time, he established himself as one with an independent bent of mind. He took suo motu action, requiring the government to explain, even take back, certain measures that in the court's view affected the general public's interest. Whether it was the poor rape victims who could not obtain justice through normal channels because influential people were involved or those who had gone 'missing' since the 'war on terror' began and the government said it had no clue of their whereabouts, or indeed the controversial privatization of nationalized industries, Justice Chaudhry established a reputation of calling the government high-ups to book. This particularly infuriated Prime Minister Shaukat Aziz and Gen. Musharraf, so the latter, upon the advice of the prime minister, decided to seek the judge's resignation by whatever means it took.

Before that happened, however, a copy of a letter sent to the chief justice by a well-known lawyer from Lahore—an open letter of sorts addressed to Justice Chaudhry—was released to the media. It accused him of derogatory treatment of lawyers, of haughtiness that did not become his office, and of misconduct and misuse of authority, including a preoccupation with receiving protocols and demanding favours to which he was not entitled. It also accused the chief justice of getting his son appointed to a job for which he was not qualified. It begged the top judge not to bring a bad name to his exalted office, and either make amends or step down. Thus, when the 9 March grilling of the chief justice took place at the president's camp office followed by his suspension, there was unexpected reaction from the legal community given the contents of the letter made public just days before the event. The lawyers, refuting by their action what the open letter by their fellow lawyer claimed, rallied behind the suspended judge and demanded his immediate reinstatement.

The month of March saw protest rallies outside the Supreme Court in Islamabad, the lawyers' boycott of court proceedings, and demands that Musharraf step down. The extreme demand by the lawyers came in the wake of the illegal way in which the chief justice had been suspended. Under pressure, the government asked the remaining Supreme Court judges to start a hearing of the chief justice's case before going for his impeachment. The case was begun behind closed doors. On 16 March, the lawyers became even more infuriated, challenging the legality of the hearing, and demanding open-court proceedings against the chief justice at a rally in Islamabad. Security forces attacked the rally with tear gas and batons, wounding several lawyers. The violence against the lawyers' rally was covered live by independent news channels; one of the channels' newsroom also came under attack

by the security forces and the intelligence apparatus operating
in plain clothes. The government–lawyers standoff became
the biggest developing story, which began to be broadcast live
whenever the lawyers took to the streets. By April, the lawyers
declared an open war on the Musharraf regime, vowing to fight
on until the restoration of Justice Chaudhry. Their demand that
the case being heard behind closed doors should be converted
into a public hearing was finally met by the government halfway,
allowing in-camera proceedings.

The lawyers, led by the Supreme Court Bar Association,
activated the district and high court bar associations across the
country, and the scenes of riot police charging against peaceful
rallies organized by the legal community began to be broadcast
live to a national audience. The legal community's protest spread
to all large and small cities across Pakistan. On 6 May, the chief
justice's defence lawyer-cum-PPP politician, Barrister Aitzaz
Ahsan, drove the top judge in a massive rally from Islamabad
to Lahore, covering the distance of 280 kilometres in a period
of over twenty-four hours. At the Lahore rally, the chief justice
again received a rousing welcome when political activists and
civil society members from a cross-section of society joined
the legal community's show of strength to press for the chief
justice's restoration. Justice Chaudhry addressed the Lahore Bar
Council, calling for a reform of the existing position by standing
up to dictatorship. The movement of sorts gained considerable
momentum within days and the chief justice embarked on a
nationwide programme of addressing the hundred or so bar
councils across Pakistan.

However, his planned tour of Karachi on 12 May was
scuttled by Musharraf's supporters. The PML-Q and MQM-led
provincial and city government blockaded all major roads and
let their armed party workers loose to block the passage of the
chief justice and his supporters into the city from the airport.
Pakistan's commercial capital and the largest city came to a
grinding halt as its arteries became battlefields of rival political

workers. The day-long violence culminated in a death toll of forty-one, 'deportation' from Karachi airport of the chief justice's non-Karachi-based supporters, including Barrister Ahsan, and finally Justice Iftikhar also opted to board a plane back to Islamabad from the airport. Later that night, Musharraf at his own rally arranged at Islamabad with the help of the Chaudhrys of Punjab, thanked the 'people' of Karachi for not allowing his opponents to enter the city. The media blasted the president's insensitive speech, and termed it as condoning violence that took innocent lives. Musharraf responded by placing curbs on the media, including a ban on certain talk shows. However, due to intense public pressure, the government had to lift the curbs after a few days.

On 2 July, the Supreme Court's full bench threw out the so-called evidence, based on government's surveillance tapes of judges' movement and telephone tapping, provided to it by the attorney general of Pakistan, declaring it scandalous, illegal and thus inadmissible. The attorney general and his team got a lot of flak from the presiding judges. They were told to furnish details about who collected such evidence and on whose instructions. The government team cut a sorry figure, feigning ignorance about the ignoble evidence's origins, and begged the court for forgiveness.

On 17 July, when a decision in favour of the chief justice seemed all too imminent, a lawyers' rally being held in Islamabad was attacked by a suicide bomber, killing fifteen participants, though the lawyers' leadership escaped unscathed. On 20 July, the Supreme Court dismissed the government's plea to indict the chief justice, reinstating him to his post and declaring Gen. Musharraf's summary suspension of him illegal and without due process—just as Musharraf's own sacking by Nawaz Sharif had been seven years earlier.

With a smug appearance and standing by his criticism of the lawyers' movement, Musharraf, however, said he accepted the Supreme Court's decision to reinstate Justice Chaudhry. His legal team informed him that now there was little he or the government could do to get rid of the chief justice while remaining within the bounds of the constitution. Immediately after his reinstatement, Justice Chaudhry formed several benches headed by senior judges to take up the pending petitions whose hearing had been deferred by the four-and-a-half-month-long judicial crisis caused by Musharraf's suspension of him and the lawyers' refusal to attend to legal business. The restoration of the chief justice did wonders in establishing a sense of justice and rule of law among the people at large and restored public confidence in the justice system which had been all but eroded. The restoration of the chief justice was also hailed by all political parties as a sign of the loosening of Musharraf's complete stranglehold over power. It encouraged Benazir Bhutto and Nawaz Sharif to think about returning to Pakistan and taking part in the 2008 elections, said their party sources. There was suddenly hope that the Supreme Court could allow the two leaders what Musharraf said he wouldn't, that is, returning home to participate in the polls. Accordingly, Nawaz Sharif planned his return for 10 September, after the court ruled that it was his right to return home as a citizen whenever he chose to do so.

Litigants seeking relief against various government acts of commission and omission made a beeline for the Supreme Court. Among these were the families of the 'missing persons', a euphemism for those who were suspected of having been picked up by intelligence agencies and held in prison or even possibly being handed over to the Americans for their alleged links to Al Qaeda and the like; labour unions whose activities were seriously curtailed and who were protesting against laws that had been recently amended to the benefit of the employer (one such law stipulated that a working day constituted twelve hours of labour, six days a week, without giving the labourers any additional pay for the extra three hours they now had to work). To this list were also added the burning issues of the so-called affected parties of the Lal Masjid operation and Musharraf's seeking re-election for another five years from the outgoing electoral college, the national parliament and the four provincial legislatures. It was to Justice Chaudhry's credit that he abstained from presiding over the cases involving the Lal Masjid operation and Musharraf's bid for re-election, for obvious reasons. It was also to his credit that he abstained from hearing a petition of contempt of court filed by the PML-Nawaz against the Musharraf regime which against the court's ruling to the contrary had deported Nawaz Sharif only hours after his landing at Islamabad on 10 September. The general, however, suspected him and the judges who had restored him of showing no less partiality against him. When a decision on his own re-election by the outgoing electoral college was imminent on 3 November 2007, Gen. Musharraf struck again. Recalling the 'dark day' a year later, the English-language *Daily Times* wrote in its editorial: 'President Musharraf transformed himself into General Musharraf and imposed martial law, called "emergency-plus", to dismiss Justice Chaudhry, along with scores of other judges in the higher judiciary.'

The new Provisional Constitution Order (PCO) passed by the general required all existing high court and Supreme Court judges to take a fresh oath of office so as to dispense justice under the provisions of the PCO now put into force rather than the Constitution of Pakistan, which the PCO placed in abeyance. This time round, some sixty judges led by the chief justice of Pakistan, Iftikhar Mohammed Chaudhry, refused to oblige the general. The majority of them might not have done that previously, as in 1999, but there was no way that they could do so again after the triumph of the lawyers' movement that resulted, with immense public support behind it, in the reinstatement in July of the chief justice. The judges' refusal to take a fresh oath threw the country into another major legal crisis, the likes of which Pakistan had never seen before. As people and opposition leaders thronged the houses of the judges in the support of their decision not to stamp their approval on the PCO, the general placed them all under house arrest, with intelligence goons sent to some to persuade them to comply. Only a few succumbed to pressure, the vast majority remaining steadfast. Politicians who tried to reach the chief justice's house in Islamabad were also arrested and placed under house arrest. Members of civil society who tried to lodge their protest by holding even peaceful vigils outside the judges' residences were also rounded up. A reign of terror was unleashed against whoever now dared to oppose the general, who had not been known for such high-handedness thus far. Prominent lawyers were also picked up; some were tortured, including the erstwhile president of the Supreme Court Bar Association, Munir A. Malik. First his house in Karachi was attacked by sniper firing; when that failed, he was taken into custody after the imposition of emergency rule, and brutally tortured, to such a degree that he had to be hospitalized for kidney failure and put on dialysis. Barrister Ahsan and the firebrand Ali Ahmed Kurd were also placed under a long house arrest lasting weeks.

Soon after their release, as the elected government took office, the lawyers kept up their demand for the restoration of the deposed judges, but the PPP-led government appeared in no mood for accommodation. On 25 March 2008, the day he took up office as the prime minister, Yousaf Raza Gilani, addressing the elected house, verbally ordered the release of Justice Chaudhry, and the directive was complied with literally within minutes by the Islamabad police. Barricades laid to the Judges' Colony were removed and within a couple of hours the lawyers and camera crews gathered to see and hear the chief justice, who appeared on his gallery, looking triumphant. The hope that the judges would now be swiftly restored by the PPP-led government was rekindled, because the party had committed in writing to doing so in an agreement signed between Zardari and Sharif days before they launched their bid to impeach Musharraf. However, in the days that followed, it became clear that Zardari had other ideas. He reneged on the promise, perhaps fearing the independent judiciary that had taken shape under Justice Chaudhry's leadership, and which had even looked the army chief in the eye and defied him.

The lawyers pressed on with their demand; in June 2008, they launched a nationwide long march to Islamabad to pressurize the government to restore the deposed judges. The week-long event saw thousands of lawyers from across Pakistan converge outside parliament, braving the heat. Barrister Aitzaz Ahsan who led the long march as the Supreme Court Bar Association president, and who was at the time a member of the PPP's Executive Committee, assured the lawyers, many of whom had come to stage a sit-in until the government acceded to their demands, that they had made their point and that the government had given the assurance that it would soon reinstate all the judges. That never happened.

Meanwhile, as Zardari eyed the presidency in the wake of Musharraf's imminent departure, the PPP brought more and more of the deposed judges round to the idea of taking a fresh oath of office under the same PCO which had sent the judges packing in the first place. With Zardari's election to the presidency, the process of co-opting the judges gained a new momentum, to the point that nearly all but some four judges, including the former chief justice, rejoined their duties. The lawyers, however, refused to relent, though the government believed that their movement had lost the steam it had before a majority of judges returned to their seats.

Thus far, though all the original sixty judges fired by Musharraf were not reinstated even much after his resignation in August 2008, the lawyers' movement will go down in history as one that changed many things in Pakistan. For one, it brought on TV and into ordinary citizens' homes, the discussion of fine legal points and debate on the rule of law and constitutionalism as against dictatorial politics, thereby educating the people. It also galvanized public opinion in favour of democracy, the people's right to know and stand up for their rights, and also distinguish the right from the wrong—even when engaging in politics. In terms of being a campaign aimed at creating political awareness among a largely depoliticized younger generation and among university students, it more than succeeded in achieving its purpose.

Some accused the lawyers' movement of falling into the hands of right-wing parties opposed to Musharraf's 'Enlightened Moderation', and also of being funded by the Sharifs in Punjab in particular, where it was arguably more popular than elsewhere. But to the majority of middle-class lawyers who put their livelihoods on hold for nearly two years, this sounds too harsh a view as grounds for the movement's dismissal. One of the charges that Musharraf levelled against the judges who refused to take a fresh oath under the 3 November 2007 PCO was indeed that the Supreme Court under Justice Chaudhry was bent on supporting the regressive agenda of the extremists. The general cited the strong line the court took on ordering the provision of relief to the affected families of the Lal Masjid operation and taking the government to task in the case of 'missing persons'; Musharraf's explanation was that those cited as 'missing' had gone off to jihad in Afghanistan and beyond on their own and the government could not be held responsible for their conduct. The general's position on the issue was somewhat vindicated by the PPP-led government months after he stepped down from office. The government's adviser on interior affairs, Rehman Malik, corroborated the assertion in parliament in January 2009 during a grilling session by lawmakers who pressed the democratic government to tell the truth about the whereabouts of the people who had gone 'missing' under Musharraf's rule. It was further corroborated by the parents of the Mumbai blast suspect, Ajmal Amir Kasab, who told journalists that their son had gone 'missing' months before he surfaced on TV screens in a surreal, gruesome scene, killing innocent people indiscriminately, as the footage released by Indian authorities showed. Kasab's parents also admitted that their son, on his last visit home, said he would be heading out for jihad, requesting his mother to pray for him. The story was broken by the Pakistani media piecemeal as journalists made their way to Kasab's village looking for his family in the aftermath of the Mumbai attacks.

Back to Musharraf's waning weeks in power and his ongoing confrontation with the lawyers, as it transpired, the judges who handed down the anti-government judgment in the Lal Masjid case and those who threatened the Federal Investigation Agency's chief of action against him if he failed to produce the 'missing' persons before the court, were among the minority of Supreme Court judges who took the fresh oath of office under General Musharraf's PCO of 3 November 2007. As irony would have it, Justice Abdul Hameed Dogar, one among them, was later appointed the chief justice of Pakistan by the PPP-led democratically elected government, which too has come to fear an independent judiciary and refused to reinstate Justice Chaudhry.

# 11

## Women's Issues

L ike his madrassa reform plan, Gen. Musharraf's stated desire to bring meaningful legal reforms in laws repugnant to women also remained a pipe dream. The Protection of Women's Rights Bill, which was passed by parliament in November 2006 with the help of Bhutto's People's Party, which surprisingly but understandably voted alongside the government, was a case of too little, too late. The rest of the opposition parties, with the exception of Sharif's PML-N which abstained, voted against the bill, with the MMA, the religious parties' alliance, threatening to resign if the bill were signed into law—something it never did when the bill was indeed signed into law by Musharraf. On the other hand, rights groups and civil society organizations which demanded a complete repeal of the controversial set of so-called Islamic laws introduced by the former dictator Gen. Ziaul Haq, rejected the bill which they said only tried to water down some aspects of the laws discriminatory to women, not take the entire sting out of them.

The Hudood Ordinances of 1979 were among the first set of laws that Gen. Zia enforced through presidential ordinances which were later ratified by his largely non-representative, rubber-stamp parliament. The so-called Islamic laws, endorsed by only some ultra-orthodox clerics interpreting the Quran, had long remained controversial within the scholarly religious circles. For instance, the twentieth-century great Muslim poet, philosopher and pan-Islamist Allama Mohammed Iqbal, who also happens to be Pakistan's national poet laureate, had rejected the traditionally formulated Hudood laws as being against the spirit of Islamic justice, and called for a rethink on all such laws which were mistakenly referred to as laws given by the Quran (*Reconstruction of Religious Thought in Islam: The Madras Lectures*). In fact, Iqbal went a step further and argued that the Quran was not a book of law, but one that propounded universally applicable principles on which laws were to be based. He authoritatively ruled that such laws should be formulated by qualified individuals for application in a Muslim society that they had the mandate to serve at a given point in time, rather than transplantation of the cited instances of certain laws as they were applied in a tribal society 1400 years ago. Justice, he argued, was the underpinning higher principle as derived from the Quran.

The supposedly Islamic laws enforced by the Zia dictatorship and pertaining principally to sex-related offences, equated rape with fornication by assuming the woman complainant guilty of having had illicit sex, by her own admission, unless she could prove her innocence by presenting four male eyewitnesses to her rape. Testimony of women witnesses to the crime was only acceptable on a redoubled discriminatory basis of equating two female witnesses with the testimony of one male witness, who must have seen with the naked eye the man being accused of rape as actually penetrating the victim. There cannot, by any stretch of the imagination, be any sense of justice being rendered at any time under such a scheme of reckoning. No wonder then that women's rights organizations had opposed the Hudood laws tooth and nail even when these were promulgated under Ziaul Haq's martial law. In fact, women who took to the streets to register their rejection of these laws throughout the early years of the Zia regime and his dubious Islamization process became the vanguard and icons of the political movement that later materialized as a formidable challenge to his rule.

The promulgation of Hudood laws nonetheless opened the floodgates of further abuse of women in Pakistan; every woman victim of rape was now assumed guilty by the law of having had illicit sex which became punishable by the state. A greater inherent evil in the law dictated that reporting a rape by a woman was actually a confession on the victim's part that an illicit sexual act had indeed taken place; if she was not able to meet the requirement of presenting before a court four male witnesses to the crime she alleged was committed against her, her consent to it must be assumed. Within months of the passage of the twisted law, thousands of women who went to seek justice for a crime committed against them, and failed to provide the prescribed gender-biased count of witnesses to prove it, ended up in jail. The patent, state-backed injustice against women continued long after Gen. Zia was dead and gone barely a decade after promulgating the infamous laws. Successive governments, including two of them led by Benazir Bhutto and her supposedly liberal, secular party, were too reluctant to repeal or even attempt at reforming the outrageously vicious laws that made a mockery of justice, Islamic or otherwise.

However, by the time Musharraf took up the issue, much water had flown under the bridge. The public stood equally disenchanted with his policies as it had been with those of his predecessors. The daily in-depth dissection of all issues confronting the nation on an independent electronic media beamed into every home had definitely made the viewers more, even if not necessarily better, informed. Live, interactive programming on prime-time TV left little unexplored or unexposed.

There was too much that was deemed to be un-Islamic and West sponsored in Musharraf's 'Enlightened Moderation' in action. Any tinkering with supposedly Islamic laws was equally supposedly an attempt at spreading un-Islamic, Western values of 'free' thinking, anathema to an increasingly Islamic society. In the case of the changes proposed in the Hudood Ordinances, it was also seen by many and voiced as endorsing 'free sex'; that is, if indeed the clause on fornication was to be watered down and made less severely punishable by negating its equation with being raped. This was poignantly pointed out by none other than Maulana Fazlur Rahman of the MMA, whom Musharraf had designated as the leader of the opposition in parliament, considering him a pragmatic politician who always seemed to prevail over his hardliner–religious persona. By the time the proposed amendments to the controversial laws were brought to parliament, the MMA had already fallen foul of the general for reneging on his promise to doff his military uniform in return for the religious parties' support of a constitutional amendment indemnifying all actions taken by the general in the aftermath of the 1999 military coup, including his appointment of himself as the all-powerful president who also retained the post of army chief.

On the other hand, the commission set up by the Musharraf regime under a retired high court (woman) judge, Justice Majida Razvi, entrusting her with the task of making recommendations on the repeal or otherwise of the controversial Islamic laws repugnant to women, had recommended an outright repeal of the Hudood Ordinances. The PML-Q government was, however, not eager to move on the recommendation. It took two long years, basically sitting on the proposal without taking any action, perhaps hoping that Musharraf too would move on to other pressing matters than bothering with the now controversial repeal of the Hudood Ordinances.

He did not, however, move on. Upon persistent prodding by Musharraf, the ruling party finally agreed to float the issue out of the cellar where it had only been gathering dust. Yet, before doing this, the PML-Q president, Chaudhry Shujaat Husain, and his cousin, Parvez Elahi, the chief minister of Punjab, went to consult a committee they had constituted of religious scholars to endorse only those changes in the laws which would not blemish them with the charge of acting against Islam. Clearly, the two politicians were already looking at life beyond Musharraf's military rule umbrella which sheltered them. By the time this was done to the satisfaction of the Chaudhrys, it was too late in terms of delivering what the rulers were ready to deliver. Even the People's Party, which had pledged its support to the bill in a bid to encourage Musharraf to seriously get talking to Benazir Bhutto for political accommodation, felt uncomfortable going along with the much-watered-down version of the bill, say party sources.

It took a lot of pep-talking by Musharraf himself with the PML-Q leadership on the eve of the passage of the Protection of Women's Rights Bill before the party hurriedly, if still reluctantly, moved the bill in parliament and got it passed within two hours without any meaningful debate being permitted. Minutes before the vote was taken, in a melodramatic move, the PML-Q president, Chaudhry Shujaat Husain, submitted his resignation in advance to the speaker of the house, saying that it would come into effect if anyone could prove that the bill his party was bringing was against the injunctions of Islam. The point that it wasn't, as it had been altered and endorsed by the Chaudhrys' hand-picked religious scholars, was the real problem that evaded everyone concerned.

Consequently, women victims of the ordinances only got a bare minimum respite in the form of a sessions court now being brought in to order a victim's arrest upon complaint of rape rather than the police arresting the victim immediately and requiring her to present witnesses to prove her innocence before she could be set free and treated as a victim. 'Alleging' on the part of a woman that she was raped also became a bailable 'offence', which it was not under the originally drafted and the existing law. The rest of the conditions pertaining to furnishing four male or double that number of women witnesses in support of the victim's 'allegation', remained unchanged. It was clear that the relief that the wronged women of Pakistan so desperately needed was still being denied to them. The Musharraf regime, however, flaunted the bill as a great breakthrough that further empowered the women of Pakistan by eradicating gender bias from the law.

The rights' groups rejected it outright. Their grievances against General Musharraf harked back to his insensitive and offensive handling of at least two women's plight, which came to light, at the hands of a social order and the state which through its laws equally perpetuated injustice towards women. The cases in point were the gang rape of the internationally publicized Mukhtar Mai under a punitive sentence passed on her by a tribal jury and the reported rape of Dr Shazia Khalid, allegedly by an army captain. While Musharraf had promised to bring Mai's tormentors to justice, he had exonerated the captain accused in the second instance even as he ordered an enquiry. Later, he was heard implying time and again that the surfacing of such cases brought a bad name to the image of Pakistan, and therefore the media should have desisted from playing them up.

While Dr Khalid was offered asylum by the UK government after she received threats for going public with her accusations of rape, Mai was prevented by the authorities acting directly under orders from Musharraf to leave on a tour of the US to address rights groups' forums there. Both had brought a bad name to Pakistan, argued the general, and were doing no service to the country. Deep down, he probably took the reporting and 'playing up' of such crimes against women as a personal insult. He was after all seen all too often on TV and in person patronizing performing artistes, mostly women. How could he allow their emancipation and victimization at the same time, he must have asked himself, and found only one answer: that his political opponents were blowing out of all proportion tales of women suffering under his benevolent rule just to bring him down; worse still, to tarnish the image of the country which only he was destined to lead as its sole messiah. Much of the criticism he faced for introducing the women's rights bill, from both liberal and conservative quarters, perhaps reminded him of his failure to effectively defend his ambivalence on the issue

that harked back to his tour of the US in connection with the
UN General Assembly's annual session in 2005.

In an interview to the *Washington Post*, he was quoted to have
remarked that apparently it sounded quite lucrative for Pakistani
women to get raped, as that would win them visas to go [and live]
abroad. Though Musharraf denied having made that comment,
the paper firmly stood by the story, making the original recording
of the interview available online for all to hear.

Soon thereafter, the general had another outrageous episode
of angry outbursts with Pakistani women rights activists who
confronted him at a conference in New York with regard to his
personal views on women as expressed in his interview with
the American newspaper. He shouted down at them from the
podium: 'You are against me and Pakistan.'

'The president allowed an event held to promote his
government's pro-women policies to degenerate into one between
himself and part of the invited audience,' as *Dawn* and the *Hindu*
quoting the story reported (19 September 2005). Musharraf
completely lost his cool in response to another question by
another woman: 'I am a fighter [and] I will fight you. I do not
give up and if you can shout, I can shout louder. I wish you
had quoted Muslim scholars [in support of your argument] as
opposed to British scholars,' he raged on. When yet another
woman raised a question, he completely lost it: 'You are a Benazir
supporter. The lady was prime minister of Pakistan twice; ask
her what she has done for Pakistan.' He carried on like a person
possessed, accusing his audience of taking sides of leaders for
whom he made no attempt to hide his contempt:

> We have introduced new leaders who don't tell lies like your
> leaders did. You have disappointed me. I am disappointed
> with people like you. You work with the people who
> looted and plundered the nation. You [act] against national
> interest; you have your own agenda [highlighting the cases

that hurt Pakistan's reputation]. I know that there are people with vested interests and financial interests who are against Pakistan.

*Dawn*'s correspondent present on the scene wrote: 'When altercations began to get uglier [Pakistan's ambassador to the US], Jehangir Karamat [the army chief preceding Musharraf], moved the president away from the podium by gently patting his shoulder. Musharraf, however, returned to the podium to say he was not against all those who worked for the cause of women's emancipation.'

Ironically, in the months that followed, the same Gen. Musharraf would engage Benazir Bhutto and reach a deal with her that would pave the way for the exiled leader's return to Pakistan, largely on her terms, but at a price that she would pay with her life.

# 12

# The Balochistan Imbroglio

This was one more ill-conceived and uncalled-for war which the adventurer in Musharraf began and also won, albeit with disastrous, lingering consequences that continue to haunt Pakistan. The petroleum-, gas- and mineral-rich south-western province of Balochistan borders Iran and Afghanistan to the west and has a 1000-kilometre-long coastline to the south, stretching from the strategic mouth of the Strait of Hormuz in the Persian Gulf to the shoreline of Karachi along the Arabian Sea. The province is sparsely populated and utterly underdeveloped, with a population barely half that of Karachi city, but a vast area marked by rocky mountains, plateaus and plains, which make it the largest province of Pakistan. Right from independence from the Raj, Balochistan has had a history of neglect by the central government in terms of development; political decision-making and provincial governments have been imposed from outside, even through military actions when deemed fit, or by playing one tribe up against another. The ethnic Baloch barely constitute a majority in the province, and are in a minority in the provincial capital, Quetta, an important garrison town near the Afghan border on the road to Kandahar. The other major ethnic group comprises Pashtuns and a much smaller number of nomadic Brahvi tribes.

After 9/11, with the presence of international troops in Afghanistan and Pakistan military's forced retreat from there, Balochistan, along with the Frontier province, became the country's frontline state within the state. The Musharraf regime embarked on an ambitious project of setting up more military cantonments there and pursuing in right earnest the development of a fully fledged deep-sea port at Gwadar, a historical fishing village, located at the far south-western end of the Balochistan coast. Earlier, during the Nawaz Sharif and Bhutto governments, a modern fishing port had been developed at Gwadar and plans to link the far-off port with Karachi through a 750-km-long coastal highway had been approved. Further north from Gwadar, Bhutto had also initiated a gold-mining project at Saindak. With the prospects of developing a deep-sea port at Gwadar and linking it by road to Karachi and upcountry through another highway, Pakistan hoped to open a lucrative trading link with Central Asia, on the one hand, and China, on the other, in the years ahead. By the time Musharraf came along, and under the changed geopolitical and strategic situation brought about by the ouster of the Taliban in Afghanistan, he speeded up the work on these projects. China was engaged for building the deep-sea port, Pakistan's third port, and the army was given the contract to lay the highways. Both the deep-sea port and the coastal highway were completed well within the stipulated schedule, though the construction of a north–south highway was still pending when Musharraf bowed out of office. This has, however, generated little economic activity, much less any trickling down of benefits of the port to the local communities. This is because things also changed for the worse in Balochistan during the eight years of the military-backed regime led by Musharraf.

With the beginning of construction of the port at Gwadar, massive irregularities began taking place from the very outset. The land around the site of the port and far beyond the sleepy town was purchased by the government and the army from the local people at throwaway prices with promises of development of a modern, future city with all amenities in the years to come. It was, however, almost instantly put up for grabs by the urban commercial land mafia operating principally from Karachi and

Punjab. Land prices were jacked up overnight, with the urban middle and upper-middle class investing heavily in this far-off 'city of the future'. Within months, a five-star hotel chain set up a luxury hotel at Gwadar which began to be frequented by investors. Cut off for all practical purposes from the large cities, the people of Gwadar for the first time came face to face with what was a known and accepted fact of life elsewhere: economic disparity. Sensing resentment among the local people, the commercial developers laying roadworks and other essential infrastructure at the many planned housing societies and commercial areas around Gwadar opted to bring in labour from Sindh and Punjab. This added further to the local people's alienation in this purely Baloch area of the province. Soon Baloch nationalists, led largely by tribal sardars (chieftains) from the north-east of the province and with a history of resisting domination from outside forces, also made their way into Gwadar. Citing the local community's grievances, they threatened the government with a great Baloch nationalist movement if it did not stop such development projects which not only aimed at uprooting but also clearly bypassing the local, long-settled, if impoverished, fishing communities. The government responded by increasing the security cover for the Chinese engineers working on the Gwadar port project, cordoning off the port area and setting up pickets manned by the notoriously high-handed Frontier Corps, still working under its colonial-era, all-encompassing mandate to maintain law and order, backed by paramilitary forces. The Baloch nationalists rekindled what was believed to be a lost cause since the last major military operation under Zulfikar Ali Bhutto was launched in Balochistan in 1974.

The three Baloch tribes of Marri, Mengal and Bugti, with their private armies, were once again found pitted against the powerful Pakistani military establishment. Old grievances, too, were revived, after two Chinese engineers working in Gwadar were kidnapped and killed by Baloch nationalists in 2005. The government warned the sardars to back off or be ready for a military confrontation. Long-dormant organizations like the Baloch Liberation Army, the Baloch Liberation Front and the Baloch People's Liberation Front were revived and the battle-lines were redrawn.

The old Nawab Akbar Khan Bugti, who had served as the governor and chief minister of the province under successive regimes in the past, took up the cause of the Baloch, and called it resistance against the outside forces eyeing the lands and the resources of the proud Baloch people. He also called off his long-running feuds with the Mengals and the Marris and invited them to join the struggle. The nawab's Bugti clan owns hundreds of thousands of acres upon which one of Pakistan's natural gas fields is located in Sui. Under an existing arrangement, the government of Balochistan got the gas royalty from Islamabad and the Bugtis collected a significant amount in annual rent for their lands. With nationalist sentiments flaring up, the running dispute in progress with Islamabad over the rent of the land, which Bugti insisted had been short-measured at the time it was first leased out to the government in the 1950s, escalated. He now wanted more rent for the additional land that was actually under the government's use, together with all the backdated arrears.

When the Musharraf government began setting up a new cantonment in the neighbouring district of Kohlu, the Marris who owned the bulk of the land there, threw in their lot with the Bugtis; not to be left out, the other major clan, the Mengals, also joined their kinsmen in resisting the building of new military cantonments on 'Baloch' land. Skirmishes began between the army and the three tribes' lashkars, called *farari*s or insurgent private armies. In March 2005, the PML-Q government formed a reconciliation committee comprising party chief Chaudhry Shujaat Husain and the cabinet minister Mushahid Husain Syed to talk things out with the disgruntled sardars. They met Nawab Bugti and clinched a deal with him, having put his political concerns to rest and also agreeing to greater development and job quotas for the Baloch as well as revision of the rent the government owed to the Bugtis for the use of their land. When weeks passed by and there was no let-up in the siege laid by paramilitary forces to the Bugti area, Nawab Bugti withdrew his 'ceasefire', and pitched battles broke out with the paramilitary forces. It was clear that the army was not willing to relent and let the political government deliver on the deal it had struck with Nawab Bugti.

Meanwhile, a highly politicized rape of the lady doctor Shazia Khalid, serving at the Pakistan Petroleum complex located on Bugti lands and alleged to have involved an army officer, took place. The Baloch across the board were flabbergasted as they considered the lady their 'guest' and a benefactor. To add fuel to the fire, Musharraf dismissed the victim's allegation, exonerating the accused army officer even before an enquiry was conducted. The doctor and her husband, a petroleum engineer at the Sui government facility, had to flee for their lives, alleging intimidation and threats from the officer concerned. Rights organizations with intervention from Western governments were barely able to rescue the couple; the UK government eventually bailed them out by offering asylum in June 2005. Musharraf responded angrily to the move, saying the allegations were politically motivated and that it was an attempt by Baloch nationalists to bludgeon Pakistan's image abroad.

By December it was an all-out war. The army bombarded Dera Bugti, the Bugtis' home town, with the aim of driving the nawab's *farari* army and tribesmen out and declaring their intention to build a military cantonment there to protect the gas fields. Baloch nationalist organizations now openly called for independence from Pakistani rule and began targeting infrastructure, power stations, gas pipelines, railways and government offices whenever and wherever they could. The provincial capital of Quetta, and even Karachi, which has a two-million-strong Baloch population, also saw a number of bombings which the government blamed on Baloch nationalists. The entire leadership of the insurgent *fararis* was now underground, following a missile attack that razed Nawab Bugti's housing complex at Dera Bugti to the ground. Musharraf threatened the sardar to fall in line or else 'he won't know what hit him'.

Seeking refuge with the Marris from continuing aerial bombardment, Nawab Bugti and his people were now on the run. In an interview from his hideout in February 2006, he said: 'Our options are clear: resist and die or die without resisting' (*Herald*, March 2006). As violence from both sides was in full swing, Bugti and the other sardars claimed that thousands of their men were picked up by security forces and were now 'missing'. The government refuted the claim, saying there were only so many Baloch 'subversive' men taken into custody as the police record showed. The independent Human Rights Commission of Pakistan corroborated the nationalists' claim.

Amidst all this, Musharraf embarked on a campaign to visit far-flung areas in Balochistan, inaugurating a dam here and a power generation project there. In March 2006, in a high-profile and heavily guarded visit to Gwadar with security helicopters keeping vigil from the skies above, he inaugurated the gas supply project for the 'new city'. True, piped natural gas did arrive in Gwadar, but a year down the road only some 118 connections were given, largely to those living within or next to the new port. The town and most of its 60,000 inhabitants were conveniently left out.

Back at Dera Bugti, the army arranged a tribal *jirga* (consultative assembly) comprising Nawab Bugti's rival clans who decided to oust the nawab from his lands, taking control of the holding as their own. On 26 August 2006, helicopter gunships pursued Nawab Bugti deep into his remote mountain hideout in a cave. According to official accounts, as the commandos descended from the helicopter at the mouth of the cave, a huge explosion took place; the roof of the cave collapsed and the old Nawab Bugti was crushed under the rubble along with his bodyguards. Bugti's son, however, alleged that the army used chemical weapons to kill his father. Six days later, the body of the seventy-nine-year-old nawab was handed over, locked up inside a coffin, to two of his clansmen. The government allowed a very short funeral prayer which only a handful of people attended and the nawab was laid to rest at Dera Bugti. No children or grandchildren were allowed to be present at the last rites.

The entire province of Balochistan, including the capital, Quetta, was completely shut down in protest for four days. Highways in and out of the province were also shut down to all traffic. Condemnation of the military action followed from across the country. All large and small parties, rights groups and civil society organizations deplored the killing of the Baloch leader. A nationwide shutter-down strike was also observed. The influential khan of Kalat, Mir Suleman Daud, whose family, though of non-Baloch origins, had ruled Balochistan under the Raj, warned: 'If Islamabad continues its anti-Baloch attitude, Balochistan will one day become an independent country' (*Herald*, September 2006). Veteran Baloch nationalist leader Sardar Khair Bux Marri endorsed the khan's view. The jailed former chief minister of Balochistan, Sardar Akhtar Mengal, also called for independence, seeking international support. Musharraf responded to this total alienation of the Baloch by congratulating his men in khaki on the success of the military operation that killed Bugti. He showered praises on five of the 'valiant' commandos, including a colonel, who had also died in the assault on Bugti's cave. However, official reaction from the Balochistan government, coming from one of Bugti's tribesmen, Razik Bugti, was: 'When there is a battle, there will be losses on both sides. Remember bullets and rockets cannot distinguish between an army colonel or a nawab or a foot soldier.'

Balochistan never fully recovered from the fissures caused by the military action. Baloch nationalist leaders remained underground for the rest of Musharraf's tenure in office; some went into exile. Targeting of government infrastructure and public facilities and kidnappings of non-Baloch in Balochistan became the norm. Musharraf blamed Indian consulates in neighbouring Kandahar in Afghanistan and Zahidan in Iran for funding and supporting Baloch insurgents. All Balochistan-based political parties boycotted the February 2008 elections. On 15 August, three days before Musharraf resigned, the newly elected Balochistan assembly unanimously passed a resolution urging the federal government to initiate impeachment proceedings against the president.

Ironically, the resolution was moved by none other than Musharraf's own erstwhile loyalist MPs from the PML-Q. It accused the general of 'exercising his powers in an unconstitutional and undemocratic manner, [launching] military operations in Balochistan in which hundreds of people, including Nawab Akbar Khan Bugti, were killed and hundreds of Baloch, Pashtuns and Balochistanis [non-Baloch residents] were kept in illegal, secret cells'. Some MPs also demanded that a case be filed against Gen. Musharraf for killing innocent people in military operations. Others also demanded that the general be 'arrested and brought to Balochistan for an open trial' (*Dawn*, 16 August 2008).

This outburst of anger and vengeful rhetoric aside, the truth was that the current Balochistan assembly comprises only those who, against the call of the nationalists, had contested the election and won, many on PML-Q tickets. Traditionally, successive Balochistan governments have been known for their corruption and poor governance. After assuming the presidency in September as the duly elected president, Asif Ali Zardari, himself an ethnic Baloch long settled in Sindh, has attempted to reach out to the Baloch by offering unconditional apology on behalf of the federal government for the 'wrongs done in the past' and promising greater autonomy to the provinces together with the transfer of administrative and financial control over their resources.

# 13

## The Bhutto Magic

One calls it magic because it works as such with the teeming millions of the poor and the dispossessed of Pakistan; the spell has demonstrated its lingering effect since 1970. Benazir Bhutto may never have been as popular as her father, Zulfikar Ali Bhutto, but there is no denying that she was the sole heir to the legacy of populism he bequeathed to Pakistan. It may shatter stereotypes in what is without question a markedly male-dominated society, but the popular acceptance of Benazir Bhutto as the heir to the Bhutto legacy is unquestionable; it is blasphemy to think, rather believe, otherwise even in the ever-increasingly Islamic republic. No other leader who has achieved popular public approval through legitimate means (credible electoral victory, public relations, canvassing, etc.) has approached Benazir Bhutto's popularity, and that includes her own late bother, Mir Murtaza Bhutto, the male and thus supposedly more bona fide heir to the Bhutto legacy. Politically a hardliner and a fierce opponent of Benazir's pragmatic politics, Murtaza Bhutto was gunned down in an exchange of fire between his security guards and the police deployed near his home (the original Bhutto residence) in Karachi in September 1996 when his sister was the prime minister. Benazir's husband, Asif Ali Zardari, was accused of having been behind the 'murder' of his brother-in-law; an allegation both Benazir and her party denied.

According to a news story entitled 'The Story behind "Benazir–Musharraf Contacts"' which appeared in *Dawn* on 22 June 2007,

quoting the *Guardian*, Gen. Musharraf's contacts with Benazir
Bhutto, seeking to reach an understanding on power-sharing,
dated back to the latter half of 2005. However, the inverted
commas used in the heading told a tale itself. It was only two
years after the fact that the media finally caught on to what two
of Pakistan's most important leaders had been up to; although
there were speculations that the two leaders may be talking to
each other, these remained just that. Neither side would confirm
or deny such reports, and both certainly sustained their mutually
antagonistic rhetoric.

The *Dawn* story was received in Pakistan as a 'breaking news'
tellip that Pakistanis were by now all too accustomed to seeing
on their TV screens. This, while Musharraf's battle continued
with an independent judiciary headed by the then suspended chief
justice of Pakistan, Iftikhar Mohammed Chaudhry. However,
even as the story of Bhutto–Musharraf contacts broke in 2007,
no one knew how close the two leaders were from striking a
deal, much less have an inkling about the dramatic events set to
unfold in the months ahead.

According to the story, Musharraf had nurtured a grudge
against Benazir that dated back to her first stint in power as the
prime minister as far back as in 1993. The general had made out
a case before the prime minister, suggesting an all-out assault
on Kashmir as an indigenous insurgency had been sparked there
in the aftermath of the rigged state elections of 1989. Bhutto,
however, rejected the idea and confronted the general as follows:
'This country is run by a civilian government. I am still the prime
minister.' When Musharraf still pressed his point, an argument
ensued between the two, with Bhutto finally asking, 'Tell me what
happens the morning after [Pakistan attacks India]?' Outwitted,
the general was reported to have abruptly left the briefing in a
huff. Having made her point, Bhutto left the matter at that.

At the diplomatic level and relying on its own intelligence
reports, the UK by mid-2004 was convinced that it could not
trust Musharraf alone for what he said and did with regard to

the 'war on terror'. It established contact with Benazir Bhutto through the then foreign secretary, Jack Straw, who tried to convince Bhutto of the possibility of her and Musharraf working together under a democratic dispensation to curb the rise of extremism in Pakistan. Bhutto initially thought the proposal 'hopeless'. Shortly thereafter, Mark Lyall Grant, the then UK high commissioner in Islamabad, conveyed a message from Musharraf to Bhutto in Dubai, seeking her help in steering Pakistan out of its many problems, and offering to release her husband who had languished in jail for years facing unproven corruption charges as a confidence-building step between the two leaders. The paper said Bhutto was still suspicious and did not agree to carry forward the dialogue. In her book *Reconciliation: Islam, Democracy and the West*, published posthumously, Bhutto dwells in detail on her on-again, off-again engagement with the general. She admits that contact between her party and the general was established soon after the 1999 coup, which pre-dated and confounded the guesswork and speculations that the media was churning out in 2004. Bhutto says they exchanged views and ideas indirectly and through emissaries, but there always remained mutual suspicion between them. However, they met face to face as late as in January 2007 in Abu Dhabi. Earlier, in August 2006, the Americans had facilitated a phone conversation between the two while Bhutto was in New York, which broke the ice with Musharraf's suggestion that progressive forces should join hands to address the challenges faced by Pakistan. Bhutto had placed certain conditions to be met before she could consider saying yes to Musharraf. He had suggested that she meet his emissaries to work out the details. Bhutto, however, also grew suspicious of the middlemen, and said she would rather talk to the general directly, so there followed a lull in contact.

When they finally met in Abu Dhabi four months later, Bhutto wrote that she was surprised at how '... the meeting was both long and cordial. We had had a one-to-one meeting for several hours ... I brought up all the contentious issues, and

Gen. Musharraf's response to all of them was positive' (p. 227). Bhutto's list of demands included: give up the post of army chief; hold transparent elections monitored by international observers and open to all parties and individuals; set up an impartial election commission; remove the ban on the election of a prime minister for a third term; and scrap politically motivated cases against all politicians who had not been convicted after years of being put on trial in what Bhutto called the 'kangaroo courts' of Pakistan.

In that ground-breaking meeting in January 2007, according to Bhutto, the general gave her everything she asked for in return for her joining the next post-election government with him staying on as president but in his capacity as a civilian and not as army chief. They also agreed on Bhutto's return to Pakistan before December 2007 and in time for her to take part in the election due in January 2008.

From this account of Bhutto's, it is clear that the general gave up all the bargaining chips he held one after the other. He had to commit to doffing his uniform and even give a date for doing so (which he did); he had to give up the condition that Bhutto return to Pakistan after the election and certainly not take part in it; he had to agree to take back all corruption cases against Bhutto and her husband (which he eventually did) against his publicly stated position that he 'would recover all the looted wealth' from politicians who had gone into self-imposed exile (the obvious reference to Bhutto could not be mistaken). In return, he was even unable to get her party's support for his re-election bid the following October before he dissolved parliament and called for fresh elections. Bhutto's surprise at how well their meeting had gone was indeed well founded, for against all her expectations she had given the general nothing in exchange for all she desired and thought she got from him.

Indeed, as the following weeks and months would bear out, everything that Bhutto eventually got the general to agree to in Abu Dhabi did not come to her nearly as smoothly as Musharraf had promised. She had little reason to take him or his word for what they were. He had hoodwinked the MMA by getting their support to indemnify all his actions through a constitutional amendment and then reneged on doffing his military uniform. The Americans and the British too no longer believed what the general said in terms of lending his support to the 'war on terror' and doing even a fraction of what he promised.

Bhutto's understanding was that the general now stood virtually isolated and needed her to bail him out. In the domestic arena, the political dispensation he had put in place had miserably failed to deliver: the electorate had come to despise the system and the individuals who symbolized it; there was nothing they loathed more passionately than the general and his impotent political sycophants whom Bhutto called 'political orphans' who needed the army to shelter them; the people wanted all of them out immediately rather than anyone staying on for a further five-year term in office. Musharraf's rash and without-due-process sacking of the chief justice of Pakistan, and the latter's reinstatement by his colleagues without even putting him on trial, was a further pointer to the general's eroding control and authority. Internationally, too, especially after the London bombings and the reluctant assault on the Lal Masjid compound by the army, the general's 'double face' lay exposed to his Western friends: the fact that he denied that the London bombers had any links with Al Qaeda operating out of Pakistan, which proved quite untrue, infuriated the UK; that he had permitted Lal Masjid to operate in the very heart of the Pakistani capital, serving as a base for terrorists planning attacks on targets in the West, angered the US. Benazir Bhutto's suspicion of Musharraf was now, at long last, being matched by the West's sudden wariness of him. She was not going to extend any favours to him without making him go down on his knees and offer her on a platter all she wanted from him, and more.

While Musharraf had time and again failed to live up to the West's and Bhutto's expectations, he never failed them on their suspicion of him. The US kept pressing him to do more: to get on the track of the wanted terrorists and start busting their gangs and strongholds; Bhutto wanted him to let democracy take its own course by stepping aside and ending the role of the army in politics. However, neither seemed to be getting too far with Musharraf other than receiving mere promises. If this view was true, then the choice Musharraf eventually made was between acceding to what Bhutto wanted from him as against what the US wanted. He gave her what he had promised, though only grudgingly and piecemeal, because he thought that doing so at the time was also meeting at least one of the demands made on him by the US: restore democracy. Also, he knew that Bhutto was no alien to the political system of Pakistan, democratic or otherwise, in which the real power always rested with the generals and not the chief executive.

The gory suicide bombing drama enacted on Bhutto's arrival home on 18 October 2007 in Karachi left even a woman as courageous as her shaken. She had least expected such a turn of events, having cast aside the many advisories passed on to her through friendly governments. However, because she knew Musharraf had also tried to dissuade her from coming home before the election, she stuck with her decision to return before the election and take part in it. He had already got himself elected by the outgoing parliament on 6 October, with Bhutto's PPP having abstained from the vote. A major opposition alliance led by the MMA had tendered their resignations hoping for the dissolution of the electoral college, but the PPP had persuaded Nawaz Sharif not to jump on the bandwagon. Over a week had elapsed since his re-election but Musharraf had not withdrawn the cases against Bhutto and her husband. Till the very last days before her return home, she had to spend 'long hours' on the phone with Musharraf, reminding him of his promise but he had already begun dilly-dallying. This raised Bhutto's suspicions of the general to even greater heights and gave rise to concerns about her security after her return. Finally, just days before 18 October, the scheduled date of her return, Musharraf promulgated the NRO quashing all cases against the Bhutto couple.

Thousands of her supporters came to receive her at Karachi airport; all security arrangements for her and her vehicle were made by the party itself, nothing being left to the government which nonetheless promised to give the broader security cover. As her nearly half-a-kilometre-long motorcade moved from the airport towards the city at a snail's pace, and party workers sang and danced in front of her truck, night fell. Party leaders in the procession, and even on the same vehicle (a custom-built bulletproof truck), complained that their cellphones were still working, hinting that the government had not jammed any wireless or remote-operated devices along the route of her procession. This was promptly conveyed to the authorities, but no action was taken. Along the route of the procession, the police were conspicuous by their absence; even the main artery going towards the airport, with only a green belt separating it from the side on which Bhutto's motorcade was inching forward, was open to vehicular traffic (I drove right up to the mouth of the procession on the parallel road as did some others minutes before the bombs went off). After nearly ten hours into the procession, street lights went out and the entire area (one of the city's major cantonments) was shrouded in darkness. The local utility and the Sindh (provincial) government were contacted and pleaded with but to no avail, say party leaders. Then suddenly a suicide bomber struck; seconds later a remote-controlled device also went off, instantly killing some 150 people and seriously wounding hundreds. Bhutto miraculously survived.

Within minutes, her personal security staff (many of whom had also been killed in the attack), whisked her away to safety. The following day, Bhutto alleged criminal complacency on the part of the government for the many obvious security lapses, and even blamed a few individuals, including the Chaudhrys of Punjab, for complicity in the attack.

The motley crowd of thousands that had come to Karachi to welcome their leader returned in as orderly a manner as they had come, some having lost close relatives. There was sadness and shock at what had happened, but no anger or lawlessness; not a stone was pelted, nor even a bush harmed. Given that there were no police present, the PPP supporters could have gone on a rampage, but they didn't. Nobody carried firearms, and there was not even aerial firing in protest, as there had been none in jubilation at their leader's homecoming only hours earlier despite the fact that carrying firearms and firing in the air are all too common in a Karachi rally.

That night it appeared that terrorists had struck out of desperation but they could never succeed in a country with a leader who had so much of her people's power behind her. The majority had spoken with their refusal to indulge in violence despite the violence perpetrated against them that night. There was enormous emotional strength and political maturity in the value system Bhutto had come to embody.

However, as an eyewitness to both the historical homecomings of Benazir Bhutto from exile, in 1986 in Lahore and in 2007 in Karachi, one observed a vast difference between the two occasions. In 1986, the Punjab government led by Nawaz Sharif, then a protégé of Gen. Ziaul Haq, had effectively sealed off the city of Lahore to prevent people from elsewhere from entering (only a minority of her supporters managed to filter in on foot to receive Bhutto). The government had also grounded all transport vehicles in Lahore to stop the people from going to the airport twenty-four hours before her arrival. The provincial Sindh or the MQM's city government did nothing of the sort in Karachi on 18 October; on the contrary, the MQM leader Altaf Hussain welcomed Bhutto's decision to land in her home town (where she, as he, was born and raised). The Karachi event saw hundreds of vehicles packed with Bhutto's supporters from across the country make their way to the airport and from there on form part of her procession into the city. While in 1986 it was an unending sea of people that thronged the entire fifteen-kilometre route from the old Lahore airport to the venue of her public meeting despite the restrictions imposed by the Punjab government, in Karachi in 2007 it was a phalanx of cars, buses and trucks, four to six abreast, that made up her procession. The rest of the city, being essentially an MQM stronghold, wore a deserted look. Even outside Bhutto's residence, in the posh seaside Clifton, and her electoral stronghold of the inner city, the utterly impoverished district of Lyari, there were few signs of public festivity. By comparison, in 1986, the entire city of Lahore had worn the appearance of a public festival for the preceding twenty-four hours despite harassment by the Sharif-led authorities. Perhaps the difference in the fervour demonstrated at the two receptions reflected the difference between the two military dictators, Generals Ziaul Haq and Musharraf. While the former was a dictator in the classical sense who employed all means to control people's minds and their actions, and had hanged Zulfikar Ali Bhutto, the latter tried desperately (through his 'Enlightened Moderation') to appeal to people's hearts but failed to elicit the reaction that he so keenly sought; even so, he had managed to facilitate the return home of their leader. More importantly, Musharraf had the grace to demonstrate that he knew how to live with his failures, and there had been many by then.

The languages heard in Bhutto's procession in Karachi were many and regional, as we call them in Pakistan; it was a motley crowd that had converged on Karachi from across the country, united only by their leader and her, even if only perceived, forward-looking and emancipating vision for Pakistan. Urdu of the variety spoken in Karachi was conspicuous by its absence, yet the national language brought the disparate PPP supporters together as they shouted in unison: *Benazir aayegi, rozgaar laayegi* (Benazir shall come and bring employment) and *Chaaron soobon ki zanjir, Benazir, Benazir* (the thread that holds the four provinces together is Benazir).

The Bhutto magic had returned to Pakistan, rekindling hope for the masses and instilling fear and awe in those with dictatorial or pro-autocratic proclivities. Zulfikar Ali Bhutto's daughter would cast the spell even as she was being propelled to her sad end in the weeks ahead. She might be gone soon but the spell would linger, as does the slogan *Jeeay Bhutto!* (Long live Bhutto)

# 14

## The Final Coup

In the aftermath of the attack on Bhutto's homecoming rally, and after accusations had been traded between her and the Sindh government as to who was responsible for the carnage, the latter placed restrictions on her movement, citing serious threats to her life. Bhutto insisted that only the government's own henchmen, her political opponents and rogue elements within the country's intelligence and security apparatus, were out to get her. She made light of the threat posed to her life by Islamist terrorists, which the government insisted was very real. The following day, *Dawn* (19 October) quoted the US deputy secretary of state John Negroponte, who had played a role in urging Musharraf and Benazir to work together, as saying: 'We would like to encourage moderate political forces, and ... we think that Gen. Musharraf is a moderate political element, and so is Ms Bhutto ... [to] to work together to try and deal with the very challenging issues their country faces.' The paper also quoted another US State Department official who condemned the threat posed to Benazir Bhutto by Al Qaeda.

However, not to be deterred by officialdom, one day Bhutto left her home in Karachi to visit her constituency of Lyari, insisting she must go to her people and not sit at home waiting for the election. Deep down it was perhaps her lingering suspicion of Musharraf that made her embark on daredevilry. Rumours were rife of the government advising the president to declare a state of emergency, and call off elections for another two years. Musharraf's re-election as president for the next five years by the outgoing parliament while still staying on as army chief had been challenged in the Supreme Court as illegal. The general feared that a hostile Supreme Court under its reinstated chief justice whom Musharraf had dismissed, might just declare his reappointment as president null and void, and the PML-Q government led by Bhutto's opponents was playing on that fear. With terrorists striking randomly, a nationalist insurgency brewing in Balochistan, and the Islamists terrorizing huge pockets of the Frontier province, the government made a case for postponing the elections, and Musharraf was said to be 'weighing all options'. Flabbergasted, Bhutto reacted with full fury, but while denouncing dictatorship as a counterweight to democracy, she never criticized Musharraf by name or implied that he would act on the misconceived advice of the government. Privately, as she writes in *Reconciliation*, she counted on the then free and independent judiciary to remove that last hurdle in the way of a full restoration of democracy by declaring Musharraf's re-election unconstitutional and thus void.

Then came 3 November, the eve of the day Musharraf had come to fear. He pre-empted an imminent negative ruling by the Supreme Court by a few hours by declaring, in his capacity as the chief of army staff as opposed to the president of Pakistan, a state of emergency, suspending basic freedoms, placing the constitution in abeyance once more. Musharraf again made another of those 'My dear countrymen' speeches. It was clear he had little cause to impose emergency rule other than saving himself from losing power, a prospect that had never figured in his vision for Pakistan under his 'leadership'. The reasons advanced by the general for imposing emergency sounded like a charge sheet against a government which acted as his rubber stamp, and which, ironically, he had chosen not to dismiss even though the constitution permitted him to do so. That was not, however, the point. The extra-constitutional step was aimed only at enabling Musharraf as the army chief to suspend the constitution, eject the judges whose adverse ruling he feared, and also teach the media a lesson for what he called 'overstepping its role', before making new rules that he could live with. There was an immediate crackdown on the media; all news channels were pulled off air, and newspapers were told to watch what they printed. A Provisional Constitution Order (PCO) promulgated by the army chief gave the president (Musharraf himself) sweeping powers under which to rule and to ask the government to take action as it deemed fit to deal with the 'challenging, extraordinary, and chaotic situation' obtaining in the country. There was to be no recourse to the court against the PCO, which required all judges to take a new oath under the new provisions or be compulsorily retired.

All political activity was banned until further notice. Benazir Bhutto, who had dashed back to Dubai over the weekend to be with her children, husband and ailing mother, rushed back home, terming the imposition of emergency rule by the general 'martial law'. On her return, she too was swiftly placed under house arrest in Lahore, this time 'surrounded by 4,000 Pakistani militia with bayonets drawn; it was clear that free elections were impossible', as she wrote in *Reconciliation* (p. 231). Musharraf had again lived up to her suspicion of him. If there was any consolation, it was in the fact that soon British Foreign Secretary David Miliband, US Deputy Secretary of State John Negroponte, and Chairman of the (US) Senate's Foreign Relations Committee Joseph Biden assured her of their governments' resolve to keep up the pressure on Musharraf to lift the emergency and hold free and fair elections.

It would not be until Musharraf was able to pack the Supreme Court with new judges, promoted from the lower levels, who would be loyal to him and not declare his re-election illegal, that he would be prevailed upon to lift emergency rule. Thus, with the courts on his side, and relenting principally to external pressure, he lifted the state of emergency and announced the date he would doff his military uniform before holding elections, scheduled for

8 January 2008. Still, there was no telling whether the general would hold free and fair elections. The restrictions placed on the media, however, were not fully lifted. News channels were asked to give undertakings to the government that they would not broadcast live the coverage given to the suspended chief justice or the still protesting lawyers, not cast aspersions on Musharraf's re-election as the president, and the like. Only those channels that complied with the new code of conduct were permitted to return to air. Two popular news channels, Geo and Aaj, owned by large media groups, stayed off the air much longer than others. Later, Aaj was restored, but Geo's broadcasts in Pakistan remained shut for many more weeks. Bans were also placed on certain anchors of talk shows with whom the general had really fallen foul.

Given such conditions, the opposition parties argued with some credibility that the government was set to rig the forthcoming elections. Nearly all religious parties, the lawyers' movement for the restoration of the judges, some smaller parties, and most regional, nationalist parties gave a call for the boycott of the election under Gen. Musharraf. However, after Musharraf swallowed another bitter pill of allowing the return of the Sharifs, his arch-enemies, from exile in Saudi Arabia in November 2007, Bhutto was able to convince Nawaz Sharif not to pull out from contesting the polls. She had argued that even if the elections were to be rigged, the general would fear incurring the wrath of the voters of Pakistan's two most popular parties, which would bring more pressure on him than boycotting the polls. Leaving the field open for Musharraf to play the game according to his own rules made little sense, Bhutto stressed on Sharif, and he listened to her advice. The two parties decided to take on the general together. While Bhutto's rhetoric in her election campaign was somewhat circumspect, in that she left Musharraf out of her criticism, her axe fell heavily on his cronies in the PML-Q. Sharif demanded the return of the army to the barracks and keeping it there if democracy were to take root. The election campaigns by the two main parties, however, lacked the traditional, festive fervour associated with election rallies. The leaders' movement was heavily curtailed by security risks posed by militants striking undeterred at the place and time of their own choosing. Even Bhutto had begun taking warnings about her safety seriously, and she heavily cut down her planned itinerary of touring the country.

Then came the fateful day of 27 December, barely ten days before the nation was scheduled to go to the polls. Bhutto's mysterious assassination by a gunshot or by the impact of the bomb blast next to her vehicle shortly after her rally in Rawalpindi, shocked the nation as never before. There was massive outpouring of anger across the country. Enraged protesters took to the streets within minutes of the tragedy, indulging in acts of mindless lawlessness. Karachi and the entire province of Sindh were worst hit. In three days of arson and vandalism by angry mobs, several hundred vehicles were torched and public and private property was damaged. The law enforcement agencies were conspicuous by their absence, as they had been at the scene of the carnage following Bhutto's homecoming on 18 October.

Meanwhile, the People's Party and the government again traded accusations. When Musharraf was asked about the apparent lack of security cover at Bhutto's Rawalpindi rally, he denied the charge, insisting that the best possible security had been provided, and that Bhutto's own 'stupid' act of standing up through the sunroof duct to wave to her supporters was to blame for the tragedy. The PPP's demand that international forensic experts be brought in and an enquiry be conducted by the UN into Bhutto's assassination was turned down. When a couple of weeks later, under immense public pressure, the government did call in Scotland Yard experts, their findings matched those of the government's own investigations into the tragedy, citing the fact that the scene of the crime had been washed clean of all possible evidence, virtually within minutes of the bombing. The PPP was now clearly on the wrong side of the government once again. Musharraf made no effort to reach out to the party in its hour of grief; instead, he further vitiated the atmosphere by issuing a biting criticism of the deceased Bhutto, basically focusing on her refusal to take the threat posed to her life by extremists very seriously, dismissing it as a figment of the government's imagination. The 'deal' signed between Benazir Bhutto and Musharraf virtually lay in tatters, at least as far as public perception went, while Nawaz Sharif stepped forward and lent his voice to the sentiment of anger prevailing among the PPP rank and file. Together, his faction of the PML and the PPP vowed to avenge the murder of Bhutto.

It was under such extreme political polarization between Musharraf and his opponents that the election of 18 February 2008, rescheduled from 8 January, was held. Surprisingly, however, no major incident of violence was reported from any part of the country on election day. One of the reasons perhaps was that against the public's expectations, no extraordinary number of security personnel were deployed, and certainly there were no army personnel in sight which would have made many voters suspicious of Musharraf's intentions and also generated anger amongst them. A 45 per cent voter turnout, high by Pakistani standards, was reported. When the results began coming in later that night, it became clear that the election had been one of the fairest in the history of the country. The PPP garnered the highest number of seats, followed by Sharif's PML-N. The Musharraf-backed PML-Q had been routed, as had been the mullahs. In the Frontier, seen as the hotbed of extremist activities, the secular, leftist Awami National Party and the PPP bagged the bulk of the votes. In Karachi, the MQM allowed not a single seat to fall to the rightist parties, many of whose candidates contested as independent candidates despite the majority of the MMA parties having boycotted the polls.

As far as Musharraf and his policies were concerned, the public mandate given to his opponents was a message that both had been rejected at the polls. Musharraf, however, refused to read the writing on the wall and vowed to continue in office, calling himself a duly elected president under the very system which had in turn resulted in the triumph of his opponents, and hence underscored his and the system's legitimacy. He was perhaps counting on the split vote of the electorate which had not given any one political party a simple majority to form the government on its own. According to the amended constitution, it was now up to the parties to show the president which particular group could forge a coalition government for the heads of that group to be invited to form a government within thirty days. While the PPP, the PML-N, the ANP and the rightist JUI agreed to sit in a coalition government, Musharraf once again tried to lobby with the MQM, the PML-Q and other elements to form a government with the PPP, hoping to salvage the power-sharing deal he had struck with Benazir Bhutto. His final disappointment came when the PPP also succeeded in winning over the sympathy of the MQM, which agreed to support the combined opposition forces against the now isolated president. Still the general was unmoved, and vowed defiantly to stay on.

By July 2008, the coalition government came under immense public pressure to impeach the president. All the four provincial legislatures passed resolutions urging the central government to impeach the general-president. Zardari and Sharif accused Musharraf of plotting to create bad blood amongst the coalition partners and the presidency of hatching conspiracies to destabilize their coalition government. In August, the coalition parties agreed to initiate impeachment proceedings against the president. Musharraf finally agreed to a loosely cut deal between him and the government, brokered by Western diplomats and under pressure from the army, that would allow him to bow out with any grace that was possible. He would not be exiled, nor put on trial for any action taken since he assumed office in October 1999.

With immunity granted to the fallen general for all his actions, he made his last, passionate, resignation speech over national TV on 18 August to an audience that now sought only to see the back of him. In his long speech lasting forty-five minutes, the general looked the defeated soldier he now was, taking pains to explain his achievements during the eight years that he had ruled the country virtually single-handedly and without being accountable to anyone for his unilateral actions and decisions. Contrary to all expectations, there was little remorse in the general's tone and tenor, and greater self-praise than ever seen or heard before. Towards the end of his resignation speech he theatrically lifted his hands up in a dramatic gesture and concluded with '*Pakistan ka khuda hafiz!*' (God save Pakistan!) as he clearly very reluctantly stepped down from office.

Thus ended the eight-year-long virtual one-man rule of a general who became known in equal measure for his liberal cultural policy and a deviant brand of politics that he, like his autocratic and self-styled messiah predecessors, practised. The saving grace: the high security Army House in Rawalpindi would remain his home until his nearby luxurious property, a country farmhouse spread over acres, was ready for occupation. The state would continue to provide the former president with the top level of security cover that he genuinely needed and enjoyed during his years in office, along with the officially entitled protocol at home and during his personal visits abroad. No other former Pakistani president, elected or self-anointed to the office, had ever enjoyed such extraordinary privileges after retirement. This perhaps had more to do with the back-door pressure exerted on the government by the army top brass. The sitting generals did not want to see their former chief and the symbol of the army's stranglehold over political power for eight long years be humiliated in any way. So, in a way, he walked away yet again with all, even in his apparent downfall.

Those who met him at social gatherings after his resignation detected little loss of oomph and zest for life in the general. He was still his boastful, daredevil self, making uncanny predictions of the fall of the elected government as being 'only a matter of time'. This, some in the media interpreted as a sign of the fire still burning in the general's belly, which may one day, soon enough, see him re-enter politics. Though an unlikely prospect, there is no telling what actually goes on in his head.

# PART II

# 15

## Hearsay

Ibrahim Zauq, the last Mughal emperor Bahadur Shah Zafar's tutor in poetry, and a great nineteenth-century Delhi poet, composed the famous ghazal that begins '*Sunn toh sahi jahan mein hai tera fasana kya/Kehti hai tujh ko khalq-e-khuda ghaibana kya* (Listen to what your story is in this wide world/ What God's mortals say of you behind your back).

As a young boy, Pervez Musharraf was raised amidst such conventional wisdom that informed his Delhi-based, middle-class, civil-servant-studded, forward-looking family, and the traditional Muslim values it espoused. However, at Independence, the one-way journey that the family took to Pakistan meant not only leaving their Neherwali Haveli in Old Delhi but also much else behind. As the family struggled to settle down in the new country, there was more to learn, more to seek, and less to guard of a past from which it had walked away. By the time Musharraf went through high school and joined the army, the past had all but become an echo. As he climbed ranks within the most disciplined and powerful institution of Pakistan, where he learnt to break rules and get away with it, he also learnt to make new ones, for himself and the country he would rule single-handedly for over eight years. Amidst all this, the old value of listening to what the people had to say behind one's back went missing. Unbridled power took the reins of his life.

This more or less frames the story of the erstwhile most powerful man in Pakistan since the reigns of his predecessors known for their autocratic tendencies which defined their way of governance. These included Gen. Ziaul Haq, a military dictator (1979–88); Zulfikar Ali Bhutto, Pakistan's only civilian chief, martial law administrator, president, and elected prime minister (1971–79), and last but not the least, Prime Minister Nawaz Sharif, whose stints in power were equally marked by dictatorial conduct.

# 16

## The Jewel

'As seventeen-year-old boys in the PMA [Pakistan Military Academy] in 1961, we were a bit different from the rest of the cadets there,' says the former Colonel Akbar Ali Shareef, Musharraf's batchmate, and a loyal friend to date.

Enamoured by and unashamedly loyal to his lasting friendship with the general, an excitable Col Shareef cannot wait to divulge the harmless details of comradeship that, he claims, has never seen any lows. The two have met and partied throughout the past many decades as and when an occasion arose; this includes Musharraf's trips home to visit his family in Karachi even during his presidency. The colonel begins recounting right from the beginning: '[at the PMA] Both of us came from Karachi, from a public school background. He and I had had exposure to the outside world at an early age, and that mattered a lot. My father had spent time in Ceylon [Sri Lanka] as the Director-General, Colombo Plan, rubbing shoulders with UN officials. Musharraf's father had served in the foreign service in Turkey. We had seen more of the outside world in our formative years than the other boys at the PMA.'

Most young recruits in the army come from modest middle-class backgrounds from the recruiting hinterland of northern Punjab and the Frontier Province, where the colonial-time physical attributes of height, chest width, body weight, together with loyalty and obedience to authority exist as traditionally qualifying personality traits for recruitment in the armed forces.

Few aspiring cadets from elsewhere make it past the initial physical exam; fewer still get past the written test followed by an intimidating oral ordeal, where a heavily northern Punjab- and Frontier-based garrison dialect reminiscent of the old British officers' arrogant mannerism is the staple fare. Apart from the first few decades following Independence, the army has very largely comprised recruits from rural areas, although there have been exceptions in the official cadre.

Col Shareef continues: 'Unlike the rest of the boys, we were very jovial, happy-go-lucky young men and full of the zest of life. We were pranksters and mischievous as boys that age are. Such memorable mischief we did that we even laugh today recalling those days. I remember that even if we had a three-day holiday, we would catch the next train to Karachi [a twenty-four-hour journey] and have our fun along the way before returning to the academy.'

Col Shareef arguably came from a least likely army cadet background, educated as he was at the elite, very westernized coeducational convent institution, Karachi Grammar School. Musharraf had attended the only somewhat more accessible St Patrick's, an all-boys convent. Both schools were known equally for their very urban-based enrolment of students coming from modern families with liberal values.

Recounts Shareef: 'Back in my school in Karachi, I was the president of the Elvis Presley Fan Club, Pakistan. Musharraf had a record-changer, which few people did in those days. Our rooms were next to each other in the academy; we were so ahead of the rest of the boys that none dared pass in front of our rooms. We were both fond of dancing. In fact I taught him how to dance the Cha-cha-cha ... he tells people even today that I am his ustad. "He taught me dancing," he says. Since then we have had a friendship and an association that has not seen any downs. All along we have had the same understanding of issues, likes and dislikes. In the academy we didn't have many boys from

Karachi; among the few that were there, we were like-minded. Our understanding only grew with time, and we did not break our association, even when we served in different areas as officers. We'd always find time to meet up.'

From Col Shareef's recollections of their time together in the forces, Musharraf emerges as a carefree, happy-go-lucky young officer full of buoyancy, who would take risks even if that meant annoying his superiors. In his memoirs, *In the Line of Fire*, the general himself makes little secret of such a tendency.

Shareef continues: 'It was me, for instance, who told him of the ceasefire in the 1971 war. We were in the Suleimanki sector [lower Punjab]; I was in the striking corps, he was in the armoured division and a commando. The commandos were to launch ahead of us the next day when a ceasefire was declared. So that morning I drove up to him to inform him that a ceasefire had been agreed upon just the night before.'

There's much pride in Col Shareef's recollections of the times past and spent together, particularly of the two men's affinity right from their formative years which only strengthened with the passage of time. Musharraf, he says, is a man who will do what he feels he has to do come what may, and anything to be with a friend: 'There has been no crack in our friendship. Ever. Once, he cut short his visit as the president to Abu Dhabi to be at my daughter's wedding in Karachi. No event in my family takes place without him being present. It just does not happen. And I know that.'

Then, recalling the day of his daughter's wedding, Shareef also points a finger at some of the people who had by then come close to the president by becoming sycophants. Referring to the bunch as opportunists, he says, 'They thought the president was in the UAE and he wouldn't come to the wedding, so they too didn't show up. And then he came.'

As a man perhaps too sure of himself and not showing any sign of insecurity (a typical serviceman trait), Shareef says, 'Musharraf has many friends around him [at most times]; he's very trusting of them. He is even weak of the ear when it comes to his "friends"; whoever gets to him first he will believe them.'

This, while the general is also known to take umbrage when advised or warned; advice solicited or otherwise, even by those he counts as his friends, is seldom welcome: 'I never wanted to be the one to tell him which friends to choose or who to keep close. It was for him to decide all along. I did not want to be seen as causing a wedge between him and his newer friends while he was in power. I did not want any doubts or friction to come between us at any point. At times the majority of us, his inner circle friends, felt that a certain individual should not be close to him. But we seldom said that to his face. He still has some "friends" close to him about whom I can only pray that they are and will remain his friends.'

While many of the general's 'friends' may have deserted him after he relinquished power because he was no longer in a position to extend favours to them, Shareef did the opposite: 'After his resignation, I took the first flight out to Rawalpindi to be with him. He would be down in the dumps, I thought. But I saw no change in him. All he said was that he did the best thing to resign when he did and that he did so "for the sake of the country". Had he not resigned there would have been a bloodbath.'

Shareef quotes the general saying so in as many words. There were concerns that if Musharraf did not leave the country after retirement, no amount of security provided to him would be deemed sufficient given that he had made many enemies, especially among the radical Islamist militants. Reports in the media suggested that despite the high threat Musharraf had turned down suggestions of leaving the country which could imply that he had gone into exile: 'He said he committed no wrong whilst in power, so under no circumstances did he want the people to think that he had something to hide and had therefore left the country after resigning. "I have nothing to run away from," he said. This was my friend, Pervez, Pallu, Mush, Sharfu ... the nicknames, we, the friends in his inner circle, variously call him by.'

Shareef has an attachment to Musharraf which more than borders on sentimentality given their long association: 'I have known him when he was nobody, then I saw him become somebody, become big, the army chief, the chief executive, and then the president. He would visit me no matter how high up he went in his career; he would visit my office, my flat ... there is a lot of humility in the man. All through his rise, I've gone and stayed with him as a friend and always found the same person greeting me. After relinquishing the presidency, there he was the very same person who greeted me the way he always did whenever I went to see him. He's a jewel of a man, a jewel of a friend and a jewel of a person to know.'

During his career in the army, Col Shareef also had the opportunity to get to know the former dictator, Ziaul Haq, from up close. The general was many years and ranks senior to him. 'I was his ADC for four and a half years. I resigned in 1985 at the peak of my career. He tried to stop me, promising I would rise much further if I stayed on. But then, on my farewell call to his house, he did not meet me. He was angry that I was seeking retirement. He treated me like a son and did not wish me gone.'

I ask him how he would compare the two generals.

'There is no comparison. Zia was a complete hypocrite. He would say one thing and do another. He once promoted a batch of officers who brought a bad name to the armed forces. They did all those despicable things to people which you were not supposed to do.' The colonel pauses and rethinks. He decides not to elaborate on the subject any further, but shares the exchange he had with Gen. Zia on the occasion. 'I said to him how come he was promoting them. And he replied, "Need is the call of the hour," meaning something like necessity is the mother of invention. All his friendships and actions were based on such values.'

Then, after a pause, Shareef returns to his friend, Musharraf, when I ask him what in his opinion went wrong with the general. Was he given short shrift by the PPP, the Americans, or both? 'He was never taken in by the PPP, or the Americans; it was the power beyond that he was taken in by. Beyond is God, below God is [worldly] power, which dictated his actions.'

The majority in the Pakistani army have traditionally been wary of Bhutto's People's Party. Many in the officer cadre continue to view it as the only challenging force, representing to a greater extent the will of the people across the four provinces than any other party, and thus posing a threat to the supremacy of the armed forces. The roots of discontent with the party also lie in its genesis. It was the brainchild of Zulfikar Ali Bhutto, who in the 1960s graduated from being a protégé of the then reigning dictator Ayub Khan to being his most potent challenger. The populist appeal that Bhutto brought to the masses changed the face of Pakistani politics. Notwithstanding his autocratic tendencies while in power, Bhutto remains an icon, the undisputed champion of the cause of the poor. The Zia dictatorship did all it could to decimate the People's Party but failed. Even during Benazir Bhutto's two subsequent terms in power, the army very grudgingly and only conditionally accepted her as the head of government, suspecting her of a hidden agenda that ran counter to its perceptions of national security. It was believed to be behind her ouster from power both times when the army sensed her popularity dipping. Both Shareef and Musharraf seem to retain that mindset against the People's Party.

'Pakistan's independence has been weakened by Musharraf's departure from the scene,' says Shareef, before he raises other questions without offering answers, questions which imply that all is not well with the People's Party being once again at the helm. 'Perhaps somebody else was groomed and trained elsewhere and told that he would serve their purpose better after Musharraf was removed. Anyone who had an inkling of this is now dead. Mehmood Durrani is a national security adviser now [Durrani was abruptly removed from the position by Prime Minister Gilani in January when he went public owning up that Ajmal Kasab, the suspect in the 26/11 Mumbai attack, is a Pakistani. Zardari was apparently not pleased with the prime minister's hasty action]. He was military secretary to Ziaul Haq, the man who hanged Bhutto. Why is he still around? There are undercurrents. Why should Mr Zardari have him? Why has he swallowed the bitter pill? Definitely for a reason.' His lips are sealed beyond that, he says.

Returning to Musharraf's own undoing of his power, Shareef thinks the bogus referendum he held in April 2002, on the basis of which he declared himself an elected president, 'was the first crack which became a fracture with the judiciary crisis [March 2007], and the imposition of emergency rule [3 November 2007] was the last nail in the coffin of his power. Whoever advised him on those occasions were not his friends, least of all [PM] Shaukat Aziz, who feared to lose most at the hands of an independent judiciary.'

# 17

## Dynamic and Scheming

Finding old-fashioned, apparently straight-talking, retired generals in Pakistan who do not gloat over their exploits while in service, do not flaunt their lavish lifestyle and refuse to look beyond their own noses is a difficult task. When I approached Lt Gen. (retd) Moinuddin Haider for an interview for the book, he asked me to choose the time. When I insisted on his convenience, bang came the suggestion: 'How about tomorrow at 11 a.m. if that suits you?' I said noon would be better, and he said he would wait for me.

After retirement from service in 1997 as corps commander, Lahore, Gen. Haider served in the Leghari–Nawaz Sharif government as governor of Sindh until June 1999. After the Musharraf coup the following October, he was appointed interior minister of Pakistan by his long-time friend who had just declared himself the chief executive of Pakistan. The appointment came to an end with the election of November 2002, over a year after 9/11 when Gen. Musharraf took a U-turn on foreign policy, becoming an ally of the US in the 'war on terror'. Turning their back on the Taliban—the ISI's and the CIA's offspring born of their communion during the Afghan jihad against the Soviet Union in the 1980s—was a major decision under which Pakistan still reels. Gen. Haider was a witness to Pakistan's support of dialogue with and the later abandonment of the Taliban.

A widower, he now lives a somewhat busy retired life, supporting a number of charity organizations, including the

Army Foundation, collecting blood and running transfusion services free of cost across the country. He is also a member of the National Public Safety Commission of the Government of Pakistan, representing the civil society seat from the Sindh province. These, and the feel-good voluntary work he does, leave him with little time for indulgence in other pursuits, though he enjoys sitting in with friends for an evening.

The generals' colony in Karachi's upscale Zamzama neighbourhood where he lives looks quite impressive from the outside. Protected by high walls and barrier gates, it is lined with palatial bungalows, with spacious landscaped lawns and swimming pools in a city where water is as precious as two square meals for a labourer in this time of high inflation and economic meltdown. No. 5, where Gen. Haider lives, however, proved to be an ordinary, perhaps a 1000 square-foot, bungalow, of which category there's no dearth in the sprawling Defence Housing Authority that is home to the city's rich and the famous, and out of which is carved the generals' colony. At the entrance to the enclave, there was no extra security as would have been expected (the general's brother was killed in a sectarian attack a few years ago). Even at the barrier, it sufficed to say whom I wanted to meet. No ID card was required to be deposited, no phone call was made to the house for permission to enter the colony, nor a visitor pass issued, as is the norm at other high-profile military enclaves in Karachi.

At the gate of the house, a domestic servant promptly showed me in. The general, looking relaxed in his T-shirt and trousers, arrived within minutes, and we began a very candid discussion on the rise and fall of Musharraf. He seemed confidently eager to divulge the details of his interaction with the former president over the years, and appeared to be one who had little to hide.

'I have known Pervez Musharraf since 1961 when he joined the Pakistan Military Academy at Kakul [100 miles north-west of Islamabad in the lesser Himalaya hills] as a cadet. I was his senior cadet in charge. I groomed him in the army lifestyle, uniform-keeping, drill, punctuality, guidance, etc. Our six-month interaction turned into a lifelong relationship of respect and understanding.'

That this would transform into estrangement between the two men in the last years of Musharraf's presidency perhaps never occurred to Haider until it happened. Over their long association in the army, they had laughed and played and fought wars together. 'We fought at Khem Karan in the 1965 war, but I was an infantry soldier on the frontline and he was behind us in the artillery.'

The acquaintance and the mutual regard they had for each other grew over the years; an intimacy of sorts developed in earnest when the families of the two began to socialize: 'In 1986 we both became brigadiers and landed at the General Headquarters in Rawalpindi. We became very close, our families became very close, for about three years, going out on picnics and playing golf, and socializing on a very regular basis.'

After that posting in Rawalpindi, Haider was transferred to Quetta in Balochistan and Musharraf to Okara in central Punjab, hundreds of miles apart, but they made time to meet up. 'I went to spend time with him; and he came with his family to stay with us in Quetta.' Back together in Rawalpindi once again in 1989, they also became neighbours. [So] we met nearly every evening and generally hung out together. I was promoted to a three-star general; he too got the promotion a year after that. Then he was sent off to Mangla [sixty miles from Rawalpindi] and I to Lahore [another hundred miles down the road from Mangla], but we were meeting all the time, with families, coming to stay at each other's houses.'

After retirement from the army in 1997, when Haider became the governor of Sindh, Musharraf came especially to Karachi to attend his swearing-in ceremony, which Haider says was very 'nice and kind of him'. Months later, Musharraf was promoted as army chief by Nawaz Sharif after he forced Gen. Karamat to resign. There weren't apparently any ripples in the army top brass, or even if there were, Haider says he was not privy to such matters, but pleased for his friend to get the top slot. Contacts and friendship with Musharraf continued. 'We would go to Rawalpindi and have dinner with him at the Army House. When he came to Karachi he and the family dined with us at the Governor House. We kept meeting as and when the opportunity arose.'

After the October 1999 coup, Haider, who had retired as governor some three months earlier, was asked to join the Musharraf cabinet as his interior minister. He readily accepted the offer. 'Then we started meeting more often. Those were tough times, what with an economic meltdown, the war on terror and the growing extremism that followed... there were many issues.'

Haider says that eventually it was because of their differences over the same issues a few years later that the two men walked away from each other. While Haider says he developed a more on-the-ground view of reality, Musharraf steadily drifted away from it. 'We as ministers travelled economy class on commercial flights which helped us mix with the people, get to know what they thought of the government. We were not political people; we didn't have a constituency, so these were the ways to read the people's thoughts, get to know about their problems.'

The emerging, and what Haider calls a pro-people, world view of Musharraf's cabinet ministers apparently began to bother him. His cabinet comprised people who had clean reputations; who were there to help their leader, their people and the country. This they had begun doing by being more vocal and candid while reporting to Musharraf. The ministers began expressing their opinions without fear of being snubbed by the chief executive who, Haider says, increasingly began to overrule them, especially after the 2001 largely bogus referendum in which the people supposedly elected him as president.

'We raised our voices in the cabinet on the issues confronting the people. Those were very eventful years. We [Pakistan] were slapped with sanctions after the nuclear tests. President Musharraf showed a lot of courage. He had his political and economic reform agenda; he imposed financial discipline in the government and carried out reforms in many sectors. He had a good vision at that time and he was very sincere about changing things around, and he was still popular.'

Then came 9/11 in 2001. There was turmoil, as Islamists came out on the streets to protest against Musharraf's decision to join America's 'war on terror'. Home-grown extremism simmered just beneath the surface. Musharraf's liberal policies, promising to open up society and the economy, became a ready target of the rightists' wrath. Sectarian tit-for-tat killings between the majority Sunni and minority Shia returned with a vengeance. According to Haider, Musharraf took many unilateral decisions without consulting his friends or the cabinet: 'He did not consult me or the cabinet on sending the Sharifs into exile in Jeddah. He held secret negotiations with them and informed me the night before they were to leave. He may have consulted the corps commanders but I am not aware of this. I told him he should have taken the cabinet into confidence, and he said we would discuss that later. This was not the time. He then told me to inform the governors of Balochistan and Sindh so they were on board, which I did. Then, the next morning he explained his decision to the cabinet; many of us were very upset that we had not been consulted. Some protested, but in vain.'

The same was true of the decision after 9/11. 'We were not taken into confidence but were informed later on. We were reassured that the four air bases given to the Americans in Balochistan and Sindh were to be used for logistics purposes only, not for flying combat missions into Afghanistan. We were concerned in the cabinet that this would not go down well with the people of Pakistan. Why should we lend a shoulder to kill our Muslim Afghan brethren? we asked, and were reassured by the president on that. We only discovered the truth later on, when the US central command disclosed that they had flown out over 50,000 combat missions from Pakistan. We [the cabinet ministers] were very upset because we had to face the media.'

Haider believes that while the 'Pakistan army was on board, the cabinet was not. He [Musharraf] felt more at ease with his military high command rather than with his civilian cabinet.' Having said that, Haider admits that because he himself had retired as a corps commander, he was privy to some of the discussions that took place among the serving army top brass: 'I was once the only minister invited to a briefing by Gen. Aziz who argued that we should not hand over everything to the Americans because we have our own security concerns vis-à-vis the US. [Gen. Aziz] talked about putting certain checks and balances in place, he mentioned Pakistan's sovereignty, the view of the Islamists in Afghanistan and elsewhere, etc. in support of his argument. The president asked him whether these were his personal ideas or those of the military headquarters. The president did not agree with him and said he had already made certain decisions. The president overruled him.'

Haider ostensibly shared the line of argument advanced by some of the serving generals while briefing Musharraf on a host of critical issues, not least on how much of a free hand the Americans should be given while pursuing the goals of their 'war on terror' with Pakistan's help.

Haider's own interior ministry came under tremendous pressure. 'The Americans demanded,' he says, 'that the FIA should be given many concessions, including going in and arresting terrorists. This cannot be done, we said. They would never understand our culture. We refused. They would only operate through us, never independently. It was our tough stance on the issue. Our own intelligence agencies are very good. Even our CID police are good. The only edge the FBI had was due to their equipment. Our intelligence people are very competent, and they follow orders. It was the police which unearthed the cases of the French marines' bombing and the murder of Daniel Pearl in Karachi. To superimpose an agency from outside weakens our institutions.'

Haider says the interior ministry under him stood up to the pressure, but he cannot say the same for the ministry under his successor, Hayat Mohammed Khan Sherpao, who headed the breakaway Pakistan People's Party faction after the 2002 election, and became part of Musharraf's cabinet. Corruption cases against the leader from the Frontier province were withdrawn by the government in exchange for his support for the Pakistan Muslim League-Q (cleverly named after the Quaid-i-Azam, Jinnah), founded by Musharraf.

When asked what truth there was in the American suspicion, and therefore, insistence that they be given a free hand because Pakistani forces might act only half-heartedly to nab terrorists, Haider says: 'It cannot be ruled out that some members of the intelligence services may have their sympathies with the other side. You see, since 1979 we had been actively directing and helping the Taliban along with the Americans against the Soviets. When suddenly a U-turn is taken, your [individual] contacts will remain. Some of the [intelligence] people in their personal capacity may be lukewarm on certain issues, but I think otherwise it is not possible that they will not follow orders. They may go slow. But if they have been given a task on which they have to report to the headquarters, they cannot go in the opposite direction. No.'

On what was right or wrong with President Musharraf's doctrine of 'Enlightened Moderation', Haider says it 'meant changing many laws which he [Musharraf] believed were not in consonance with international opinion. He would be convinced in his heart and mind on what is the right action to take but when he came under pressure from Islamists and rightists he would give in and take a step back. He would revise his strong decisions, calling it pragmatism.'

Haider also attributes the reversals on such issues to the kind of people Musharraf chose as his political deputies to enforce his agenda after the 2000 election. 'It happens after second-rate politicians and opportunists lend their political support to a military man,' he says, referring to Chaudhry Shujaat and Pervez Elahi of the PML-Q. The party was highly favoured by the civil–military bureaucracy to win the polls.

'Even then they could not form a government, so the president bypassed the constitution on floor crossing and held parleys with the PPP to win over their members. They were told that corruption charges will be pursued against them [if they refused to lend their support] or they were promised ministries; they were rewarded.'

Haider believes that after the 2002 elections, expediency came to define the way Musharraf conducted his quasi-democratic regime. 'My suggestion before the 2002 election was to put Pakistan on the road to democracy. [I advised Musharraf that he] might as well rise above everything and invite back the big party leaders like Benazir Bhutto and Nawaz Sharif.'

The two leaders, each having been prime minister for two terms, albeit cut short by their sacking by respective presidents, were barred from premiership for a third term through an amendment to that effect in the constitution inserted by Musharraf. He hoped to get the incoming parliament to endorse the ban, which it did.

Haider, however, says, 'Referendum [and the amendments] apart, Musharraf was still quite popular. There were many people with him. Of the three leaders I mention, he was the most popular. [I told him to] work out a political reform in the three years the Supreme Court gave him; that he should implement certain reforms within the political parties too, engage their leaders by inviting them back to the country and ask them to support him in greater national interest. They would have willingly shared power with him, as the president, as a father figure.'

To Haider's dismay, however, Musharraf did the very opposite. 'He thought the people here would make a new party. In the latter part of 2002 he stopped listening to advice. On my farewell call, I told him that banning a third-time premiership was not right; genetically engineered political parties and breaking major parties would weaken the federation. The lesson should have been learnt from [the breaking away of] East Pakistan [Bangladesh]. Then, how can you call back certain [other] corrupt people from abroad and offer to make them ministers, as he did after the 2002 election? He didn't listen to me and called me an idealist. "You don't understand realpolitik. We have to be pragmatic in our approach. You have no experience in these matters," he told me. I confronted him by saying that his and my experience was the same. "I meet more people than you and know they won't like it," I told him. What he eventually did was like serving old wine in new bottles.'

By 'old wine' Haider means exchanging one bunch of corrupt politicians for their predecessors equally blemished with corruption charges. In spite of everything, Haider frankly admits that Musharraf on occasions continued to seek the views if not advice from his old friends in the army: 'After the 2002 elections, he called a session of serving and retired generals and we discussed the situation for three hours as to why he should not keep the political company he did. We warned him of politicians he was working with, who were corrupt, but he wouldn't listen. In 2005, at the centenary of the Staff College we met again and had interactive sessions for two days to discuss the country and the issues it faced. We said, "Sir, we don't know why you're sitting with those people who have a very bad track record"; but by then he was playing into the hands of those very politicians.'

As a last recourse to warn Musharraf of his erroneous behaviour, a group of prominent citizens, among them the general's friends and confidants from his first years in office and ex-servicemen, wrote him a letter which was subsequently leaked to the media. Moinuddin Haider recalls: 'In 2006 I was a signatory with some seventeen other people to a letter we addressed to him. After this our relations became strained. Between 2004 and 2006 we had excellent relations. But already in 2003 I felt whenever you gave him a suggestion for the good of the country he didn't like it. He felt irritated. So I decided not to irritate him. Our conversations steered on to other issues after he enumerated his successes, say on the economic front. I would just listen without offering a comment.'

In July 2006, some eighteen individuals, including retired generals, politicians and intellectuals wrote the said letter to President Musharraf advising him to strengthen democracy by separating the offices of the army chief and the president and establishing an independent election commission, besides refraining from seeking re-election by the outgoing parliament. The signatories included people from a cross-section of public opinion, of both liberal and rightist hues, two former ISI chiefs, Generals Hameed Gul and Asad Durrani, besides Musharraf's erstwhile supporters and former ministers, Moinuddin Haider and Javed Jabbar.

'The letter we had written contained nothing that he hadn't said and committed himself to. We suggested that he bifurcate the army chief's and the president's office, form an independent election commission and improve governance. He received the letter. It sat on his desk for fifteen days, but he would not read it,' Haider says.

When the letter was leaked to the media, Musharraf was furious. 'He gave me a very long call the next day. We spoke for a good three hours. He mentioned that he was sorry to see me, Gen. Naqvi and S.M. Zafar, his legal adviser, as co-signatories. He said he considered me a friend and was sorry to see my name on the letter. After that our relations were strained. This was in August 2006.

That was the last time the long-time friends spoke to each other. From then on, the break seemed to have been final. Haider elaborates: 'Later he used certain language in the media about me in person which I did not appreciate. It did not behove the president of Pakistan. Soon after the letter episode, he withdrew the guard he had offered and sent to protect me after my brother was killed by sectarian murderers. The National Defence College

in Islamabad also stopped inviting me as a guest speaker, which
it had been doing for some seven years.'

In his final analysis of the rise and fall of Musharraf, Gen.
Haider records the following: 'He thought he was too powerful.
He could do anything and get away with it, change the
constitution, throw this person out and so on. There are people
who advise you, but the buck stops at the boss. He could have
said, "Sorry, this will not happen. I do not accept it."'

Was it a tussle between Musharraf's outgoing cabinet in 2002
and the new one that took office under a democratic process
which he had personally crafted to his satisfaction that led to
the falling out of long-time friends?

Asked to define Musharraf using an adjective or two, the
word that readily emerges from Gen. Haider's lips is 'dynamic'.
He elaborates further: 'He is on the move, sleeps little, enjoys
physical activity, swimming, golf, etc. He's fond of music and
bridge, for which he finds time even under the most difficult and
critical circumstances. Then, almost as an afterthought, Haider
adds: 'This for me is rather odd. But he did so, taking out three
to four hours [a day] even during the Kargil crisis. Probably that
was the way for him to relax mentally. He schemes also, and
sometimes doesn't rise above himself, like a statesman, to mend
fences in the larger interest of the country.'

Asked what he made of Musharraf's pardoning of Nawaz
Sharif by commuting his sentence and giving him a safe passage
into exile and the implementation of the controversial NRO, of
which Benazir Bhutto and Asif Zardari became the beneficiaries,
Haider says: 'He didn't pardon Nawaz Sharif. He got rid of him
by banishing him for ten years. As far as the NRO and Zardari
are concerned, it was part of a power-sharing arrangement:
that he'd continue as president while political support will be
provided by the PPP.'

Then, like a schoolboy who has just broken up with his
best friend, Haider complains of other lapses that Musharraf

committed in the course of his career as a soldier. The general's memoir, *In the Line of Fire*, gives him more fodder.

'He should have avoided mentioning the unauthorized leave he took during the 1965 war. [As I recall] The commanding officer was furious. It sent the wrong signal to young officers, like "do whatever you like". Such casual remarks [in his memoirs still] give wrong pointers. Also, he should have avoided saying what he mentioned about Ali Quli Khan; that he [Musharraf] was the best man who should have gone to Sandhurst. But they sent a general's son instead; that [Quli] was a mediocre man. This is not true. The same system that promoted Ali Quli also promoted him and Gen. Abdul Qadir whom he accused of being a man of low IQ. On the nuclear issue, too, he shouldn't have given details about A.Q. Khan. He should not have boasted that we handed over so many of our own people to the Americans. This shows that he sometimes does things the implications of which he cannot foresee. He went wrong with the Lal Masjid [operation] in Islamabad, with [the killing of] Bugti [veteran Baloch nationalist leader].

I ask Gen. Haider to narrate a candid instance from his long and close association with one of the most powerful men in Pakistan. A childlike smile returns to the general's face, as his thoughts rush back to the good, cheerful time spent together. Circumspect about what to divulge, he narrates: 'I was sent to see Mullah Omar three times. One time he [Musharraf] advised me to take two ladies with me from our cabinet, Zobeida Jalal and Attiya Inayatullah. I knew the Taliban would not appreciate meeting the ladies. Mrs Inayatullah was known for working on family planning issues and Ms Jalal for girls' education. He said there was no harm in suggesting opening a girls' school and a women's clinic in Kabul or Kandahar. I said if you want to get rid of the ladies do something else, don't hand them over to the Taliban. And we both laughed. There is this side to him. For instance, he wanted marathon races for women wearing shorts and running in the streets. This is not acceptable in our society, but he would say that those who don't like it can look the other way; the marathon will happen. Zahir Shah tried to do this in Afghanistan and the Shah in Iran—effect change in a very fast manner. It doesn't happen like this. When my mother came here from India at independence, she wore a burqa. Then she wore a chador, before doffing both in good time. Change doesn't happen by order. It happens gradually and slowly.'

# 18

## Affable, but ...

'My relationship with Musharraf is not what it was. But I am still a well-wisher; perhaps, for some perverse reason, I don't wish him ill. He is an affable, forward-looking gentleman, without necessarily possessing an understanding of the complexity of issues he was dealing with.' These are the words of the multifaceted Javed Jabbar, an old-time friend and a former minister in Musharraf's 1999 cabinet, who resigned from his post after just eleven months in office. Adman-turned-film-maker, writer, politician, former senator and social activist, Jabbar has worn and continues to wear many hats, with the only constant remaining his intellectual cap that he never doffs.

'Three days after his resignation we exchanged a phone call after a lapse of four years. I hoped for his safety, and sent a message through an intermediary, a common friend. He was kind enough to call me back. I've known the gentleman for two decades. Our families have known each other for nearly half as long. We've had an empathetic relationship, sharing views on Pakistan over the years, having common friends. We met socially, and struck it off well individually.'

Jabbar has also interacted with the armed forces as an institution since the 1980s, regularly visiting army training colleges and professional defence institutions to deliver lectures to the officer cadres. He claims that in the course of his long informal association with army institutions and his interaction with officers, he got to know how the military mind worked. At the same time, he also stresses, 'It's not a homogeneous mind. The military is very much a part of the larger entity that is Pakistan and therefore, I suppose, I understand it as well as Mr Musharraf understands the civilian political sphere, and that is a lot [of understanding] there.'

Jabbar has the knack of thinking in layers even as he speaks off the cuff. His low-key, diplomatic, yet convincing tone and tenor continue to be guided by the bigger picture that he has conceived and saved in his head of the subject at hand. There are unmistakable glimpses in him of the 'old world', when many politicians were truly literate and informed; they were expected to be astute individuals; leaders who had manners and a presence suiting the occasion; they had the confidence to know and guide their people to what they had carved out as their destiny as a nation.

The only difference is that in Jabbar you also meet a contemporary man of intellect; he's a thoroughbred democrat who believes in consultation, as opposed to individual, unilateral decision-making howsoever well founded or well intended it might be. He is somewhat cautious and circumspect about what he says, preferring to consider the shades of grey rather than seeing the world in black and white: a trait on which his friend Musharraf would not score very highly. What then brought them together?

'Amongst our commonalities, we both believed in modernity or a sense of the contemporary. Karl Marx said it well: "Modernity can also be a contradiction of progress because sometimes modernity is so disruptive of how humanity is supposed to evolve in its own way." [Otherwise] Modernity can be a false imposition or suppression of something that would have [taken time and] evolved. It can be likened to a forced birth of something.'

This is perhaps how Jabbar looks back at Musharraf's years in power, without saying it in so many words, because he says, he's 'not at liberty' to discuss certain aspects of what he knows of Musharraf's years in power. Then, taking a breather, he goes on to define where he and Musharraf were coming from at the time of their meeting and parting of ways, their careers evolving in their respective fields. He rebuffs the public perception that he and Musharraf ever went to the same school or college.

'We are from very different backgrounds, and only met socially, as fully grown adults. While I was in the political sphere and making sense of the morass there, he was making steady progress, from the rank of brigadier to major general and finally general. We kept in touch through family and friends. It was not a work-oriented relationship; over time, we became very good friends. I was in and out of government. I was in the caretaker government when he was the corps commander at Mangla. He came to visit us in Islamabad. Later, in 1997, when President Leghari [under pressure from Nawaz Sharif and the army] resigned, and I joined him to set up the Millat Party, after having earlier resigned from the People's Party in 1995, we kept meeting, but only socially. Me becoming the office-bearer of a political party and Mr Musharraf being in the services, we kept the two things separate. But I could sense that he was disturbed at the direction the country was taking.'

This was long before Musharraf became the army chief and developed differences with Nawaz Sharif. However, unlike Moinuddin Haider who terms Musharraf as 'scheming', Jabbar stops himself there, refusing to venture any further.

Jabbar and Leghari's Millat Party proved to be a non-starter, unable to muster the requisite public support it went out to seek even though it represented an apparently popular, secular political strand at a time when the rightists were defining secularism as akin to godlessness, and thus anathema to an Islamic republic that they view Pakistan as being. The party was perhaps hampered by the fact that it included many of Benazir Bhutto's old supporters who had left the party after accusing her of corruption and malpractices, which in turn made them stand with the rightists on the other side of the political fence. Jabbar, however, has a more complex analysis to offer.

In the February 1997 election overseen by a caretaker government in which Jabbar was a cabinet minister, Nawaz Sharif's Muslim League won a thumping majority. There was little love lost between the government which oversaw the election and Sharif, but Jabbar says, 'Sharif got the heavy mandate because of the general view among the public that Benazir's second tenure had not been used for the purpose for which they had given her the mandate. There was widespread corruption and malpractice [in her government]. Some election results here and there could have been manipulated in the 1997 election, like in any other election before that, but Sharif got the windfall also partly because the Supreme Court was anticipated to give a verdict justifying the Bhutto government's dissolution by the president; the PPP voters also didn't go out to vote in large numbers; perhaps the candidates did not click. Still, some members of the cabinet were surprised at the result because the magnitude of the PPP's defeat was not expected.'

Thus, having held the election, the caretaker government transferred power to the newly elected Sharif government in March 1998. In October that year, Musharraf was promoted as general and chief of army staff by Nawaz Sharif, superseding two senior major generals. 'It came as a delightful surprise to the family and friends that he was made the army chief. There was no change in our relationship now that he had a higher responsibility.'

Then, in May 1999, came the Kargil crisis. 'I felt that public perception that Nawaz Sharif was not informed of the Kargil operation was not well founded because it was not possible for the prime minister to be unaware; if he was unaware it was a major omission or lapse on his part. He should have made sure he asked the right questions or followed through after the briefing given to him [by Musharraf and the army high command] and made sure that the army was sticking to the policy line that he [Sharif] had defined.'

There are others who differ with Jabbar's perception of the Sharif–Musharraf interaction on Kargil. Aftab Gul, for instance, has a different story to tell on the episode in the pages that follow. Meanwhile, Jabbar was also privy to what else had begun pulling the prime minister and the army chief apart.

'There was that glitch between the prime minister and the army chief because of Mr Sharif's deliberate delay in announcing Musharraf as the chairman, Joint Chiefs of Staff Committee. This caused a lot of misgiving. Musharraf thought the delay was not justified because he had gone out of his way to help the new civilian government dig in its heels; he made qualified personnel of the armed forces and their expertise available to the government across various sectors. The tendency in Sharif to act as if he were an anointed messiah began to annoy everyone, not just Musharraf. By mid-1999, tensions over Kargil really began to set in; especially how it was allowed to be interpreted by the media. The failure of the civilian government to rebut the negative campaign, including advertisements launched against the Pakistani army, in *New York Times*, for instance. This continued for several days, and there was no response from the government. It was incumbent on the Nawaz Sharif government to rebut the negative campaign in a very forceful way. But it did nothing.'

Speaking passionately and reflecting back, Jabbar continues: 'The Sharif government's commitment to genuine democracy was also questionable. We [the caretaker government of the pre-February 1997 election] had formulated a freedom of information ordinance and laws governing the independent electronic media. These were allowed to lapse when Sharif could have got them passed into laws, in minutes, through parliament. It pains me that even Mushahid Hussain, then Sharif's information minister and himself a man from the media, didn't do anything. Then with Kargil and all the negative backlash in the media, instead of rebutting the allegations against the army, the prime minister and his party also attacked the national institution [the army].'

Having said that, and pausing to collect his thoughts, Jabbar makes the following allowance: 'Even if the army was involved in some way [in] subverting Nawaz Sharif's political authority, outside of Pakistan it was incumbent on the government to defend the army. That failure I think also had a fallout on how the army generals viewed the government and how they reacted on 12 October 1999. Towards the end of his second tenure, Nawaz Sharif had retreated not merely to his kitchen cabinet, but to a corner of the kitchen. If I am not mistaken even his younger brother and the then chief minister of Punjab, Shahbaz Sharif, who was in the PM House at the time of the military coup, was not privy to Nawaz Sharif's final decision to change the COAS; only their father and Gen. Ziauddin Butt, the new COAS to be, knew of the decision. There was resentment in the army ranks that the government had "not stood by us on Kargil the way it should have", regardless of whether the army leadership acted responsibly or not.'

This, in Jabbar's view, brought down the Sharif government. At the time of the October 1999 coup, Jabbar says he was in Washington. 'Within a few hours [of the coup] Musharraf called me and asked when I was coming back. I cut short my visit. I was eventually inducted into the cabinet; by mutual agreement we delayed it to November. I gave him advice informally until the third week of November. I was formally inducted as adviser on national affairs, with the specific charge of information and broadcasting. This was the first time we were working together. We worked well, initially.'

However, a few months into the working relationship, Jabbar says, 'I could sense that over the long term or even mid-term what he and his colleagues wanted to do was very different from how I saw the process should have evolved. I now interacted with him very frequently. I also attended meetings at the [army's] General Headquarters and listened to how they [the generals] were viewing the situation. I gave them my views on what I thought it was and how we should act.

Frustration in dealing with a 'military mind', which Jabbar says he knew well enough, was beginning to set in as the days passed. The dramatic events involving the hijacking of an Indian Airlines plane did not help either. In December 1999, an Indian Airlines plane was hijacked from Kathmandu and taken to Kandahar, with the hijackers demanding the release of the jihadist Maulana Masood Azhar and others of his ilk in return for the safety of the passengers on board. 'There was intense activity; I had to face the media,' says Jabbar. Masood Azhar, after being released by India on the demand of the hijackers, was allowed to walk free in Pakistan; Syed Salahuddin, another Kashmir jihad leader, was allowed to hold a press conference. 'There was no justification for what they were allowed to do in Pakistan ... Salahuddin held a press conference with guns around. He made a weird spectacle of himself in front of the world media at such a hypersensitive time.'

Such lapses or deliberate actions on the part of the army, allowing embarrassing things to happen under Gen. Musharraf's undisputed and direct command, pushed Jabbar to gradually but decisively distancing himself from the emerging system. 'I was particularly deferential to the Supreme Court [12 May 2000] verdict which had gone beyond what one had expected, giving Musharraf the power that he hadn't even asked for, to amend the constitution [after validating the October 1999 coup]. [The former] Chief Justice Irshad Hasan must at some point answer as to why he had given such remarkable powers to Musharraf.'

The Supreme Court had given Musharraf three years in which to effect a transition back to democratic rule. In so doing, however, it had also conferred blanket powers on the army chief to amend the constitution to facilitate the smooth running of state affairs. This was unprecedented, and proved a riddle to people like Jabbar, who wanted the extra-constitutional rule of the army to end as soon as possible.

'The regime having got such formidable powers for itself from the Supreme Court, I looked for a well-defined plan ahead;

but the clarity that I looked for in the regime's thinking wasn't coming through to me. I stayed for eleven months, and finally resigned in October 2000. I would have been out earlier but it was on his [Musharraf's] kind insistence that I didn't. In fact I had accepted the formal title of minister of information in June only on his insistence. But already by July–August I felt it would be better if we parted company. I thought it was not fair on him that his friend and his own cabinet member should be in basic disagreement over his long-term objectives.'

Jabbar again holds back from spelling out what these long-term objectives were and why he thought they were long term when the court had given Musharraf only three years in which to restore democracy. He articulates the general's objectives at the time as broadly as possible: '[Our] disagreement was over how soon to restore the normal democratic political system, how quickly to implement the new media framework, and to what extent accept the unavoidable load of criticism and scepticism that comes with media freedom.'

Having said that, Jabbar recoils, again giving Musharraf his due: 'He was a liberal and a modernist but when you're in power you react to what is said about you. He showed the capacity to take a lot of criticism. I wanted to frame a freedom of information law which he was in agreement with. Yet our differences in the cabinet, in the public domain, put him in an awkward position. Remember, I was his friend.'

Even after his resignation, Jabbar says, he met his 'friend' periodically, and did his bit to help the country eschew the poor image it was projecting of itself. 'When the Indian parliament was attacked in December 2001, I did a series of programmes on the state-run PTV. He [Musharraf] was very appreciative. I did that on a voluntary basis every two to three days, putting across Pakistan's viewpoint on the issue, rebutting what the world thought about our involvement in the attack. He called to thank me for the effort.'

Earlier too, soon after the 1999 coup d'état, Jabbar had taken it upon himself to appear on PTV, time and again, to offer what can only be termed a de facto defence of the military coup. He argued that the classical British-style democracy did not suit Pakistan, because, with some benefit of hindsight, it could be said that it had not served the cause of sustaining a democratic order in the country. But by the same token of learning from recent history, military interventions in the past that had tried to reinvent the wheel of democracy also failed in transplanting an indigenous brand of democracy. The argument is as old as the one first advanced in Pakistan back in the 1960s by the military dictator Ayub Khan who said that Western-style democracy did not suit the 'genius of our people', and set about putting together a de facto presidential form of government. Whether Jabbar's line of thinking echoed the thoughts of Gen. Musharraf in 1999–2000, or whether this was one of the many 'commonalities' that Jabbar and his 'friend' had developed on many issues over the years of their acquaintance, is not clear. The truth perhaps lies somewhere between the intellectual honesty expected of Jabbar and his unshakeable sense of patriotism, which on critical occasions may perhaps have taken the better of him.

In 2002, Jabbar says, Musharraf attended his son's wedding. Then, where did the two 'friends' part company, one might well ask. 'In February 2003 he promulgated a law which I thought was outrageous. It said that those who did not win in the 2002 election were disqualified from standing for [the] Senate. I challenged it in [the] Supreme Court and won the case. I told him before going to the court how wrong I felt the law was. Losing an election in a democracy cannot disqualify you from contesting another election. He said I must do what my conscience told me to do. The Supreme Court had the courage to overturn the presidential ordinance. Sheikh Riaz was the chief justice. In the course of the argument, the chief justice asked if we were challenging the 17th amendment to the constitution which, passed by parliament at the president's behest, also gave the president the power to promulgate laws through ordinances. I told the judge, yes, we were challenging it. The moment that went out as a signal to Musharraf, something very basic changed in our relationship and we stopped communicating. By then I also felt he was going on perpetuating his power to an unhealthy degree. Subsequently, we met one last time at a conference which he had come to inaugurate, in 2004.'

Asked whether Musharraf, like the American neo-cons speaking on the 'war on terror', had also begun to believe that one was either with him or against him, Jabbar says, 'I am not at liberty to share some of my thoughts. He assumed that perhaps because such and such person had challenged his power, therefore, he was no longer a friend. That was a fundamental error.'

Or was it? Jabbar was after all on the list of the eighteen prominent persons who wrote that letter to Musharraf in 2006 asking him to stop what he was doing and start doing what in their opinion was right for the country. 'I was chosen as the chairman of the drafting committee which upset him,' says Jabbar. Not all the signatories were well inclined towards the general. A group of ex-servicemen, comprising some elements of the Military Intelligence of Gen. Ziaul Haq's Afghan jihad days, and largely a group dominated by Punjabis and Pathans, wanted to see the liberal, Urdu-speaking Musharraf out.

In the final analysis and without elaborating, Jabbar says, 'Despite all the colossal blunders and errors that Musharraf has made, I wish him well. I hope he comes to realize where he went wrong. This terrible spectacle of him having to leave office the way he did saddens me. I wish he had done it a few months earlier, on 21 February, when [the] official results of the election were declared.'

Commenting on Musharraf's extended, elaborate parting speech over national TV on 18 August 2008, Jabbar says he should have done that with a three-line resignation speech, saying, 'I have done my best for my country. The result is clear. I resign from the post.' Full stop. Nothing more should have been said. That 'what I did and what I achieved' is part of historical record; let history speak for itself.

As Jabbar maintains that he still wishes his 'friend' well, I ask what advice he would give Musharraf if he had the occasion to do so now. He responds instantly: 'Only if he's given the level of security given to a head of state, I recommend he stay in Pakistan. If not, he should leave the country.'

As Jabbar had said at the beginning of this interview, he perhaps now only hopes for Musharraf's safety, and little beyond that.

# 19

# The Adventurer, but No Traitor

'Musharraf is part of the praetorian tradition in Pakistan where the military assumes power under one pretext or the other. But he had the leanest of excuses. You don't overthrow a government merely because the chief of army staff feels threatened that his life may be in some sort of danger,' says Aftab Gul, discounting the fact that there were nearly 200 other people on board the commercial flight that nearly crashed on 12 October 1999.

A well-read man-in-the-know with leftist views, if self-admittedly 'despairing' in his world view, Gul is a lawyer from Lahore. A former student leader, Pakistan Test cricketer (1969–71), a Zulfikar Ali Bhutto confidant, a close friend and colleague of the late Mir Murtaza Bhutto, the elder son of Bhutto who ran the guerrilla organization Al Zulfikar in the aftermath of his father's overthrow by Gen. Zia in 1979, Gul was tried in absentia for his alleged involvement in abetting Al Zulfikar's activities. He was, however, found not guilty by a court of law which cleared him of all charges of terrorism. He is known in the civil–military establishment circles as an insider, and is well connected with the who's who in the army and the bureaucracy. Gul is, however, more of a historical overview man, a leftist ideologue who has seen his dream of Pakistan go sour over the years, and represents the disgruntled elements in Pakistan's most developed and traditionally politically influential Punjab province.

'One good thing that Musharraf did was break the ice on Kashmir. Musharraf alone was responsible for making a dialogue situation between India and Pakistan acceptable in Pakistan. He was prepared to go the extra mile ... for whatever reason. Maybe he thought he'd have a place in history if he succeeded. He was a president who was prepared for a compromise and to go back to the original Pakistan position in 1947, which said "let the Kashmiris decide their own future".'

When Aftab Gul utters these words, he is probably also aware of the shift in the larger public mindset in Punjab that has taken place vis-à-vis India during Musharraf's years in power. The people of this most populous and prosperous province, which is also the recruiting ground for the Pakistani army, have consistently, even if surprisingly, supported the efforts made by Nawaz Sharif in 1997–99 and subsequently by Gen. Musharraf, to bury the hatchet with India. Punjab has been warming up to the economic gains that can be garnered by normalizing relations with India, of which it would be a primary beneficiary as it shares a longer border with India than any other province. Punjab is the first land of call for the territorial trade route 'passage' that India needs to access Afghanistan and the Central Asian republics through Pakistan.

While Gul credits Musharraf with really cutting the ice with India, he also sees him as embarking on a road that pulled him in the opposite direction simultaneously. 'Kargil was a contradiction because if that's what you wanted you should have known that you couldn't run with the hare and hunt with the hounds. I will always hold him in some kind of regard [for his detente with India policy] but for Kargil.'

Yet in his circumspection, he apportions the blame for the Kargil crisis equally on the shoulders of Musharraf and Nawaz Sharif. 'From talking to army generals involved, including my own brother, Imtiaz Shaheen, who was one of Musharraf's corps commanders, I don't know of any official briefing on Kargil that was given to Sharif by Musharraf. However, the prime minister was said to have once casually remarked to his army chief something to the effect that "the Indians are bugging us; do you have some contingency plan in place to deal with them?" And Musharraf said, "Yes, we do, but the political government won't back us." Sharif said his government was different; it would back the army all the way, and so Kargil happened. This was wrong because Sharif was also shaking hands at the time with Vajpayee in Lahore.'

Gul also believes that there was a personal reason for Musharraf's Kargil misadventure. 'He had to establish his command on the [predominantly Punjabi and Pashtun] armed forces.' Gul says that many an eyebrow was raised when Musharraf was appointed as army chief. Questions were asked whether he would be able to take the army along because he did not belong to the traditional recruiting belt in north-western Punjab and the adjoining Frontier province districts.

'Musharraf believed that he had to somehow prove that despite not being one of "them" he would be able to command them. My brother was the director-general, Rangers [a Border Patrol Force often required to help with law and order in Sindh cities] in Karachi. The MQM demanded his removal. Consequently, Gen. Imtiaz Shaheen was asked to leave by Musharraf. He had argued that terrorists and criminals should be dealt with regardless of their political affiliations. But Musharraf had allied with the party [MQM] a long time ago. He had asked my brother to make a list of "my own people". The army had no such system of knowing this [ethnic background of officers]. True, most of them [Urdu-speaking officers] were qualified people but that's not how you run the institution. Musharraf met Altaf Hussain in London, who is wanted in many criminal cases in Pakistan. Meeting him granted Altaf legitimacy. He's an absconder. You don't do that.'

Gul is equally critical of Musharraf's promulgation of the National Reconciliation Ordinance, which gave blanket immunity to Benazir Bhutto and her husband Asif Zardari. 'It was a big sell-out. Look at Nelson Mandela. For twenty-two years the man remained in jail. Asif Zardari was in [an] "A" class prison where he had all the facilities, including machines and gadgets. The Truth and Reconciliation Commission which gave relief in South Africa was only confined to people who were charged with political offences. But here people charged with corruption, with making millions of dollars illegally, were given relief. The cases were withdrawn, nothing had been proved against them but the cases were still in court, not only here but also abroad, and these were withdrawn.'

Scathing in his criticism and with an eye on the historical process, Gul digs up the past, tacitly absolving Musharraf of any possible charge of breaking the established tradition of abiding by the law, or seeking short cuts to achieve perceived national goals.

'That's also a problem that we have had and where I find Mr Jinnah to be responsible. There was a struggle against colonial rule but the people who fought for freedom and paid the price were largely non-Muslim, starting from Bhagat Singh. Ours was only a so-called struggle where nobody went to jail. Jinnah Sahib never went to jail; he made speeches and spoke to the British, so whenever we have a political problem our people run to the courts. Zardari is not to be judged by the courts alone but by public opinion. Ask the people and an overwhelming number will tell you "yes, he's corrupt". We have suffered all sorts of colonization; we were not only colonized by the British, we were also colonized by our emperors and our caliphs before that. We have a masochistic tendency; even our scriptures tell us not to stand in the way of [one] whom God has given power [over the people]. What could be more damaging than that? To say that because Zardari was not convicted betrays a mindset which looks for excuses to mix the good with the bad. The process [of his accountability] was thwarted halfway; the legal process takes long but it should have been allowed to run its course. In 1986, when Benazir had come back, a lawyer student had asked her how she supported herself in exile. Where did the money come from to maintain the lifestyle she did? Income from her land could not support that. We have one set of standards for the ordinary people and another for the rulers of this country. There are rulers and there are the ruled. Leaders switch parties and remain leaders. There's something seriously wrong with us.'

To drive home his point, the Marxist lawyer picks on another one of the ruling People's Party stalwarts: 'Makhdoom Amin Fahim [Benazir's trusted deputy whom Zardari sidelined] might be a good man but in his constituency [in impoverished semi-urban Sindh] perhaps 80 per cent don't have drinking water and education. If he contests from an affluent Islamabad constituency I can understand that given his political savvy, people would elect him. What I can't understand is how come the poorest of the poor should vote for him when he does not resolve their problems. Such people go to parliament and we congratulate ourselves on the restoration of democracy. What democracy? Such leaders have different aspirations and plans, they take their holidays in France and Florida; their children go to Harvard and Cambridge. They can't think for the poor. I am not blaming them for the way they are. It's a distortion of reality to say that they represent the people who vote for them.'

Getting back to Musharraf, Gul says he 'was like the rest of the dictators. It was like playing by the script; the Muslim League had to be pressed into power, some sort of political elements had to be brought in. Then he rigged the election [2002] and tried to stay in power. He also sought some kind of legality for his actions through the Supreme Court.'

However, the same compliant Supreme Court also turned on Musharraf, with the former Chief Justice Iftikhar Chaudhry refusing to give in to any further pressure. The illegal removal of the chief justice, as also candidly admitted by Musharraf in one of his speeches, sparked a lawyers' protest movement. The chief justice was reinstated in July, but Musharraf fired him again, along with dozens of his fellow judges at the Supreme Court and the four high courts when he imposed emergency rule in November 2007. The lawyers' movement picked up from where it had left off. Zardari himself as president, for personal reasons, refused the reinstatement of the former chief justice sacked by Musharraf. Speaking of the continuing but much mellowed-down movement for the reinstatement of the chief justice, Gul does not spare his own colleagues in the legal community: 'There was no ill-will in the civil society movement against Musharraf; they were for the rule of law. The lawyers meant well. If they could have sustained the movement for a few more weeks it would have brought about some change. But they let the steam out. We have a great disrespect for words. You can't sit in a Land Cruiser, have orange juice and say you are on a long march to Islamabad.'

This is a dig at the PPP stalwart Barrister Aitzaz Ahsan who, as president of the Supreme Court Bar Association, himself drove the chief justice on his long road journeys. It was Aitzaz, also a member of the PPP's central executive committee, who had dispelled the impression that the lawyers were going to stage a sit-in outside parliament in June 2008, and ensured that they disbursed peacefully after the rally.

That indeed was what in Gul's opinion had taken the steam out of the lawyers' movement, as within hours of reaching Islamabad in large numbers from across the country (10–14 June 2008)], the lawyers dispersed without so much as staging a sit-in for a few hours.

During the second of the fairest elections ever held in Pakistan, on 18 February 2008, Gul says with a touch of cynicism that 'the people vented their anger by voting for those who were opposed to Musharraf's policies. But now the misery of the people has been extended for another five years. The people who supposedly have the solution to our problems are part of the problem.'

Politicians are not, however, the only group of people whom Gul derides: 'The army too had the chance to clean up but it didn't. If there is corruption, the army accounts for 90 per cent of it. This process is not going to resolve the people's issues. It won't sustain the poor.' However, to be fair to Musharraf, Gul

believes that 'he got sucked into the process. So when he lost his
utility, he was thrown out. Pakistan on the whole has receded
into anarchy; we will not explode, we will implode. There will
soon be food riots here. People who talk about civil society and
the lawyers' movement [as a watershed] in their drawing rooms
include many who either have foreign passports or have applied
for immigration abroad.'

Having said that, Gul also believes that 'Musharraf's coup in
1999 brought about a situation whereby no civilian government
can now function without the help of the army. Unless the military
goes back and sticks to its professional role, Pakistan as a civilized
polity cannot exist. Look at our mindset. Now that the Americans
have launched hot pursuit inside our borders, everyone's looking
to Gen. Kayani and wondering what he has to say. Why? Who's
Kayani but a Grade 22 officer subordinate to the secretary, defence,
and to the orders of the president?' he asks rhetorically.

'I despair for this country. You may call me a cynic and a
pessimist, but I simply despair. There's only destruction ahead;
we're not on a roller-coaster ride, we are on a downward slide,
going downhill. The middle class is shrinking even further.
There are only haves and have-nots. We're still where we were
in 1974 when a wave of hijackings took place and people like
Edward Said wrote that to stop such acts we need to address
the causes. We're still there. Musharraf was threatened with
[Pakistan] being bombed back to the stone age. He reluctantly
agreed to help America, so we became a frontline state and a
global ally in the "war on terror"; then came democracy and we
called it our own war. I ask: if it is your own war, what have
you done to get ready for it? We want to bring the poor to the
negotiating table; those who see their children's bodies blown
to pieces? Where is morality? If they respond with violence, we
call them terrorists.'

As a Marxist, Gul has no love lost for the rightist elements,
so I ask him: 'What's the solution? Did we ever try to search
for a solution?'

Gul promptly responds: 'Musharraf did, and for that we cannot dismiss him. He tried solving the issues in the beginning but then he went into his own myth, which every military ruler does. Over time he too came to consider himself the law, master of all. But he was a product of his institution. He ignored and sidelined the major political forces. At least the PPP was quiet when he came to power; it didn't make any noises against him. Yet he set about marginalizing it. When you do that it creates a vacuum which is then filled by alternative forces. The Frontier and Balochistan provinces were made over to the maulvis who did not have modern education. Our basic issues and problems did not start with or after Musharraf. They started in 1947.'

It's difficult to keep Gul focused on the present or the recent past.

'Mr Jinnah may have been very sharp and witty, but he didn't know much of, well, really, anything. The post-Second World War world was afloat with ideas; there was communism on the one hand, and nationalism was gripping the world. Little did he think in terms of taking stock of the global thinking, and based the idea of a new country on religion. The language of political mobilization that Jinnah evolved was not secular. He said, "Your mosques would shut down" [if India remained united]. Look at his team: all the landed aristocracy from Punjab and Sindh [and their counterparts from India's Muslim-minority states] who embraced the idea of Pakistan and ran with it. Daniyal Latifi [a senior advocate of the Supreme Court of pre-Independence India, known for his reformist ideas] gave him a land reform programme which he threw out.'

Having laid the blame squarely on those who created Pakistan without having a game plan in mind as to how to run the new country, Gul acquiesces: 'Even then if we were learned and knew enough, the country could have been run by evolving a civic nationalism based on the rule of law. But when you get talking about serving Islam and passing the "Objectives Resolution" [1949], declaring Pakistan an Islamic republic, much is already lost. You are a multi-ethnic country, and a nation bound only by faith; then there are extra-territorial aspirations. Why should we look to Mecca and Madina for state building or governing our country? Why should we look to religion vis-à-vis the polity? Pakistan's knot cannot be untied that easily; it can only be untied in our Anglophile drawing rooms and not in the real world outside.'

So what's the solution?

'This soil needs the blood of some 500,000 or so who are its exploiters. This parliament comprising landowners and land-grabbers will only make laws that suit their purposes, not the people's cause. The Altaf Hussains and the Zardaris will come and go but no one will have the courage to question such basic premises. Wrong is right and right is wrong. And Aftab Gul is an aberration,' he avers passionately.

His final verdict on Musharraf: 'He was an adventurer, more so than even Zia. Musharraf did not know where he was heading. There was no resistance to his takeover. He made few promises but failed to deliver even on those.'

This was perhaps because Gul believes that Musharraf, like many in Pakistan, had his world view skewed by his preoccupation with India; a view that Khaled Ahmed also shares in the pages that follow. Says Gul: 'The only identity we have is in relation to India; we are what they are not. We believe the Red Fort will one day be ours. Despite this flawed thinking, this country will not fall apart easily. Many an Indian I know is happy we opted out in 1947; imagine what trouble we would be causing India if we were part of it. This wound will continue to fester. Somebody has to take a quantum leap.'

On the issue of Pakistan's nuclear arsenal, Gul says he is very clear: 'Our nuclear weapons are safe. No two ways about it. The army will not surrender them. They are like the Israeli army. They won't listen to the Americans if it comes to that. And Musharraf, despite all his failings, was not a traitor.'

# 20

## Ambivalent and Reckless

Khaled Ahmed is a senior editor with the liberal English-language *Daily Times* and the newsweekly *Friday Times*, which have nationwide circulation. He has come to be known as one of an increasingly rare, and to many, shockingly honest, breed of journalists in Pakistan. His frank, original, unapologetic, liberal–democratic views as an immensely well-read editor and opinion leader, and as a peacenik in the Indo-Pakistan context, make his genre of writing controversial, not to say intellectually challenging for many. His views on Musharraf and the general's legacy live up to this reputation.

'When Gen. Musharraf came he evoked in us very positive feelings. Pakistan had made a blunder when Prime Minister Nawaz Sharif tested the nuclear device in 1998 and paid no attention to the economic plight of the people. Our state is weak and revisionist and cannot control its passions. It is true of all states that have the agenda of a challenger. They become destabilized by their own emotions. When Musharraf came he reversed the trend. He started looking at the economy more realistically. Then he made the decision of joining the US-led war on terror which went against the emotion of the people. I don't think people knew that Pakistan was complicit in what happened on 9/11. Musharraf's policies were realistic and he saved the economy which was belly-up.'

Having said that, Ahmed is equally cognizant of Musharraf's own mistakes. 'He was no messiah in all fields and at all times.

He made a blunder in Kargil, which all army people, given the chance, would do. He had fantasized about setting up a defeatable enemy [India] for a state [Pakistan] which had suffered a number of defeats and tested out its nationalism, from which it should have retreated but didn't. There were the 1965 and the 1971 defeats at the hands of India which Musharraf did not take into account or admitted as such, and that was the flaw that persisted with him. Also, I don't think he let go of his Afghan policy. He did not want to give up on the Taliban after he saw the failure of the Americans there in reconstruction and nation-building, post-9/11. It was Rumsfeld's phase when warlords were created with American money and he saw the Taliban as Pakistan's proxy. That was bad for us. The Taliban were pushed into our areas. And Musharraf helped them. The seeds of what happened later on lay in the fact that while the intelligence agencies helped train the Taliban again, Musharraf told the Americans that we were wiping them out. They settled down in our areas. The Taliban headquartered in Quetta [Balochistan]; their backers and Al Qaeda came into the tribal areas. Yet, there was much that Musharraf did for the Americans for them to believe that he was okay. What he did for us in the process is to be measured later when we develop some objective distance from him.'

As for the media and the environment created for it by Musharraf before he imposed emergency rule in November 2007, Ahmed believes that 'he gave us a lot of freedom that even the so-called democrats before him had denied us. He offset some of the restrictions on expression that the Islamization of Gen. Ziaul Haq had imposed on us. I don't think any democrat[ically elected leader] would have done that.'

On the failure of the Agra Summit, Ahmed says: 'India was not in a position to make big decisions. There was nothing on the ground that convinced them to give up Kashmir. A part of the BJP leadership was perhaps willing to take a smaller decision on land adjustment. But Musharraf played up to their press. He should have kept quiet. It was a back-channel thing that took him to India and which had come to fruition so he should have kept a low profile, realizing that India was not going to give up Kashmir.'

Ahmed then speaks about some of the general's obsessions and limitations as a military man that hampered the broadening of his vision. 'After 9/11 he made a remarkable statement when in an address to the nation he said he was going along with the US because India was going to get there first if he didn't. India had set up an air base in Tajikistan. I don't think he let go of the India obsession of the army. The war [on terror] in Afghanistan became a war with India. He kept saying India was going into Balochistan and they were funding the Taliban and Al Qaeda in the tribal areas. This is uncanny but he said that. The war [in his thinking] with India continued; he did not let it go. He did not take note of the role India was playing in Afghanistan. When the US decided to let India play the bigger role in Afghanistan, it was understood the Americans did not want Pakistan to come back in. The conflict or the schizophrenia within Musharraf was on the point of having to deal with India in Afghanistan. The army never conceded that.'

Despite what Ahmed calls the Pakistani army's 'India obsession', he gives Musharraf the credit for trying to break out of it. 'He was more inventive [than his predecessors] on the India policy. He wanted to normalize relations because the world was telling him to do so. He switched off the jihad in Kashmir and the Indians were very pleased, but then he drew a line and that's where his decline set in and he began losing support in the West. The West realized that he wouldn't let go of the Taliban as Pakistan's proxy and also that he was not sincere in normalizing relations with India. His conduct was perhaps not based only on his personal conviction but reflected the thinking in his institution. His base was the army. He had or sought little political support; he was content with his base, he gave them a lot of jobs, he placated them. If the army thought his India policy was heretical, he gave them more jobs and privileges. Later on, they rebelled against him. But all the rebels were big names. They got the jobs all right, but still they rebelled.'

On the very controversial privatization process under the Musharraf regime and then its cessation, Ahmed says that the privatization commission got cold feet after 'they [the army] saw Indian investment coming into Pakistan, which was wonderful. It would make us safe. But most people think it is wrong; it is infected money. The general resisted it. Another general who rebelled was very incompetent. He shouldn't have been made the chief of the Federal Public Service Commission.'

Ahmed blames the collective mindset in the army for a lot of the ills that Musharraf tried to tackle but in vain, because he himself was only an offshoot of that mindset. Even where he tried to break loose of it, he didn't quite succeed.

'Most of our generals are low IQ people. When they speak they don't realize they're making fools of themselves. But they are received well. Even today the people who dominate are people from the ISI, like Hameed Gul and Asad Durrani; they are particularly moronic. Musharraf was cleverer. His values were liberal. He connected with the world much better than these rather retarded people. Living in cantonments can be a great retarding factor in life. These people are wedded to one world view which is India centric and that retards. People more Catholic in taste will bow out of the army without speaking too much. But [the] more popular, more assertive, who rise to the top jobs are mostly retarded people who are tactical in their thinking and meticulously non-strategic. Because if you are into strategy then you question: "Okay, I have to fight India but do I have the economy on my side? The intellectual background? Is my education okay?" Confronting India doesn't mean going out and wrestling with them. Their generals look like clerks and ours like champions but whenever we go out to fight them we lose. A strategic mind will be totally unfit in our army. This happens when a small state becomes revisionist vis-à-vis a larger undefeatable state. Our military strategy is a very incompetent formulation. It says, and generals have said it in their books, that India is an unstable country with lots of uprisings inside it. If we keep knocking it from outside it will collapse.'

Ahmed goes on to attempt laying down an alternative strategy which could work wonders for Pakistan as an economic bridge between India and the world beyond Pakistan's western borders—something that eluded Musharraf because of his Pakistani army mindset, despite his desire to make peace with India.

'Your true geo-strategy should be that of [giving] passage. Pakistan succeeds only as a corridor of trade, which means importance is given to you when you give passage to others to pass through. Once you do that, you not only enrich yourself but also protect yourself. That's where the army [mindset] comes along and says, "Okay we are geo-strategically very important; we can open up provided you give us Kashmir or else we'll block passage.' If you block for too long people go around you. This happened with the Iranian pipeline plan which we blocked for too long and India lost interest. When we finally delinked it from Kashmir it was too late. They [the Indians] bring in LNG through their fleets bypassing Pakistan.'

Reverting his focus to Musharraf as I pester him on his judgement of his years in power, Ahmed says, 'He was okay as a military person but dangerous as a civilian ruler [for his own good?]. He thought freely. He didn't have to seek anyone's approval. Taking on the judiciary was also one of the reasons for his downfall. It was the same [mistake] as Kargil. Not even a stupid man would go to Kargil and try to defeat India there. Then the freedoms he gave to the media. In the aftermath of the judiciary crisis, a perpetual constitutional debate was allowed on TV. The Lal Masjid in Islamabad was nursed as a snakepit by the agencies. He knew it was there; it was an Al Qaeda headquarters. Then there was doublespeak on his part. He doubted his relationship with the US and its realpolitik. He retained some of the wrong thinking of the military man that he was. He thought he could relocate himself in a free-thinking and deeply analytical civil society, which was not the case with Pakistan.'

As regards the very controversial National Reconciliation Ordinance that permitted Benazir Bhutto and her spouse Asif Ali Zardari to contest the 2008 election by withdrawing all cases of corruption against the couple, Ahmed says it was far too politicized. 'The NRO has a moral ground. You don't keep someone [Zardari] in jail for eleven years without a bail and without a conviction. Something more dubious happened in the case of Nawaz Sharif. There is no point of law in how Nawaz Sharif went away and came back with the help of the Saudis. The Supreme Court [under Justice Iftikhar Chaudhry] pronounced quickly on the NRO which is responsible for the PPP going back on its promise to reinstate the judiciary fired by Musharraf on 3 November 2007. No party would commit suicide just for being popular.'

To define Musharraf and his years in power, I ask Ahmed to use a couple of adjectives. He responds: 'Ambivalence and recklessness would have to be used. He was not corrupt. He was self-built, not very clear on where he wanted to go. Finally, we're too emotional: we all hate him today but his were the best years. As a journalist these were my best years. You could stand up and say whatever you thought and he took it. Nawaz Sharif never took it; he would pick up the journalist, and throw him in jail and say he doesn't have him. The freedom and the liberal environment that Musharraf gave us were marred by Al Qaeda's entry that he allowed into Pakistan. It rolled back whatever good he did. And he did plenty.'

# 21

## Rise and Fall by the Same Means

Retired Major General Saeed Zaidi lives in Rawalpindi Cantonment's upscale West Ridge district in a somewhat modest house by the standards of ex-army men from the top cadres. He has known Musharraf and his family for some four decades through their long association as course-mates; at one point early in their careers they were also room-mates. The story of a Musharraf he has known from close quarters until his rise to the post of army chief is one of an innocuous soldier, a buddy, and a person full of ambition and a zest for life, one whose company is enjoyable in a harmless way. After taking premature retirement in 1998, Gen. Zaidi contested the 2002 election from his home constituency, Jhelum, a garrison town where his family had settled after migrating from Uttar Pradesh, India, in 1947. He contested the election on a People's Party ticket, which in those days was clearly out of favour with Gen. Musharraf, and that perhaps added to his estrangement with Musharraf. Nonetheless, Zaidi has a long tale to tell of their forty-year association. He begins at the very beginning:

'Actually in his family the first person I knew was his elder brother Javed Musharraf who was with me at Government College, Lahore, though he was three years older than me. They both come from the same *thaapa* (lookalike mould) but Pervez and I became more friendly because in the PMA it's all about your platoon. Then Musharraf came to artillery in Nowshera; we did the course together. After the course we both went to

Kharian; I went back to my own unit and Musharraf came to
16. Then we realized that *idhar to larrai ka koi maza nahin aya*
(there wasn't much fun in the fight here), and so we went to
SSG together. In his book [*In the Line of Fire*] he has mentioned
Bilal, who was also there with us on the course. There were small
rooms; very bad accommodation, but Musharraf decided to stay
with me and then we were room-mates. He hasn't mentioned
me in the book but I am not surprised. He was close to Bilal,
all right, but he decided to be room-mates with me for some
reason. Then he went to East Pakistan [Bangladesh] and I was
sent to Attock Fort.

'We have done most of our courses together. He did a few
courses in which he didn't even qualify. That happens to
everyone. We also went to the Staff College together. There you
get homes strictly according to your PA (or peer) number. But
the houses we got were incidentally next to each other. We were
together and so I know his children from the time they were
born. Then they went to Karachi, but we weren't apart for very
long. When he was in Karachi I went there to meet him, and
he came all the way to Sialkot just to say hello. We have been
exceptionally close. In fact people used to say ours was a special
relationship. Like I was his shadow or he was my shadow. This
remained so till he became the army chief.'

Here I interrupt the general to ask him if he was surprised
by the promotion, because, according to Aftab Gul and his
sources in the army, many senior officers from Punjab were
caught unawares at Musharraf's elevation to the top slot. Zaidi
responds: 'No, I wasn't surprised. In the military system it
becomes very clear who might get where, because basically it is
a process of elimination for many reasons. And in the run were
Generals Khalil, Khalid Nawaz and Musharraf. I thought he
was the best choice.'

I ask Zaidi if their contact was severed just because Musharraf,
as the army chief, became less accessible or if they had a falling
out of sorts.

'Not that I know of. A mutual friend, Inam Bari, said [to me to] "patch up" [with him]. I [said] I have nothing to patch up. I was with him on all issues. One time he said he was very fond of me. Then he said that he had been all his life trying to protect me and everybody laughed; and then he said he didn't say it. But I thought that was routine among friends. I said, what have I got to patch up for? I don't see any rift between the two of us.'

I ask him about the time when there appeared 'rumours' of their falling out as friends. The general responds that it was shortly before Musharraf was promoted as the chief, around 1998. I ask him if he was privy to the tensions that began developing between Gen. Musharraf and Prime Minister Sharif soon after Musharraf became the chief.

'Once he became the chief I was not privy to just about anything. When he was a nobody I was always around him. Even if I am an idiot, even if he is everything, I said I would not increase my distance. But this happens when a chap rises to such heights, with new people gathering around him who make sure that old friends are eliminated.'

'Is Musharraf given to flattery, then?' is my next question.

'Oh, yes. He's got a lot of qualities. In *desi zabaan* we say *jo makhhan laga de udhar yeh slip bohat asani se ho jata hai*. In fact, I warned him of his so-called new friends. Once he said of someone "meet my old friend". I had never seen that person in our forty years together. But one time I was not well and as soon as he found out he showed up at twelve-thirty in the night. So it shows he has a lot of regard and compassion. Or I can say that when you become too close you get taken for granted so you may not even meet up ... One time he said, "It's been fifteen–twenty days and we haven't dined together." A lot of people were there so I didn't say anything. Then when we were alone I said it had been a year. So it could be genuine because he is a genuine chap. When he became the army chief our contact decreased.'

Gen. Zaidi fixes his gaze on the wall and reflects before he speaks again.

'When on 12 October 1999 I found out that Nawaz Sharif had sacked him I had to sit down to calm myself. I had seldom been that broken. I always used to tell him that he was big time into the social factor and he loved to roam around. He had been to the Maldives [and Sri Lanka], and he was dismissed while he was away. I was very upset. But later at night that day the situation became clearer. I even got a phone call from him that everything was okay.'

Even though meetings between the two old friends became rare, Zaidi says that they meet each other's children and families just as warmly wherever and whenever they can.

'Even he and I have met a few times. For instance, at his *samdhi*'s son's wedding in Lahore, in 2005 or so. I saw him sitting in the dark. He got up to receive me and then I had to meet all his family because in forty years I know just about every one of them. He kept standing and all the corps commanders were giving each other the look, wondering who this was, for whom was the president standing.'

Clearly, following the edicts of seniority with a generous measure of flattery thrown in, whereby you look up to your boss in an all too obviously unbecoming manner, is deeply ingrained in the army's officer cadre, perhaps a hangover from colonial times. Zaidi goes on to reveal more of his friend's personality: 'He is good company. Light hearted. Very fond of kids. My children used to climb over his head. One time he said to me, "We are going to Cherat; why don't you come with us in the helicopter?" We sat in the chopper, he was to my right and Sehba Bhabhi sat opposite him. He said we will chat but when I looked at him he looked very tired. I said to him, '*Yaar*, just sleep, we can chat later. He went off to sleep in a second. Like a switch had been turned off. When we landed after thirty-five or forty minutes, he gave his head a shake and he was totally fresh. So he catches up on sleep when he is travelling. He is interested in sports and running. He has a lot of drive, and he likes to be in the driving seat. Very ambitious. He had to be, to be the chief.

'He carries a lot of influence of his formative years in Turkey. He was very impressed with Turkey [and its modernity]. The way I see it, you rise and fall by the same means. He was the hero in a non-heroic age [in a country where] we don't have a concept of legitimacy [in governance]. Whoever sits [comes to power], sits indefinitely till he sorts himself and the country out. He should [have] just stayed and carried through his seven points when he came [but that didn't happen]. This country can be put right in one year if you have the right intentions and if you have the *himmat* [courage]. But anybody who gets there wants to stay there [as long as] he is alive.'

Zaidi says he retired in 1998 soon after Musharraf assumed charge as the army chief. 'I still had a year and a half but I retired a little early because we had been so close, wherever I'd go I'd be taken as Musharraf's man. I am nobody's man. What is right is right and what is wrong is wrong. He didn't have to protect me. And he was very angry [at my retiring prematurely]. He said that I should stay on. Then I said, where would I go after one and a half years. He said I could go to the ministry [of defence]. I said I didn't want to be a liability. He was annoyed and took two months to sign the paper.'

I ask him if Musharraf sought him out after retiring in August 2008.

'Our relationship since he became the chief was switched off. In between he got in touch a couple of times. A month before he resigned he called me up at four-thirty p.m. asking what I was doing. "Are you at home? I am just coming," he said. At five o' clock he was here. Then, a couple of days before his resignation it was his *samdhi*'s daughter's wedding. We met there. There were very few military people and I was surprised because his *samdhi* is also a brigadier. There were very few course-mates; I think four or five of us. After that he resigned. After the resignation we called him up a couple of times; they gave us time fifteen days after that. My wife and I went to see them for an hour at the Army House. We are still very fond of him.'

I ask Zaidi if he found Musharraf in good spirits.

'At that time I thought he was preoccupied. He had something on his mind. Both he and his wife looked thinner. Otherwise there was nothing that stood out.'

'Where do you think he went wrong as a president?' I ask.

'Like I said, you rise and fall by the same means. Ambition took him there and ambition brought him down. Had he stayed just for four to five years, the problems would have been tackled. Today your constitution is a *khichrri* [mishmash]. Respect for the constitution has further deteriorated in these past eight years. There is no respect for law and unless there is respect for law, society decays very rapidly. Someone asked me the key reason for America's greatness and I said one word, the "constitution". What is our constitution? We amend it in minutes. And I think we have a world record of amending a constitution in thirteen minutes. I think that was the key reason for Musharraf's downfall. The time for one-man rule was over.

'One time we had a meeting and I said to him, remember these things ... be very careful about the advisers you select. And he gave me the look that said, "What do you mean?" I said I meant exactly what I was saying. I asked him, "Should I give you a *desi* [local] example or a *vilayati* [foreign]? You are a *vilayati* man so I will start with a *vilayati* example." I told him that Winston Churchill once wrote an article on Adolf Hitler in which he said that the course Germany would adopt depended largely on the advisers Hitler would select for himself. The point is that even Hitler was dependent on his advisers.

'The other thing is that Musharraf is urban and simple. The tribal people are more *mard shina*s [better judges of people]. He is a simple Karachiite and he is unable to figure out these people. So ambition is one reason he went up and came down. Second, he has always had this problem which I tried to address but without success. He only sees things in black or white, which is not practical at all. In my perception there is no such thing as black and no such thing as white. Everything operates in shades of grey and we keep sliding *oopar neechay* [up and down] on that.'

At this point I ask Zaidi whether he shared any opinions with him on the political process in Pakistan, For instance, who in their opinion as generals was good or bad for the country?

'We had [a] discussion on the subject before he became the army chief. He used to get annoyed with me because I said the civilian establishment was [represented by] Nawaz Sharif since Ziaul Haq's time. He also did martial law duty under Zia which I refused to do. I was detained twice but I said no. I am very lucky that I got promoted because in Zia's time if you didn't do martial law duty you were done for; he [Musharraf] was always leaning [towards the establishment], whereas I used to say that the point you yield to should be right. For him Benazir was a traitor and then later Nawaz Sharif was also one. *Wah, wah,* what an idea! This I thought was bad. Where Sharif was right I would say he was right, where Benazir was right I would say she was right. Because what is right is more important than who is doing what. It is not to say that a person does not matter. Mr Jinnah matters. The Prophet [of Islam] matters. But in day-to-day activities what is right is more important. I think his black-and-white view of reality isolated him more; so did his new friends.'

'So when the Americans said to him, "You are either with us or against us," you think he went with them because he thinks in a similar way?" I ask.

'Julius Caesar first used this phrase. I was very sad when the choice for him was that either he resigns or be impeached. I was very sad because of our long association. His advisers were not right and there was too much American pressure on him at the same time. His advisers were bureaucrats and that reminds me of Lyndon Johnson who said that Nixon had selected the most remarkable people as his staff but they were not politicians; they would get him into trouble. And they did. So did Musharraf's advisers.

'Now take the [shortage of] wheat problem. You may try to justify that the electricity shortfall was because so many air-conditioners were being used, that the country progressed under his rule so the electricity consumption increased. But they should have also seen to it that in eight years half a dozen new power generation plants should have come up. So [it denotes a lack of] vision. There is a problem with the army mind also. We are basically channellized or funnelled into a sphere. It's happened before. Ayub Khan went when the wind turned against him. With Yahya Khan you know what happened and with Zia everyone was unhappy.'

I ask Zaidi if there was any unhappiness under Musharraf's rule within the armed forces.

'As I said, I was soon out of the army, so I don't know the inside story. The rest is hearsay. Then there were his personality issues, for instance, if he saw the world in black and white how come he didn't also see it in terms of right and wrong?'

At this point I insist that Gen. Zaidi illustrate his point in detail. He offers to narrate an anecdote from his time at the Staff College:

'I was giving a talk on leadership in 1980 or 1981. A student asked me what the minimum qualities in an officer were. I said there are two things an officer must have: intellect and will. Till the lieutenant year it is more about will, supported by intellect. An officer must understand the system by the time a brigadier becomes a general; but for a general and above it is mind before will, though both are essential. If you can eliminate the weaknesses then your overall rating is fine. There are three weaknesses: ambition, greed and hypocrisy. I said avoid these three. Most people agreed with this but three boys disagreed with the ambition part. During the break, Musharraf also said to me that my whole lecture was fine except for this point. I asked why. He said ambition was the only driving force in life. I didn't quite understand what he meant. I said that if ambition was the prime motivating force then one got it all wrong. I said when your ambition becomes the main driving force, your conscience would be relegated. Then you would be willing to do anything for your ambition. Of course we didn't agree.'

I then ask him what the general feeling within the army was about Nawaz Sharif, a very ambitious man himself, at the time when Musharraf became army chief. 'Were they okay with him?'

'I think the bulk of our senior lot was definitely okay because of over eleven years of Ziaul Haq's military rule, and Sharif being his protégé.'

I then ask why the military so hated the PPP.

'In the eleven years of Ziaul Haq, the officers were totally brainwashed. The Bhuttos were the devils and everything bad was attributed to them. This was drilled into us: that they would sell the country and that they were traitors.'

I ask Zaidi how much of that opinion of the PPP Musharraf shared.

'He was anti-PPP. Definitely, despite being a liberal in his personal life, and their ideologies being similar; he did two to three years of martial law duty and was quite close to the inner circle around Gen. Zia. He was definitely hostile to the PPP. The other reason is that the PPP is the only party with a popular base, so there is a clash of interests [between the army and the PPP over power sharing]. The third reason is that the PPP is seen as a non-status-quo party. Our culture is for status quo and our military is the worst of the lot in that respect. The army is extremely for maintaining the status quo.'

On the allegation that Benazir Bhutto levelled against Musharraf's intelligence and security apparatus after her return to Pakistan, that they were harassing her, Zaidi says: 'There are always those who are more loyal than the king. The fact remains that despite all these years of military rule, since Zulfikar Ali Bhutto came on the political scene, politics has been either pro- or anti-Bhutto. There are no other forces. Whenever you are in power by any means other than by public support, you will

have an issue with anybody who has that support. Junejo was
picked up by Zia [as his prime minister] because he was a simple
sugarcane grower—a nobody. He was Sindhi. The PML-Q was
breathing only because of Musharraf. Nawaz Sharif's too was a
created [by the army] party but over time it has acquired a life of
its own. Now it is a political force that can confront the PPP.'

I ask him about his foray into politics and his being given a
ticket by the PPP to contest.

'I thought that the PPP was at the receiving end. Basically
from my young days I have had a lot of sympathy for the
party. Sometimes we would go to the remote and impoverished
mountain valley, Chitral, as soldiers, and my sympathies have
always been with the downtrodden. In my perception the answer
to all ills in Pakistan lies in a simple sentence: your social policy
should be changed to social justice and not status quo. The
only people who at least pay lip-service to this are the PPP.
In March–April 2001 I met Benazir Bhutto in Dubai. I said to
BB, "You are picking your own candidates [for elections]; you
should let the *awam* [public] decide because you call yourself
an *awami* [masses] party. You should let them decide their own
district candidates, their tehsil, town presidents; your workers
should decide that, who have been at it for twenty-five or thirty
years. They must decide. Not you sitting here calculating. This
only promotes sycophancy." And she listened.

'She was very kind. I was very impressed with her. I thought
she was a very articulate and sharp lady. And she had charisma.
She asked me: "General Sahib, if I come to Pakistan how much
difference do you think it will make?" I said, across the board
at least 10 per cent. But I also said that let us make the systems
grow. I said whoever comes and goes, Benazir and Nawaz Sharif
will remain [forces to reckon with]. When I said this she had it
written down. She made me a member of the Central Executive
Committee [CEC] as soon as I joined the party. She gave me the
ticket to contest from Jhelum. Now the party leaves me out. In
the entire year they have only called me three times. Later I was

told that I had been appointed a CEC member by invitation. But I remembered that she had appointed me as a permanent member of the committee who attends all meetings.'

Having been closely associated with the People's Party, Zaidi must have had the opportunity to gauge where feelings within the party cadres stood vis-à-vis the army and its chief, Gen. Musharraf, having been aware where the general stood vis-à-vis the party and Ms Bhutto.

'I found the PPP hostile to Musharraf and the army. At a dinner in Dubai with some of Benazir Bhutto's relatives, I could see their venom against the military. Some of it without reason, without basis. And there was venom against Pervez [Musharraf] also. I butted in, being a soldier; I am not a diplomat. I got very hurt. I said, having a difference of opinion is something else but Pervez has been my buddy for forty years and I am a soldier. He may leave me but I will not leave him as long as I am alive. We have this thing called comradeship—you have buddies. Pervez was my buddy from the earliest time in the army, till he became the chief; although culturally we are totally different but by design we were always together. I didn't ask for the party's ticket in the 2008 election. There were various reasons, but primarily, I was disappointed with the whole system. However, I met Benazir a year or a year and a half before her death. She was more accessible than the present-day people. And I found her very open to my suggestions.'

'When did you become aware that there were contacts between Musharraf and Bhutto?' I ask him.

'When I went to meet her [for] the first time in 2001, she was very surprised that if she and Musharraf thought the same way, why was there so much venom against her. So I gave her my reasons. She was very keen for a rapprochement with Musharraf. But I had seen him on TV being very hostile towards both of them [Sharif and Bhutto]. Somebody said that he heard the general say "I will boot them out". I thought that was in bad taste, because she was keen. Then I came to know that a lot of people thought

I was the go-between. After he became the army chief, he used to remove my name wherever he saw it!'

'Was he so upset with you because you resigned when he had asked you to stay on and then you went off to join the PPP?' I ask.

'That shouldn't have been the case. In forty years of association, there are so many ups and downs anyway. A lot of people say that we were so different we could not be friends. Like I said, we are culturally very different; you know, I would avoid the company of ladies. I would just look or go the other way. I do not drink [alcohol]; I only drink 7 Up and Pepsi, and a lot of people wondered what kind of a general I was!'

I ask him whether he knows of any occasion when he thought that Musharraf was planning to eventually rule the country one day.

'I don't know, to tell the truth, but he never said anything like that to me, though he was very ambitious. In our culture the worst is the power game. Our people have legitimized it. You may murder, destroy anything, but as long as you can grab power you are legitimate. It is un-Islamic. You saw the fraud in the referendum that Gen. Zia held, for instance. I covered the subject when giving a presentation to him and everybody asked, who is this *bad-tameez* [ill-mannered man]? But Zia was the only chap who understood exactly what I was saying. Although it was well known that Ziaul Haq never forgave a person who crossed his path, I am the only exception. We were discussing legitimacy of power. I gave examples from the Quran.'

'Do you think that by comparison Musharraf's reign was more benevolent and less hypocritical?' I ask.

'What happens is that when you have one-man rule it reverses the process of political intimidation. Power is a hub [for intimidation]. And you can see that in what Musharraf did in the manipulation of the judiciary. But this has been happening for 1400 years [in Islamic history], so why blame Musharraf? Why don't you blame the big ulema who have been passing the laws?

Why don't you blame the successive chief justices of Pakistan who legitimized [usurpation of power]? If you single out Musharraf in this, I would definitely be against you.'

'In the last eight years we suffered because of those who acted more loyal than the king himself to his cause. Musharraf's [dilemma], I would say, was that he was a hero type, who did not live in the age of heroes. Very likeable person, a lot of drive in him; the sort who would be irritated if anyone excelled over him. Because of this, he could never be second. Even where he may be second, he perceives himself to be first. That is why he became the chief.'

I press Gen. Zaidi to tell me why they fell out notwithstanding the kind words he still has to say about his close friend of forty years. 'I don't think he ever enjoyed my company. I am far too serious, introvert[ed], and when he had a choice he would not like to spend his leisure time with me,' he responds, taking a deep puff of one of the many cigarettes he has smoked during our interview.

'What is his legacy?' I ask him.

'I would say he tried but in a different way. I don't think his advisers were sincere with him. I think his legacy is "Enlightened Moderation" which should have gone down much better but the way it was applied was incorrect. If you take the Quaid-i-Azam's example he was more of the Bombay [elite]/ London [mould person], nothing to do with this area. But after the [passage of the] Pakistan Resolution [1940] we never saw him in a suit. He had a Doberman and a Spaniel when few in the subcontinent knew what those breeds were. When Musharraf came on TV with his dogs, I spoke to his wife, asking what the two pocket dogs were doing in his armpits. It doesn't go down well in our culture. "Enlightened Moderation" was not bad but the way he put it across was. Like when you say the Quaid was secular, I say I don't know of a single Muslim who is secular except for Kamal Ataturk. The Quaid-i-Azam was a born Ismaili. In 1937, when he went to see the Aga Khan to seek permission for his sister to marry a Sunni, he converted to [the mainstream] Shia faith, and Iqbal says that he [Iqbal] was nothing but a soldier of Jinnah, with all his [Iqbal's] intellect. He wouldn't say that for a secular man.'

General Saeed Zaidi is clearly more of a social thinker than your stereotypical general in the Pakistani army, who dwells on strategizing. Soliciting for socio-economic justice as the essential basis for legitimate power, thus making a case for a guided pursuit of ambition rather than ambition as the principal driving force behind political power, Zaidi contrasts sharply with Musharraf. But Zaidi's is also a view of politics informed by the classical Shia doctrine of justice and legitimacy of temporal power as the basis of governance, while Musharraf's remains thoroughly secular, even if one sought to be justified by political exigencies. Both being professional soldiers, they stuck to their respective guns even if that were to be at the cost of chilling their forty-year-long association. Ironically for both, Musharraf's lack of political pragmatism whereby he failed to distinguish between what was right and wrong despite his seeing the world in 'black and white', and Zaidi's refusal to accommodate ambition as the basis of power-wielding, notwithstanding his insistence on seeing the world in grey, made them grow apart.

# 22

## Brash!

Renowned political and military analyst, and the author of *Military Inc: Inside Pakistan's Military Economy*, Dr Ayesha Siddiqa, who now calls herself a 'gypsy scholar', often on the road for lecture tours, appears in equal measure to be fascinated and repulsed with all that General Musharraf stands for. His unique mix of personality traits and actions make him a fascinating subject for Dr Siddiqa's specialization as a military analyst; the 'disastrous consequences that his eight years of military-led rule has left behind' leaves her with cold feet. She is a scholar of few but very precise words; she doesn't beat about the bush, nor minces her words. I ask her if Musharraf is a product of his institution or one of his own making.

'I think as a person he is both a product of his institution and responsible for his own actions. Something which caught my attention once when I went to Bangladesh was the inspiration to study the stereotypical Bonapartist general [generals who decide to come and take over and I thought they all had something in common]. An extra nerve, an extra instinct that makes them do it. I mean, if you look at Generals Ziaur Rehman and Hussein Ershad of Bangladesh, and compare them with Pakistan's Ziaul Haq, Ayub Khan, Yahya Khan and Musharraf, you see that these are different products from the rest of the institution. They have this immense capacity to do things and go wrong with them. They have a fire in their belly. If you look at their careers, they have greater fire than what would help them survive in a bureaucracy. So it is a very self-serving, individualistic thinking they have which is compounded with their ability to have a sense of ownership of their organization and communicate it back to their soldiers, which eventually helps in staging a coup d'état. Both the arguments apply equally well to Musharraf. He was a product of his organization. His power was centred in that institution; yet he was a Bonapartist, a general who doesn't really think about institutions, [he thinks] only about himself as the centre of the universe.'

I ask Siddiqa whether she would blame the coup of 1999 on Nawaz Sharif, another very ambitious man, or Musharraf as the army chief who was equally ambitious, with gunpower behind him to translate his ambition into reality. Was the general waiting for an opportunity to strike as and when it arose or did it just happen like that?

'It was both. Because, I believe there is no strict civil–military divide here as far as personal ambition to rule goes. We have a dictatorial system where people change faces but the behaviour remains the same: dictatorial. So technically Nawaz Sharif could have removed the army chief but I think one knows that he erred. He had his own power and ambitions and Mush[arraf] too was driven by his own personal instinct as well as the character of the army, which has developed in the past sixty-odd years and that character is one of being an autonomous institution. It should not be questioned, and anybody who tries to challenge its power is cut down to size, and that's what Musharraf did with Nawaz Sharif. It was ultimately an issue of his own autonomy and not just for him, but for the generals around him, like General Mehmood, and the guy in charge of the Ten Corps in Rawalpindi [that carried out the coup]. The issue was that the army could not allow a civilian guy, even if you thought he was in the right, to question the autonomy of the military. And here perhaps Nawaz Sharif was not even in the right.'

'What has Musharraf's legacy been?' I ask her.

'One is the "war on terror". Then there are greater divisions within. From the Ziaul Haq days we inherited the liberal versus conservative divide. This has been further sharpened under Musharraf. This is his legacy. Plus, in many ways his legacy is the same as that of any military dictator: further weakening of the state and society.'

On whether Musharraf had any choice at all after 9/11 to take another course, Dr Siddiqa clarifies: 'I do not hold him responsible when I say that his legacy is the "war on terror". I am not suggesting that he shouldn't have helped the Americans. I am not suggesting that at all. What I am saying is that the manner in which he tried to sell a liberal agenda can be likened to Ziaul Haq's selling of jihad to the Americans; that is what has divided this whole debate about "Enlightened Moderation" and conservatism or radicalism. That is how he has defined it. I am not referring to the operational matters of the "war on terror".'

I ask her what Musharraf's greatest mistake was while he was in power. She snaps back: 'To be in power [in the first place]. Then he did it without trying to acquire legitimacy. Because the problem with both civil and military governments in Pakistan is their lack of legitimacy and whenever they run out of legitimacy they tend to look outside for their approval in office. I think Musharraf's greatest problem was his desire to stay on. All generals make this mistake. He is not the first one. Once they are there, they are caught in the game forever.'

'What about Kargil? How much personal responsibility for the ill-conceived venture do you assign to Musharraf?'

'As a general he was completely and totally responsible for it. And even if, let's assume, his generals below were hatching a plan, he was squarely responsible for allowing them something like that. So I hold him responsible.'

'Why do you think he didn't try to build for himself some kind of legitimacy with the support of certain popular political parties?'

'You can't. If you become autocratic, the structure of power of a military dictator is such that he starts seeing less as time passes. And the less you see the more mistakes you make until you completely run out of legitimacy.'

'So everything stemmed from the wrong action of his being there in the first place, and then prolonging his tenure, or was it circumstances that caused him to commit one mistake after another?' I ask.

'It's not simply circumstances alone. You make certain choices, you select your team, so you make your choices. And here is a guy who is not even trained for politics. His basic training was not in politics.'

'Why was he so popular with the international media?'

'Because, one, he was popular with the Western governments. Secondly, I think what got him the media's attention was his boyish, open attitude. In my view that attracted them to him.'

'Did the boy grow up?'

'The boy never grew up. He has still not grown up [after his resignation] from what I have heard.'

'Where did he leave his institution? Has the army been weakened professionally?'

'Of course. No doubt about it. When you engage in military adventurism, when you engage the military in doing politics, you create problems for the institution.'

'Do you think Musharraf had a game plan for Pakistan or was he just biding his time all along?'

'When he took over in 1999 he didn't have a game plan. They [the army top brass] thought they could cobble something together but they couldn't manage to do that. And that state of affairs continued. Unfortunately, our political parties don't have a plan either. That's why I was saying that we have a dictatorial system; once you are at the top you dictate regardless of whether you got there through the ballot or the bullet. Nobody has a plan.'

Does she think Musharraf was sincere in taking the peace process forward with India?

'He was forced into it. He went forward, but that didn't mean that he had changed his thinking. I remember interviewing him in

1994 when he was the DG, military operations. He said, "What makes you think that once Kashmir is over there will be an end to the conflict with India?" That's what drove his thinking and that's what drives the thinking of most of our generals.'

'What are the next frontiers of war with India?'

'Look at water. There is a crisis there already. Let me also add that every Pakistani general who has started on an adventurous path with India has eventually learnt from bitter experience that he has had to make peace with the bigger partner. This is the pattern that you find repeated with Ayub Khan, with Ziaul Haq. I mean, remember the great cricket diplomacy of Ziaul Haq? Musharraf also tried different ruses.'

'Where does it all lead?'

'It doesn't go anywhere because the whole strategy is based on biding time. It is conflict management rather than confidence-building or conflict resolution.'

'Was he truly enlightened and moderate in his own thinking?'

'Culturally, behaviourally, if you define moderation and enlightenment in simply cultural parameters, then, yes, his claim that he was enlightened [was correct]. He drinks, he's fond of women, habits that go back to his early days. He was not conservative like Ziaul Haq, but for me enlightenment is more in political terms and there he wasn't. Look at his entire rule. Initially he gagged all the opposition parties, and exiled leaders. He wouldn't allow them to return. Then there was his selective gagging of the media. A journalist from *Dawn* got beaten up after he asked a tough question of Musharraf, and you had the Okara military farms controversy while he was there; you had the fisherfolk of Sindh and Balochistan protesting under his rule. All of these conflicts emerged even at local levels while he was there, which goes to show that politically he was not enlightened.

I ask her whether she would consider him enlightened as a military man, someone apparently willing to go the extra mile to make peace with India.

'He had some assumptions that he could sell a certain project. Under pressure he realized that he couldn't force the solution of Kashmir on the Indians. It was after making a lot of blunders, like Kargil, for instance, that he understood that a war couldn't be fought, especially in a nuclear environment, in South Asia. But it doesn't mean a transformation of his thinking, and so from his point of view he did go the extra mile to suggest taking Pakistan away from its traditional position of following the UN Resolutions on Kashmir. But he was not making a corresponding change in his organization's thinking. He was the man at the top with an idea that was probably not being shared with the rest of the organization. Or not being shared in a manner that he could convince his other officers, his officer cadre that, yes, a change was needed.'

At this point I suggest that it was India that called his bluff, not his own people or the generals...

'Yes, but within the army establishment nobody can call their chief's bluff. Within that discipline he had his own way but only so far and no further.'

'What do you think of the "creation" of the religious parties' alliance, the MMA, by the military intelligence?'

'Again, the same story: divide and rule. That's what they know how to do best.'

'Is our army done with Afghanistan?'

'No, I don't think so.'

'Are they done with Kashmir?'

'I don't think that either, because again it goes on and it's still a dispute. The only difference now is that while there is a genuine resentment among the Kashmiri people who are protesting in the Valley, and the fact that the Hurriyat Conference boycotted the last election held there last year, Pakistan, because of the military's political involvement in our internal affairs and because of our own political chaos, is no longer in a position to capitalize on what's happening in Kashmir. There may be some diplomatic assistance and some other; but perhaps not, otherwise the Indians would have been shouting from their rooftops.'

I ask Dr Siddiqa why she thinks Musharraf went the way he did, having to resign under pressure from the political forces and from his own organization, the army, which refused to prop him up.

'Well, because the point at which he left, like his predecessors, he had lost all political legitimacy and credibility. And if you can't have political legitimacy you can't run the show indefinitely. The military gets its reports from the soldiers as well, who go home on leave and come back and talk about how resentful the people were feeling. The army decided to distance itself from the former chief. Plus, there was a change of guard [which he made]. There was also external pressure from the United States. So a combination of factors forced him out; not just that he wanted to leave.'

'Which is one adjective that you would like to use to describe Musharraf?'

'Brash!' is the instantaneous response from Dr Siddiqa.

# 23

# A Modern Dictator

Seasoned senior lawyer, a leftist leader, social activist and writer, Abid Hasan Minto is widely respected for being consistently upright, precise and level-headed in his thinking, attributes that rarely coalesce in a single individual in a country such as Pakistan where so much is in flux. He is not given to the so-called normal proclivities of accepting or rejecting political attitudes or the prevalent influences without systematically analysing them and then making up his mind on where he stands in relation to particular issues. He is least taken up with personalities, and in that remains a dispassionate, original analyst and thinker.

In the interview that follows, focusing on General Musharraf's years in power, Minto provides the historical and the contemporary overview of the issues at stake—a contextual and theoretical framework of sorts through which he analyses Musharraf's rule and his ouster. I begin on a more philosophical note by asking him whether Musharraf is merely a part of a historical process or did he stand out individually as someone who mattered.

'Well, he is both; a part of the historical process and someone who stood out because the history we have lived is a history composed mostly of military takeovers, of direct and indirect martial laws, which have controlled society. The imposition of martial laws has had the effect of even impacting the civilian mindset, so the people cannot get out of that thinking and they always look for some kind of a dictatorial, arbitrary authority to "control" the situation. From that perspective, Musharraf and his takeovers, one after the other, two martial laws, one in October 1999 and the other in November 2007, are part of history itself. But it is quite obvious that all takeovers are led by one individual or the other, so, starting from Ayub Khan and coming down to Musharraf, individuals also do matter.

'He was the first dictator who openly and publicly came out with some kind of a liberal attitude. The liberalism he actually demonstrated was liberalism not only in social attitudes but also in politics itself, regarding notions which were actually controlling the mindset of the people, the politicians, and society as a whole. He had some ideas that broke that mindset to some extent. Relations with India, for example, in spite of what he did in Kargil. When he became the ruling dictator he perhaps thought otherwise; and thought it necessary to break the straitjacket in which Pakistan and India had been placed for a long time. Then, again, back at home, he tried to grapple with a society based on an Islamization process modelled by Ziaul Haq, and which our middle class and upper class readily accepted when Ziaul Haq was in power. He also made some effort to break that mindset. So in some ways he had his own characteristic personality and that was in line with modern thinking. But such modern thinking, if it is not part of a democratic set-up, goes to the back seat under an arbitrary rule based on authoritarianism.

'So the dictatorial part of his personality is something we ought to forget altogether and make it a part of history. His legacy of some kind of liberalism has to be broadened and become part of the vision for a modern, democratic state.'

'How can religion be detached from the social discourse now that it is so deeply entrenched?' I ask Minto.

'That's quite difficult in Pakistan and in all Muslim countries, to a great extent. Muslims all over the world are still not free from their obsession of the empires that they had in history and the kind of authority that they wielded till the end of the

Caliphate in the early twentieth century. So they are still in that mindset in the Indian subcontinent also; one that is reinforced by the kind of authority that they wielded over 800 years of their long domination of the subcontinent in spite of the fact that they were in a minority and they had come from outside; the majority of the ruling class did. Yet it controlled the destiny of the whole subcontinent. So that is the mindset. Although it is, strictly speaking, a political and historical situation which has to be analysed differently but the common man's mindset is that as Muslims and people who adhere to the Islamic point of view they are the people who should be controlling society. It is difficult to uproot such a mindset and bring it on a par with modern thinking.

'Doing so will require a full effort, right from the educational institutions and at all cultural and social levels as also on the legal level, because the law, including the constitution, insists on some kind of an Islamic polity and Islamic society. This is a long-drawn-out struggle. Efforts have to be made not in an arbitrary, dictatorial fashion [as in the case of Musharraf] because when you impose things from above, the people react. They tend to defend themselves against new ideas and they tend to fall further back into their entrenched mindsets. Any change has to be brought in democratically. For this, new democratic forces must emerge; they must be secular and forward looking.'

'What about the lawyers' movement against Musharraf's suspension of the judges? Do you agree with Aitzaz Ahsan that it did a lot and achieved a lot, or was it just a result of the freedoms or the so-called freedoms that Musharraf allowed?'

'I think it is not just Aitzaz who thinks that. It is obvious that occasions and causes give rise to spontaneous movements and that there was a cause for this one too. I think there is a full history behind the kind of suppression that gives birth to such spontaneous movements. The suppression of democratic forces was there; but no political organization, no movement, and no occasion arose to lend it a voice until at that point in time when the chief justice was suspended arbitrarily. What was the issue? The issue was, and is, the court, its independence. Its chief justice. The violation of the constitution. These were the issues that were brought out into the open, and who brought them up? The lawyers who are mostly from the middle class, bordering on the lower-middle class. And these are the backbone of the movement ... not the people who are in a higher [economic] class. The lower and the middle classes are the ones affected by all kinds of arbitrary actions, not only politically but also socially and economically, particularly because whenever there are arbitrary actions and the supremacy of the law or the application of the law is violated, it affects the legal profession directly.

'When it is a straight martial law, it takes away the authority of the court and therefore the legal profession is affected directly. It was not the first time the lawyers came up with this kind of movement. In the previous martial laws, the first step taken against the imposition of a martial law has always come from the lawyers. In Ayub Khan's time, and particularly in Ziaul Haq's time, I was myself a part of one such movement as the president of the Lahore High Court Bar Association [at that time there was no Supreme Court Bar Association], and there were no cementing associations of lawyers in the country. Therefore, the principal bar association which was the Lahore Association, took action at that time and violated the martial law; it opposed the martial law and took out processions at a time when martial law was in full swing and people were being flogged in the streets under military tribunal judgments. Zulfikar Ali Bhutto had been hanged. There was a stifling kind of awe and fear of the military at that time. Despite that, lawyers came out in the streets. It was the lawyers who gave birth to the Movement for the Restoration of Democracy [MRD] against the Zia regime [MRD was a broad-based, long-drawn resistance movement centred in Lahore, and based on defying Ziaul Haq's regime through street protests and courting arrest, which eventually resulted in bringing Benazir Bhutto back from exile in 1986]. There is a long history

of lawyers in politics. Also, remember that at the time the total
number of lawyers in the country was 40,000. Now it is about
100,000. At that time there was little media presence. In spite of
that, the movement was a success. This time the additional fact is
that the lawyers' movement generated some kind of influence on
civil society also. Again, civil society is mostly composed of the
middle class, so this is an influence. One hopes that out of this
movement a new political structure will emerge. If that doesn't
happen, then perhaps this struggle is also lost.'

At this juncture, as Minto doubles up as a political, socialist
thinker and one of the best legal minds in the country, I seek
his opinion on the National Reconciliation Ordinance, which
absolved Benazir Bhutto and Asif Ali Zardari of all corruption
charges brought and pursued against them equally by the Nawaz
Sharif and the Musharraf-led governments. The NRO was
the last of Musharraf's many critical moves that would shape
subsequent events leading to his downfall.

Minto replies: 'I am opposed to the NRO. It is a law which
was specifically devised to cater to the kind of situation which
now prevails in Pakistan. I mean, everyone who is a beneficiary
of the NRO is now controlling the political scene in our
country. The NRO is a law that is opposed to the constitution,
notwithstanding the latest Supreme Court judgment [as validated
by the Supreme Court constituted post 3 November 2007]. It
is a law which is unethical and discriminatory. If you want to
have some kind of a reconciliation, then it is always political in
nature, providing relief across the board, not selectively to such
and such individual; there should have been blanket immunity
for everyone.

'The South African reconciliation was a totally different
story. It was a true political reconciliation by people who
were successful in their struggle and after being successful they
said, "Now we want to cement our forces and there will be
no more antagonism and apartheid in the country." That was
a different reconciliation which also revolved around a probe

into the truth. There was no scope for ascertaining the truth in the reconciliation under the NRO [in Pakistan]. From all angles this is a law I reject.'

I prod Minto further, and he elaborates: 'I reject it because it is arbitrary and it did not come through consultation. First of all, the basis of the NRO is not any real reconciliation but giving benefit to a certain group of people who have not been proved guilty in a court of law. Therefore, there is no justification for this kind of law. I know several people who have been summarily indicted by the National Accountability Bureau; why should they not benefit from this law if people accused of corruption have to be given any benefit.'

I ask Minto to sum up Musharraf and his role while he was in power in a broader perspective.

'[I look at him as] a dictator who was modern in his outlook and in a country which has known dictators before him. He tried to fit in, in the kind of system that now prevails in the world. He did not contribute directly to the chaos at the global level, but by becoming a part of the system he played a role which aggravated the situation.'

# Afterword

Even as the book is being readied for press, a series of dramatic events necessitate this 'Afterword' as a means of tying up the narrative that has gone before and providing an update on the rapidly changing political situation in Pakistan, which leaves even the most hard-boiled observer dizzy trying to make sense of it all. It is uncanny to see how Pakistan so readily lends itself to clichés like 'history repeats itself', that 'those who cannot learn from history are condemned to repeating it', or, indeed, 'absolute power corrupts absolutely'. We have seen these hold true in the past. In the absence of stable democratic institutions and those of justice and accountability, the fear remains that this dubious political history will continue to repeat itself in Pakistan—unless better sense prevails all around.

To begin with, the military action against the Taliban in Swat was abandoned halfway when the Frontier government was prevailed upon (likely by the army) to strike a deal with the warring Taliban. The so-called peace deal struck in February 2009 saw the government buckle yet again under pressure from what many regard as a mullah–military combine. The government even agreed to enforce Islamic Sharia law in Swat. Interestingly, this had been agreed to under the Benazir Bhutto government in the early 1990s but was never implemented because Bhutto stood on the wrong side of the army which actively worked to thwart any political understanding she might reach with a belligerent group that might give her government any cushion. The PPP, under Asif Ali Zardari, may yet again be walking into a similar trap. If and when (and many believe it is only a matter of time) the agreement reached with the Swat Taliban collapses for whatever reason, the PPP will get the flak for it, for having given the Taliban the opportunity to regroup at a time when they were on the run. If, however, it works, it will continue to be censured by rights groups and civil society for giving in to the Taliban's demands, to the detriment of the people of Swat who, in the 2008 elections, gave the secular ANP and the PPP the mandate to rid them of the menace of Taliban, not accommodate them.

Still to recover from the embarrassment of the capitulation in Swat, the government was soon hit by another crisis with larger and immediate international ramifications. On 3 March 2009, the Sri Lankan cricket team, on its way to the stadium in Lahore, was attacked by gunmen who appeared to be as well trained as those who held Mumbai hostage in their November 2008 attacks, leaving the country and the cricketing world in shock. After initial investigations, the government sheepishly, if surprisingly, blamed it on Indian intelligence agencies in what seemed a tit-for-tat counter-allegation, clearing the prime accused Lashkar-e-Taiba and its allied militant groups of any involvement. In the bloody assault in which about a dozen well-armed and trained gunmen took part with near-precision targeting, seven policemen were killed and an umpire, a Sri Lankan coach and a few cricketers were injured. It is such mind-boggling acts of violence that many analysts in Pakistan regard as part of the legacy left behind by Musharraf's policies.

This brings us to the government's imbroglio with lawyers. As irony would have it, Justice Abdul Hameed Dogar, who was one among the post-3 November PCO judges and who had forcefully taken up the case of the 'missing persons', had been appointed the chief justice of Pakistan by Musharraf and confirmed in his new post by the PPP-led, duly elected government. President Asif Ali Zardari, it was said, also came to fear an independent judiciary and refused to reinstate Justice Chaudhry, until 16 March 2009 when events took an unexpected, dramatic turn.

The lawyers' movement gained new momentum in March as the leaders of the legal community gave another call for a long march to Islamabad to stage an indefinite sit-in outside parliament until the restoration of Justice Chaudhry. Days before, the Dogar-led Supreme Court had declared the Sharif brothers ineligible to stand for any public office, upholding the ban imposed by Musharraf. Within minutes of the controversial decision, Zardari responded by packing up the Shahbaz Sharif-led Punjab government, imposing direct governor's rule in the province. There was nothing now that could hold back the Sharifs from taking on Zardari; the brothers called for joining the lawyers' long march.

On 11 March, the government responded by cracking down on the lawyers' leaders and opposition politicians to prevent them from joining the long march. Arrests were made across the country; some TV channels covering the event were taken off the air. Sherry Rehman, Zardari's information minister and a close confidant of Benazir Bhutto, resigned in protest against the gagging of the media by her government. The ill-advised measures were a re-enactment of Musharraf's 3 November 2007 emergency rule without, of course, the government having declared a state of emergency this time round.

However, the march began in Lahore in right earnest on 15 March 2009. As the city was put in a state of siege by security forces, Nawaz Sharif broke the cordon at his residence and led a handful of party workers out on the street. The police did not resist him. Crowds began to swell as the day wore on. By the time Sharif left Lahore for Islamabad in the late evening, his rally had swelled to mammoth proportions. Barely 40 kilometres out of the city on the 280-kilometre trek to heavily barricaded Islamabad, the government relented, with Prime Minister Syed Yousaf Raza Gilani finally announcing the unconditional restoration of Justice Chaudhry to avoid a showdown with the massive crowd that accompanied the lawyers and the Sharifs. The march was called off immediately and the jubilant crowd dispersed peacefully. Populist politics had once again won the day against the high-handedness of a government, however representative.

Justice Chaudhry resumed his duty as the chief justice of Pakistan on 24 March after Justice Dogar retired from the coveted post. Misgivings remain as to President Zardari's intentions ahead, and there are rumours that he is waiting to clip the wings of his prime minister who, together with the army chief, General Ashfaq Parvez Kayani, reportedly forced Zardari to agree to the restoration of Justice Chaudhry. True to Pakistani tradition, the army chief had backed out of defending the government's decision to stop the long march in the face of mounting public pressure. The army never wishes to be seen as being on the wrong side of public opinion if that runs counter to government policies. This was the second time within months that General Kayani reasserted that position. The first time was when he refused to facilitate Musharraf on the eve of the February 2008 elections by ensuring that the army was not used to rig the polls, to avoid being seen as defending an unpopular president.

With the reinstatement of Justice Chaudhry for the second time since his dismissal by Musharraf in March 2007, demands to bring the general to justice have been raised again. However, lawyers' leader Barrister Aitzaz Ahsan, who was suspended by Zardari from the PPP's Central Executive Committee for his role in the lawyers' movement, has been rather circumspect. He has said that if any case of Musharraf's accountability were to be brought to the Supreme Court, it was only natural that Justice Chaudhry would abstain from the panel hearing it. The same would apply to the petition being heard by the apex court, pleading for the annulment of the controversial National Reconciliation Ordinance issued by Musharraf in his last weeks in office, and whose beneficiaries were Benazir Bhutto, President Zardari and several MQM leaders and activists. All criminal and corruption cases filed against these leaders only were dropped and a selective blanket amnesty was granted under the NRO.

In the social circles of Islamabad, Lahore and Karachi, and among average men on the streets of Quetta and Peshawar (courtesy the media), comparisons are already being drawn between the current democratic dispensation and the one tailor-made by General Musharraf to suit his exigencies, but which it eventually failed to serve in the final analysis. Just as the brutal killing of Benazir Bhutto left Pakistanis in a state of shock, what has followed in terms of President Zardari's politics in action so far has certainly left many dismayed.

With the benefit of hindsight, it can be argued that the People's Party, known and cherished for upholding its original democratic ideals and its pro-people line of thinking, has reverted to its role of the mid-1970s when its founder-leader, democrat-turned-autocrat, Zulfikar Ali Bhutto, did everything within his means—and there were mighty means at his disposal—to hold on to his slipping grip on power. When the political crunch came, Z.A. Bhutto even went against his stated convictions. This started with the purges within the party of committed middle-class, enlightened elements, who were replaced with the so-called, self-styled landed aristocrats and tribal, feudal lords. Then came the high-handed tactics of curbing all dissent, which, when it failed, gave way to the exigency of appeasing the extreme rightist elements. This was done, again going against his own and the party's convictions, by declaring the Ahmadi Muslim community as non-Muslim, for instance, and opening up a barrage of discriminations against the minority sect; banning liquor and changing the weekly holiday to Friday from Sunday followed suit. By the time these ill-advised decisions came, the rightists, with tacit support from the CIA, pressed for much more, i.e., the implementation of Sharia law, even as they ironically championed the cause of more democratic freedoms to exercise their right to protest and dissent. Confusing? But true of the Cold War years in which Z.A. Bhutto, counting on his popularity with Pakistanis, had fallen sorely foul of the US.

Back in 1967, Bhutto's Pakistan People's Party was born in Lahore, of desperation and frustration among the people of the then West Pakistan (present-day Pakistan). It was also born of the failing grip on power of the military dictator, the self-anointed Field Marshal, General Mohammed Ayub Khan. The best of Pakistan's thinking minds went into carving out a charter for the new party clandestinely, offering the people the promise to redeem a sinking ship, or at the very least to salvage what was left of it. Z.A. Bhutto, despite his oratory skills and shrewd mind, knew he couldn't have done it on his own. It was a team of dedicated secular, left-leaning ideologues who put together the magic formula for him that went out to the people to rally them behind the dream of bare basics: roti, kapda aur makaan (bread, clothing and shelter). The people bought it instantly, just as they had bought the dream of Pakistan from Jinnah in 1947—from a man who didn't even speak their language. Bhutto broke the elitist mould of Pakistan politics and chose only to speak in the vernacular. The magic of his charismatic words has lingered ever since. The people have bought it over and over again, that is whenever they have been given the chance.

Pakistanis may be emotional people but they also have long memories. When Z.A. Bhutto's popularity graph began to dip in the run-up to the 1977 elections, trucks painted with popular images of the preceding dictator Ayub Khan began appearing on the roads of Pakistan. Travelling from the port city of Karachi in the south to the Hindukush Mountains of the Khyber Pass in the north-west, many identified with the imagery and the symbolism as they represented a popular regret. Ayub Khan's painted picture was almost always inscribed with a line from a popular Urdu song: 'Teri yaad aaee tere jaane ke baad' (you were missed after you left). When General Zia hanged Zulfikar Ali Bhutto after an engineered trial, Pakistan did not go up in flames. Zia was able to control the dissent in good time for him to rule happily for eleven long, though very dark, years, until he was killed in a mysterious plane crash in 1988.

Just then the people re-invoked the Bhutto magic, one that had failed to work only a decade earlier. Z.A. Bhutto had been made to pay for his omissions and commissions with his blood, and many believed wrongly so. Despite the civil–military establishment's resistance and arguably rigged elections, and in spite of a decade of Zia's indoctrination, Z.A. Bhutto's daughter and political heir, Benazir Bhutto, triumphed, winning the public mandate to rule. Even those who had been against the Father Bhutto, started with a clean slate with his young, charismatic daughter who had been tormented and victimized by an evil-minded ruler who patently abused Islam for political benefit.

But when two years down the road Benazir Bhutto was sacked by a pro-civil–military establishment president who levelled corruption charges against her and her husband, Asif Zardari, there was little public hue and cry because, to many out there, the charges weren't all too incredible. Many had watched with disappointment and disbelief the daughter's fall from grace in a fraction of the time her father took to become only somewhat unpopular. Morality, thus, did ring home with Pakistani voters, howsoever disenfranchised they might have been given the complete lack of democracy over the previous decade under General Zia's military rule.

After Benazir Bhutto's forced ouster from power in 1990, Sharif and Bhutto took turns in the prime minister's office in 1990 and 1993 respectively. With the dismissal of Benazir Bhutto's (second) government in 1996 on similar corruption charges, Sharif made his way back into premiership in 1997, and stayed in office until the 1999 military coup.

Each time with the sacking of the prime minister by the president, there was little sense of wrongdoing felt by the people. But speaking of national memory, Pakistanis did cross vote. In the four elections held between 1988 and 1997, the line between traditional party loyalties of voters were blurred—many PPP voters voted for the Muslim League, especially in Punjab, and vice versa. The voters did so each time according to their conscience, coming out strongly on the side of the wronged party at the given time. Pakistanis may lie low for a while but they never condone what they believe is wrong.

Eight years of Musharraf's one-man rule was no exception. In the return of Benazir Bhutto in 2007, the people saw hope again. When that hope was snuffed out with her murder, the election boomeranged on Musharraf with full public fury. His henchmen were defeated. Then entered Zardari, rather unexpectedly. But within months, his popularity graph began to fall rapidly as he routinely reneged on political promises made before and after the February 2008 elections.

In the light of Benazir Bhutto's murder and Zardari's subsequent ascent to the presidency as the most powerful man in Pakistan—thanks to Musharraf's tinkering with the constitution—what we saw on the streets of Lahore on 15 March was nothing short of a peaceful revolution against everything the man in the presidency stood for on that day. Sharif has never been a crowd-puller or a people's man even in his home town. When he had landed in Islamabad after ending his exile in September 2007, for instance, Musharraf had him packed back to Saudi Arabia literally within minutes, and there was no public outcry anywhere. This, even though Musharraf was already and arguably at the lower ebb of his popularity at the time. It is startling to see how Zardari managed to do within months what Musharraf could not in seven long years until 2007, despite all his failings. Nonetheless, comparisons being drawn today between Musharraf and Zardari are being drawn for a reason. Both have shown a penchant for political recklessness.

Having said that, if the past is an indicator, it is only a matter of time before Nawaz Sharif will also start drawing flak from the public—with or without help from Zardari. As the pattern goes, and because of a lack of any guarantee on the continuation of the democratic process in the post-Musharraf years, give Zardari a free hand and he will self-destruct sooner than later, and make

Sharif soar. Conversely, give Sharif's government in Punjab (now restored by Justice Chaudhry-led Supreme Court) a free hand, and the result won't be much different.

The obtaining situation has led Musharraf to finally break his silence. After returning from his lecture tours to the West and India in March, he was candid enough to talk to the media, as a crisis of governance, a worsening law and order situation, and the threat of economic meltdown stared Pakistan in the face yet again. 'I will consider a role in government if made an offer,' Musharraf boasted in his typical gung-ho style. After the assault on the Sri Lankan cricket team in Lahore earlier in the month, he regretted that no 'armed' citizen stepped forward to kill at least a couple of the terrorist gunmen who apparently walked free in the heart of the city after targeting the Sri Lankan convoy. The only issue on which Musharraf refused to speak to the media was how he relinquished power and under what terms and conditions, if any. 'When the time comes, I'll tell you,' he responded to the queries with a smile.

The road ahead is no highway to democracy. It's one infested with potholes for want of upkeep and repair all these years. Unless politicians like Zardari and Sharif show the will to learn from their mistakes, and respect the public mandate given to their respective parties to rule in accordance with the law, while at the same time empower parliament to carry out the much-needed and overdue reforms in the basic law, an Ayub, Zia or a Musharraf will keep waiting in the wings to pounce on them.

With each military coup and derailment of democracy in Pakistan, the country has been pushed back decades in terms of political sustainability and economic stability. The politicians' urge to bring out the rival's skeletons from the cupboard must be resisted. The tragedy is that even the Supreme Court under its restored and duly, if unnecessarily, politicized chief justice Iftikhar Mohammed Chaudhry, cannot be hoped to provide non-controversial solutions to the mammoth political problems that have piled up.

General Musharraf alone cannot be held responsible for all the ills plaguing Pakistan today, though he had quite a long time at the helm to have contributed significantly to such ills. That the politicians following him should manage to outdo him in a much shorter span of time will be truly tragic for Pakistan.

# The General and His World:
# A Timeline of Events

*Compiled by Shahrezad Samiuddin*

11 August 1943: Pervez Musharraf is born in the Daryaganj area of old Delhi, India, to a working mother and a family of civilian servants.

14–15 August 1947: At independence from British rule India is partitioned into two sovereign countries, India and Pakistan. Musharraf's family chooses to cross over to Pakistan, settling in the then capital, Karachi, where Musharraf undergoes early schooling. Father as a diplomat is assigned to Turkey where the family accompanies him. Musharraf spends his formative years in Turkey and Pakistan.

October–December 1948: First India–Pakistan war over Kashmir.

October 1958: General Ayub Khan stages the first military coup in Pakistan.

1961: Musharraf joins Pakistan military academy at Kakul in northern Pakistan.

1964: Commissioned in elite artillery regiment.

1965: Takes part in the second India–Pakistan war over Kashmir.

1969–70: Ayub Khan relinquishes power, handing over a country in the grip of political turmoil to a fellow general, Yahya Khan, who holds Pakistan's first elections on the basis of adult franchise but refuses to hand over power to the Awami League which bags a thumping majority, but only in East Pakistan. Street agitation ensues as Zulfikar Ali Bhutto's win in West Pakistan and Sheikh Mujibur Rehman's in East Pakistan give way to tensions between the two wings.

1971: Third India–Pakistan war breaks out over East Pakistan, which is 'liberated' from a largely West Pakistan-based armed forces, and Bangladesh is born.

1972–73: The first elected prime minister of Pakistan, Zulfikar Ali Bhutto, calls on Pakistani scientists to build the atomic bomb. Pakistan acquires its first democratic, consensus-based constitution.

1974: India carries out its first nuclear test. Bhutto vows to match the capability.

1977–78: After allegations of rigged elections by Bhutto, Gen. Ziaul Haq deposes him in a military coup. Bhutto is hanged after a closed-door trial on trumped-up murder charges.

1979–1988: Gen. Zia strengthens his hold on power backed by the US, as Iran sees the Islamic Revolution triumph and Soviet tanks roll into Afghanistan. Zia introduces controversial Islamic laws. The ISI and the CIA fund the Afghan mujahideen who are fighting a proxy war against the Soviet Union, eventually forcing the Soviets to retreat from Afghanistan. Zia is killed in a mysterious plane crash with some army top brass and the US ambassador to Islamabad in what is believed to be an inside job.

1988–1999: Benazir Bhutto and Nawaz Sharif take turns as prime minister in two terms each, as they fall in and out of favour with the civil–military establishment.

January 1991: Musharraf rises through the ranks to become a
   major general in command of Pakistan's infantry division.

October 1995: Musharraf is promoted to the rank of lieutenant
   general, now assigned the command of the strike corps.

1994–1996: The Taliban rise to power in Afghanistan, aided
   by the ISI. Islamabad accords diplomatic recognition to the
   pro-Pakistan Taliban regime, alongside Saudi Arabia and the
   United Arab Emirates, the erstwhile backers of the Afghan
   jihad against the Soviets.

May 1998: Pakistan carries out nuclear tests in response to
   India's testing of its nuclear devices earlier in the same
   month. US imposes sanctions on India and Pakistan as they
   go nuclear.

October 1998: Prime Minister Nawaz Sharif appoints General
   Musharraf army chief.

February 1999: Prime ministers Atal Behari Vajpayee and
   Nawaz Sharif sign the Lahore Declaration between India
   and Pakistan, pledging to remove irritants in bilateral
   relations.

April 1999: Musharraf is belatedly and reluctantly appointed
   as the chairman of the Joint Chiefs of Staff Committee by
   Nawaz Sharif. Rumours are rife about their being at odds.

May–July 1999: Pakistani and Indian troops clash in the Kargil
   sector of Kashmir. India calls it an all-out war. Sharif, after
   consulting with the US, orders Musharraf to withdraw. The
   prime minister and the army chief trade accusations over the
   Kargil conflict.

October 1999: Nawaz Sharif removes Gen. Pervez Musharraf
   from the position of army chief in absentia. Within hours,
   the army responds with a coup d'état, arresting the prime
   minister. Upon return from Sri Lanka the same day,
   Musharraf declares himself the chief executive of Pakistan.

The military coup is condemned internationally but a majority of Pakistanis welcome it.

December 1999: Pakistan-based anti-India extremists hijack an Indian Airlines plane from Kathmandu to Kandahar to press for their demands on India to free fellow militants. India accedes. As the freed militants make their way into Pakistan, Musharraf refuses to take any action against them, saying they were not wanted for any subversive activities in his country.

May 2000: The Supreme Court indemnifies the general's post-coup actions, and gives him unprecedented powers to amend the constitution and restore democracy in three years' time.

June 2001: Musharraf appoints himself as the president while he still occupies the post of the army chief.

11 September 2001: Al Qaeda attacks New York and the Pentagon. US Secretary of State Colin Powell tells Musharraf to help the US bring the perpetrators of the attack to justice or face Washington's wrath. A few days later, Musharraf announces joining the 'war on terror', making a U-turn on the Taliban regime, and opening up Pakistan's airspace and military bases for action against the Taliban. The move enrages Islamists and they vow revenge on Musharraf.

October 2001: Musharraf supports and facilitates the invasion of Afghanistan; Pakistan is rewarded with promises of military and economic aid. The lifting of sanctions follows.

December 2001: Indian parliament attacked by Islamist terrorists purported to have operated out of Pakistan. A stand-off with India follows.

January 2002: Musharraf condemns terrorism in most unequivocal terms for the first time, vowing to resist the growing menace of Islamic extremism in Pakistan.

April 2002: Consolidates his grip on power by extending his
presidency to five years in a referendum held to be deeply
flawed.

July 2002: Bans former prime ministers Benazir Bhutto and
Sharif from contesting any future elections or becoming
prime minister for a third term.

October 2002: Holds general elections to put his hand-picked
deputies in parliament and in government.

December 2003: Survives two allegedly Al Qaeda-inspired
assassination attempts in Rawalpindi. Low-ranking army
and air force personnel are implicated and indicted in the
first of the attacks.

January 2004: Takes vote of confidence from both houses of
parliament and four provincial assemblies.

January–July 2004: Musharraf and Atal Behari Vajpayee agree to
begin a peace dialogue after the two nations pull back from
the brink of a nuclear war. Composite dialogue begins.

December 2004: Musharraf goes back on his word to give up
the post of army chief. A pro-president parliament endorses
him as president and military chief until 2007.

May 2005: Appoints Iftikhar Mohammed Chaudhry as the chief
justice.

October 2005: Musharraf's popularity graph rises as he
galvanizes the army to carry out Pakistan's largest ever relief
operations in the aftermath of a powerful earthquake which
kills 73,000 people in northern Pakistan and Kashmir.

2006–2007: Pakistan army and US drones carry out raids on Al
Qaeda compounds in the federally administered tribal areas
(Fata) along the Pakistan–Afghanistan border.

March 2007: Musharraf suspends the chief justice of the Supreme
Court without due process, accusing him of gross misconduct

and abuse of his powers. Lawyers rally behind the suspended judge. A pro-democracy civil society movement takes shape amidst police high-handedness against peaceful protesters. Lawyers boycott court proceedings.

12 May 2007: The pro-Musharraf Sindh and the MQM-led Karachi city governments prevent the chief justice from driving into the city after he lands at Karachi airport. Road blocks are erected and street violence kills 44, mainly anti-Musharraf activists. Musharraf hails the action by his loyalists.

6 July 2007: Extremists launch a rocket attack aimed at bringing down Musharraf's plane as it takes off from the Rawalpindi airbase. They miss the target.

11 July 2007: After a week-long siege of Lal Masjid, Islamabad, which extremists have been using as a hideout, the military storms the mosque to end the violence. Over 100 madrassa students and their Al Qaeda-sympathizing teachers are killed.

20 July 2007: A full bench of the Supreme Court throws out the government's petition to dismiss Chief Justice Chaudhry. Musharraf bites the dust.

27 July 2007: Musharraf meets Benazir Bhutto in the UAE to strike a power-sharing pact apparently brokered by the US and Britain.

10 September 2007: Nawaz Sharif is arrested after landing at Islamabad from London and swiftly deported back to Saudi Arabia in defiance of the Supreme Court order that allowed him to return unhindered.

18 September 2007: Musharraf's legal team assures the Supreme Court that he intends to doff his military uniform after he is re-elected as the president by the outgoing assemblies.

October 2007: Musharraf designates the former ISI chief General Ashfaq Pervez Kayani as his successor as army chief. He signs the controversial National Reconciliation Ordinance granting amnesty to Benazir Bhutto and her husband, Asif Ali Zardari, by withdrawing all pending corruption and criminal cases against them.

18 October 2007: Benazir Bhutto, ending her self-imposed exile, lands in Karachi to a mammoth welcome. Suicide bombers strike her rally; she narrowly escapes but around 150 of her supporters die. Musharraf is accused of not providing Bhutto with enough security. He rebuffs the charge and blames the carnage on her lack of judgement in leading a public rally when it was a prime target of terrorists. Bhutto and Musharraf continue to trade charges.

3 November 2007: Musharraf imposes a state of emergency fearing an adverse judgment on his re-election for a second five-year term in the presidency, as endorsed by the outgoing parliament, blaming the judiciary of interfering in governance. He accuses extremist militants of destabilizing Pakistan, and suspends the constitution. The entire Supreme Court and high court judiciary is suspended unless they take a fresh oath of office under the new emergency rule. A defiant Supreme Court annuls the emergency as illegal; Musharraf strikes back by putting the judges under house arrest. Sixty of them refuse to take a fresh oath.

8 November 2007: Benazir Bhutto is placed under house arrest as her criticism of emergency rule mounts and she vows to restore the independent judiciary.

25 November 2007: Nawaz Sharif is allowed back into Pakistan under Saudi pressure.

28–29 November 2007: Musharraf steps down as army chief, but retains his civilian role as president, taking a fresh oath of office.

15 December 2007: Ends the state of emergency after getting his actions indemnified by judges who took a fresh oath under the emergency rule.

27 December 2007: Benazir Bhutto is assassinated after a rally in Rawalpindi. Her party and Musharraf trade accusations as to the responsibility for the security lapse. Angry protests across Pakistan, with Sindh, Bhutto's home province, facing the worst violence in years. Election is postponed from 8 January to 18 February 2008.

18 February–25 March 2008: Pro-Musharraf parties and the religious right are routed in the fairest polls held since 1970. A coalition between Bhutto's Pakistan People's Party, Sharif's Muslim League (N) and the Frontier-based Awami National Party begins to take shape. Musharraf is accused of trying to drive a wedge in the emerging coalition. The erstwhile pro-Musharraf Muttahida Qaumi Movement switches sides by lending its support to the popular ruling alliance in the offing. PPP swears in Yousaf Raza Gilani as the prime minister.

7 August 2008: The ruling coalition agrees on impeaching Musharraf if he does not step down.

16 August 2008: In a final ultimatum, the ruling coalition asks Musharraf to resign by 19 August or face impeachment.

18 August 2008: After hectic negotiations between the ruling coalition, the army and Western diplomats in Islamabad, Musharraf agrees to step down on the tacit condition that he would not be held accountable for any of his actions since the military coup of 12 October 1999. Stays on in Pakistan under complete security protocol at the Army House in Rawalpindi, pending the completion of his sprawling farmhouse residence in a hillside suburb of Islamabad, embarking on lecture tours which take him to the US, Europe and India.

# Index

Vajpayee, Atal Behari, 11, 40, 41–42, 51, 62–64, 176

Wahabis, 83
war on terrorism, ix, 4, 7, 45–46, 48–49, 68, 94, 122, 124, 150, 153, 154, 172, 183, 185, 204. *See also* United States of America
wheat shortage in Pakistan, 196

women's rights issue in Pakistan, 105, 109–10

Zahir Shah, King of Afghanistan, xii, 162
Zaidi, Major General (retd.) Saeed, 189–97
Zardari, Asif Ali, xiv, 34–35, 100, 119, 136, 149, 160, 176–79, 182, 188, 214. *See also* Bhutto, Benazir

# Select Bibliography

Advani, L.K., *My Country, My Life*, New Delhi: Rupa & Co., 2008

Bhutto, Benazir, *Reconciliation: Islam, Democracy and the West*, New York: HarperCollins, 2008

Iqbal, Allama Mohammed, *Reconstruction of Religious Thought in Islam: The Madras Lectures*, Lahore and Madras, 1928

Musharraf, Pervez, *In the Line of Fire: A Memoir*, New York: Simon & Schuster, 2006

Powell, Colin L., Secretary of State, 'Written Remarks Submitted to the National Commission on Terrorist Attacks Upon the United States', http://www.fas.org/irp/congress/2004_hr/powell_statement.pdf

Siddiqa, Ayesha, *Military Inc.: Inside Pakistan's Military Economy*, London: Pluto Press, 2007

Talbott, Strobe, *Engaging India: Diplomacy, Democracy and the Bomb*, Washington: Brookings Institution Press, 2004

# Acknowledgements

This is to thank all those who agreed to share their opinions and insights with me, and gave graciously of their valuable time at short notice. Without their inputs this book would not have materialized in the short span of time in which it took shape.

This is also to acknowledge and thank my editor(s) at HarperCollins, India, led by Karthika V.K., whose very timely idea it was to get this book out only weeks after President General Pervez Musharraf resigned in August 2008. Sincere thanks are due to her team for the meticulous editing, and value-adding inputs and suggestions.

I must also take this opportunity to thank my colleagues at *Dawn*, whose encouragement allowed me to undertake this project. Thanks are due to my organization for sanctioning frequent travel leave over the six-week research period, and to those who generously offered to share my workload.

My inspiration remains the refreshingly honest Dr Mubarak Ali, noted historian and a mentor, who taught me the value of trying to document history from a people's perspective as opposed to a ruler's.

Gratitude must also be expressed to all family members at large and many dear friends who encouraged me to undertake this project and excused my absence even from must-attend events and social gatherings.

Lastly, I must acknowledge with much respect and love the contribution made to this project by my best friend and dear wife, truly a 'Super Mom' and my very own 'Resident Editor'—all rolled into one strong, admirable person having nerves of steel—Shahrezad Samiuddin. Without her valuable inputs, editorial, logistical and emotional support this book would not have seen the light of day. She braved the challenge of working from home and deftly dividing her time and energies to single-handedly run our home and manage three lovely, but very demanding daughters, Maya, Priya and Dina, as I took time off from all worries to finish this project. Thank you, Shahrezad.